THE ANALYTICAL FAILURES OF LAW AND ECONOMICS

The law-and-economics movement remains a dominant force in American private law, even though courts and commentators recognize that many of its assumptions are implausible and that efficiency is not the law's only goal. This book adds to the debate by showing that many leading law-and-economics arguments fail on their own terms, even for those who accept their most important assumptions and goals. Adopting an analytical approach and using some law-and-economics methods against the leading arguments in that field, Shawn Bayern shows that economic thinking fails to explain or justify most rules in common law. Bayern masterfully surveys leading law-and-economics arguments in tort, contract, and property law and shows them to be fragile, self-contradictory, or otherwise problematic. Those who accept that efficiency is important should not be persuaded by the kind of law-and-economics arguments that have remained in vogue among legal scholars for decades.

Shawn Bayern is the Larry and Joyce Beltz Professor at the Florida State University College of Law. His research focuses on common-law issues, primarily in contracts, torts, and organizational law. He also has a deep background in computer science, with specialties in computer security and the development of programming languages. Professor Bayern is the author of *Autonomous Organizations* (2021).

The Analytical Failures of Law and Economics

Shawn Bayern

Florida State University

Shaftesbury Road, Cambridge CB2 8EA, United Kingdom

One Liberty Plaza, 20th Floor, New York, NY 10006, USA

477 Williamstown Road, Port Melbourne, VIC 3207, Australia

314–321, 3rd Floor, Plot 3, Splendor Forum, Jasola District Centre, New Delhi – 110025, India

103 Penang Road, #05–06/07, Visioncrest Commercial, Singapore 238467

Cambridge University Press is part of Cambridge University Press & Assessment, a department of the University of Cambridge.

We share the University's mission to contribute to society through the pursuit of education, learning and research at the highest international levels of excellence.

www.cambridge.org
Information on this title: www.cambridge.org/9781009159210

DOI: 10.1017/9781009159203

© Shawn Bayern 2023

This publication is in copyright. Subject to statutory exception and to the provisions of relevant collective licensing agreements, no reproduction of any part may take place without the written permission of Cambridge University Press & Assessment.

First published 2023

A catalogue record for this publication is available from the British Library

Library of Congress Cataloging-in-Publication Data
Names: Bayern, Shawn, author.
Title: The analytical failures of law and economics / Shawn Bayern, Florida State University.
Description: Cambridge, United Kingdom ; New York : Cambridge University Press, 2023. | Includes bibliographical references and index.
Identifiers: LCCN 2023010581 | ISBN 9781009159210 (hardback) | ISBN 9781009159203 (ebook)
Subjects: LCSH: Law and economics. | Torts. | Contracts. | Property.
Classification: LCC K487.E3 B39 2023 | DDC 343.07–dc23/eng/20230712
LC record available at https://lccn.loc.gov/2023010581

ISBN 978-1-009-15921-0 Hardback
ISBN 978-1-009-15922-7 Paperback

Cambridge University Press & Assessment has no responsibility for the persistence or accuracy of URLs for external or third-party internet websites referred to in this publication and does not guarantee that any content on such websites is, or will remain, accurate or appropriate.

For my mother, who taught me epistemic caution,
and my father, who triumphed over inefficient markets

CONTENTS

Preface . . . . *page* ix
Acknowledgments xvii

1   **Introduction and Background** 1
    1.1 Why Critique Legal-Economic Arguments Analytically? 8
    1.2 Some Patterns of Analytical Failures 12

2   **Tort Law** 25
    2.1 Negligence and Strict Liability 27
    2.2 The Neglect of Alternatives and the Inability to Isolate
        Microeconomic Features of Problems from Broader
        Economic Concerns 67
    2.3 Least-Cost-Avoider Arguments 76
    2.4 More Focused Questions of Tort Law 78
    2.5 Conclusion 82

3   **Contract Law** 84
    3.1 The Theory of Efficient Breach 86
    3.2 Other Remedial Matters 94
    3.3 Contract Interpretation 99
    3.4 Unconscionability 132
    3.5 Excuse for Unexpected Circumstances (Impossibility,
        Impracticability, and Frustration) 144
    3.6 Disclosure 148
    3.7 Conclusion 150

4   **Property Law** 153
    4.1 The Structure of Property Law: Numerus Clausus . . . 155
    4.2 Conceptual Classification of Legal Problems as an
        Influence on Law and Economics 160

viii　　　　　　　　　　　　　　　　　　　　　　　　　Contents

4.3 Adverse Possession 163
4.4 Dead-Hand Control. 165
4.5 Conclusion 167

5　Afterword: Ways Forward 168
5.1 A Review of the Problems 168
5.2 Alternative Legal-Economic Approaches 171
5.3 Studying Humanity 174
5.4 Conclusion 176

Index 179

PREFACE

There have been many general criticisms of the correctness, coherence, or application of economics as a social science generally. This book contributes to that criticism by means of what I would like to think is a sensitive legal analysis of the leading theoretical economic conceptions of private law. Its particular method is to highlight analytical problems or incompleteness in the economic arguments themselves, rather than only to question their assumptions.

I am interested, here, in showing the weaknesses of theoretical economics as applied to common-law subjects; my concern is not specifically with other types of "economic" analyses of legal doctrines, like, for example, empirical economic analysis of the effects of legal rules or processes. That said, those analyses too face an appropriate concern about the colonization of other subjects by economic-style thinking – by reductive *social scientism*, as it were. For example, though I don't particularly critique the applications of empirical studies to law in this book, one could apply methods similar to those shown within to question the forceful application of empirical studies to concrete questions of legal policy.

It may also be worth saying that epistemic and prudential caution shouldn't stop with social sciences; legal policymakers should be similarly skeptical of grand arguments from (for example) analytical philosophers as well, at least when those arguments purport to dictate legal policy. As my own teacher and mentor Mel Eisenberg once put it, "It is ... clear that law generally [has] too many rooms to unlock with one key."[1]

★ ★ ★

[1] Melvin Aron Eisenberg, *The Responsive Model of Contract Law*, 36 STAN. L. REV. 1107 (1984).

ix

x   Preface

As I was finishing this book, I was struck by the views of a former UK cabinet minister describing the general personal dispositions of those close to then-new (but even then doomed) Prime Minister Liz Truss: "[T]here is an intellectual arrogance .... They genuinely do think they are cleverer than anyone else and that other people's views are slightly tiresome."[2] The same thing is true of the Chicago school of law and economics and the overly aggressive application of theoretical economic reasoning to private law. And it is true for exactly the same reasons: at least the early proponents of law and economics presented their conclusions as if everyone else was either dull or tiresome, as if they couldn't reason correctly or had nothing to offer the world except supposedly fuzzy notions of justice. The UK government's odd lurch toward extreme libertarian policies in the name of "growth" was a strikingly clean example of how adults in positions of serious power can, strangely to the rest of us, take high-school-level economics too seriously.[3] The range of ideas that people can commit themselves to is staggering – spanning the realm of cultism, religious fanaticism, and so on – and one recurring failure mode in human psychology, particularly among academics, politicians, and those who work in think-tanks, appears to prioritize callous, senseless, inhuman policies in the name of supposedly hard-hitting theoretical economic reasoning. It is encouraging, in a way, that this lurch had the immediate reaction it did in the UK – partly because it was so politically unpopular and partly, ironically, because the financial markets themselves rejected it. I have no doubt financial markets could similarly reject analogously bad economic reasoning in private law.

That said, this book is not about politics but about particular rules in private law. I do not say much in this volume on "neoliberalism" or speculate much about where the ideas I critique have come from – and I don't even, for the most part, discuss their political dimensions. I am more interested in the arguments' intellectual features than their political ones. But the law-and-economics movement is not unique

---

[2] Rowena Mason & Aubrey Allegretti, *Kwasi Kwarteng: An Eton Tough Nut with Legendary Self-Confidence*, THE GUARDIAN, Oct. 1, 2022, theguardian.com/politics/2022/oct/01/kwasi-kwarteng-chancellor-profile [https://perma.cc/JH8C-ZPEZ] (quoting a "former cabinet minister who worked with Kwarteng as business secretary").

[3] For a similar critique of US politics, see JAMES KWAK, ECONOMISM: BAD ECONOMICS AND THE RISE OF INEQUALITY (2017).

Preface

as a movement of hyper-rationalism – that is, the notion that everything may be analyzed in a relatively straightforward fashion and, as two education researchers have put it, the impulse to "behave as though even if we cannot fully meet the requirements [of universal "scientism"], we should nevertheless try to get as far down this road as we can."[4] Offering a specifically analytical critique of legal economics may seem like a strange way to fight a tide of excessive rationalism, but as will become clear throughout this book I think much is to be gained by using the tools of hyper-rationalism against itself. If nothing else, that is perhaps the only way, practically, to make progress in the particular debates in my legal fields. But perhaps more interestingly, I think that showing the analytical failures of legal-economic arguments may be the clearest way to show that the language of social scientism is just a thin veneer over the substantive debates that need to occur anyway in law. Speaking about legal problems only in economic terms changes the language of the debate, perhaps unduly and destructively, but it is largely a linguistic translation.

A simple way to make the same point is to say that "economics" is clearly not determinative in contract law, tort law, or property law. "Economic" arguments can easily defend both a legal rule and its opposite (or its absence). Indeed, far from being decisive and important, economic legal argumentation may in many cases amount to sleight of hand. I have read whole judicial opinions – at least one of which is discussed within – that frame as an open-ended cost-benefit analysis something that earlier judges could have described instead simply as a variety of real-world factors to consider. Maybe there is no harm in saying "cost" every time we mean "potential problem," but there is also little benefit. At worst, the limitation in our language encourages a limitation in our thought.

★ ★ ★

One problem with the impulse to reduce problem-solving techniques to simple, supposedly rational analytical ones is that every reduction diminishes the decision maker's sensitivity to context. In that respect,

---

[4] PAUL SMEYERS & RICHARD SMITH, UNDERSTANDING EDUCATION AND EDUCATIONAL RESEARCH 16 (2014).

this book – like most of my work – is a critique of legal formalism, or the notion that the law should rely on rigid forms and concepts rather than being receptive to contextual facts.

People have become far too credulous of supposedly sophisticated but reductive analyses; this credulity isn't limited to economics but extends throughout the social sciences. For example, it includes the rush to accept the hypotheses of so-called evolutionary psychology even when they have not been, and in some cases could not be, empirically tested. I'm not clear if some ideas are popular because they play to a sort of inherent cultural conservatism in the United States – so that, for example, economics purportedly justifies notions of personal responsibility and evolutionary psychology reinforces traditional gender roles – or if people are simply being awed by complexity and craving rationalistic explanations in a complicated world. There is some evidence that people are persuaded by *any* argument that purports to provide reasons; whenever I encounter pure legal formalism and often when I encounter law and economics, I think of Ellen Langer's famous "copier" study,[5] in which people showed themselves to be persuaded in some situations by *any* reasons regardless of whether the reasons even added any new information.

In general, it is surprising how much people believe without any legitimate basis for doing so. This phenomenon is now more evident to people because of widespread specific and targeted misinformation about science, but it is pervasive even in mainstream thinking about nonpolitical matters. People often speak as if "rationality" demands specific actions – in the context of, say, investing or altruistic donations – when what they mean is only that an arbitrary model they've adopted, with detailed assumptions they've made up, demands those outcomes if the assumptions are correct. As a minor example, people commonly believe particular asset allocations for the individual investor's portfolio are demanded by rationality when that is true only if the future is modeled as a specific random variable based on specific past data – an assumption that echoes a problem I'll discuss in Chapter 3

---

[5] Ellen Langer et al., *The Mindlessness of Ostensibly Thoughtful Action: The Role of "Placebic" Information Interpersonal Interaction*, 36 J. PERS. & SOC. PSYCH. 635, 637 (1987) ("May I use the xerox machine [before you], because I have to make copies?").

Preface

xiii

in critiquing a formalistic defense of formalism that conflates probability with uncertainty. Among even very sophisticated people, there is a marked absence of epistemic caution, perhaps just out of a desire to fill in uncertainty with *something* that has the veneer of rationality. An alternative would be to fill that gap with intuition, experience from life and from humanistic subjects, and so on, but that is commonly rejected out of hand by people who purport to be acting scientifically even though their professional or academic work barely resembles science in any of the details.

There is always opportunity to add context, new perspectives, new information (and new whole classes of sources of information), and new degrees of epistemic or interpretive caution. Rarely does data mean something unless we ask why we are looking at it; rarely is analysis useful without judgment.

★ ★ ★

Simple observation of the world is sufficient not to take formal economics too seriously. Pricing in the real world is actually quite bad. The fact that real-estate agents in the United States can persistently charge 6 percent of property values, for example, suggests a persistent lack of a competitive marketplace (in which the agents' prices should approach their costs, which would not correlate perfectly with home prices) despite significant amounts of competition. Insurance prices can be absurd; the prices I was recently quoted for insuring the same house reflected a margin of error of something like 400 percent. The public equity markets erratically swing on a moment's notice without enough new information to rationally justify large price changes. It doesn't take a lot of real-world experience to reject strong assumptions of the perfect rationality of markets.

That set of observations is not meant to criticize markets, necessarily. Maybe they are about as good as we could expect them to be. But it is sufficient to reject the notion that markets and their participants are anything close to being perfectly rational – or that they could not be improved with better regulation.

As I describe within, starting right away in Chapter 1, a lot of the day-to-day arguments in law and economics in private law are premised in subtle ways on the notion that markets are not just useful

xiv   **Preface**

but that they are perfect. Without being able to assume the perfection, some leading law-and-economics arguments collapse entirely as an analytical matter.

★ ★ ★

I realized early in writing this book that it should not simply be a catalogue of all the detailed problems with every law-and-economics argument I could find. If it had been, the book might have turned into the same sort of unintentional parody of a picaresque novel that Arthur Leff saw in the first edition of Richard Posner's *Economic Analysis of Law* volume.[6] Instead, after an introduction that surveys the field and tries to draw a number of tentative conclusions and paint a few categories, the book covers the highlights of problems with the leading forms of economic reasoning in tort, contract, and property. I go in that order mainly because the economic analysis in tort happens to be conceptually more foundational, so some of the material later in the book depends on it. Often people think that property law should come first because tort and contract operate on concepts in property, but I think that impulse highlights a very common pedagogical error, which is to let conceptual order rather than clarity drive exposition. Moreover, the chapter on property is relatively short because the law and economics of property is, when considered carefully, surprisingly thin and focused less on legal questions than those of political theory.

★ ★ ★

As Grant Gilmore put it almost fifty years ago – perhaps too strongly, but he was more right than wrong:

> For two hundred years we have been in thrall to the eighteenth-century hypothesis that there are, in social behavior and in societal development, patterns which recur in the same way that they appear to recur in the physical universe. If the hypothesis is sound, it must

---

[6] Arthur Allen Leff, *Economic Analysis of Law: Some Realism about Nominalism*, 60 Va. L. Rev. 451, 451 (1974) ("I smelled a familiar genre …. A manual of possible uses, the kind that comes with a new chain saw? A text on herbal healing? Not quite? But what? I was more than half way through the book before it came to me: as a matter of literary genre (though most likely not as a matter of literary influence) the closest analogue to [Posner's] *Economic Analysis of Law* is the picaresque novel.").

Preface

xv

> follow that, once the relevant developmental sequences which have
> led us to our present state have been correctly analyzed, we will know
> not only where we are but where we are going. Our understanding of
> the present will enable us to predict the future and, within limits, to
> control it. Once the forces at work are known, they can be channeled
> or harnessed to serve the needs and wants not necessarily of mankind
> at large but at least of those who are in a position to manipulate them.
>
> We have never had to face up to that frightening possibility for the
> excellent reason that no historian, social scientist, or legal theorist has
> ever succeeded in predicting anything. After two hundred years of
> anguished labor, the great hypothesis has produced nothing.[7]

Despite what was obvious to Gilmore even then, little has stopped
the enthusiasm for applying excessively reductive methods to human
behavior. Whether through the more mechanical forms of "effective
altruism," law and economics, social-scientific punditry, strange faith
in the made-up numbers of political-poll aggregators, or extreme libertarian theory, people think they can predict what they cannot – that
we have the technology or intellectual capacity to understand things in
formal terms when we cannot. We persist in our faith in models and
regularities, and when the models fail, as they frequently do, we say
that a one-in-a-billion "black swan" event must be the cause.

We ought to know better by now.

---

[7] GRANT GILMORE, THE AGES OF AMERICAN LAW 99–100 (1977). Gilmore's original
formulation of this passage was published as part of *The Storrs Lectures: The Age of Anxiety*,
84 YALE L.J. 1022 (1975).

ACKNOWLEDGMENTS

For whatever reasons, this book has taken an exceptionally long time to write. It would be impossible to name all the people who contributed helpfully over the last ten years to my thinking on this subject. Conversations with and feedback from Rob Atkinson, Mel Eisenberg, Mark Seidenfeld, Joseph Singer, and Sam Wiseman stand out the most. I also thank Erin O'Connor and Don Weidner for their continuing support as my deans over the past decade.

It's once again been a great pleasure to work with Matt Gallaway at Cambridge, and the rest of the staff there, including Jadyn Fauconier-Herry and Chris Hudson, have been very helpful as well.

This book draws in part from some earlier work I have written in academic journals:

- *Rational Ignorance, Rational Closed-Mindedness, and Modern Economic Formalism in Contract Law*, 97 CALIFORNIA LAW REVIEW 943 (2009)
- *The Limits of Formal Economics in Tort Law: The Puzzle of Negligence*, 75 BROOKLYN LAW REVIEW 707 (2010)
- *False Efficiency and Missed Opportunities in Law and Economics*, 86 TULANE LAW REVIEW 135 (2011)
- *Contract Meta-Interpretation*, 49 U.C. DAVIS LAW REVIEW 1097 (2016)
- *Methodological Failures in Leading American Economic Analyses of the Private Law*, 5 CRITICAL ANALYSIS OF LAW 19 (2018)

Thanks to the publishers of those journals either for agreeing to let me draw material from them or for having standard agreements under which new formal permission was not needed.

1 INTRODUCTION AND BACKGROUND

The law has always cared about efficiency. That many law students, legal commentators, and judges imagine that the law's concern with efficiency should be credited to a handful of University of Chicago scholars over the last sixty years is a testament more to academic marketing than to the solidity or persuasiveness of the underlying research. Fundamentally, the law-and-economics movement, which is now so entrenched in American legal scholarship (though not that of other countries) that it hardly seems like a movement anymore, is a limited form of legal argumentation dressed up in impressive, and to many people intimidating, theoretical instrumentation. Contrary to the way it is commonly understood within the legal academy, the application of economic reasoning to law usually does not dictate particular results; properly conceived, it is as flexible as legal argumentation itself. To put it differently, nearly any legal argument can be couched in economic, or putatively economic, terms. That economic argumentation in law has been taken to promote a particular set of (usually politically conservative) legal rules is an unfortunate byproduct of relatively arbitrary recent history.

There are many ways to explain the law-and-economics movement's marketing success among American legal academics. As with the drive toward metrics in organizational management, the elaboration of clear, singular goals that purportedly can be measured seems to capture people's attention and divert their effort. Compared to apparently hard-hitting, measurable notions of allocative efficiency, fairness and justice can seem by contrast fuzzy and unworkable – even naive. Similarly, the notion that economics is a science appeals to our

2   Introduction and Background

craving for logic and progress; its promise of dispassionate certainty, compared to other approaches to law, appeals to our need for order. The mathematical basis of economics seems hard to dispute, particularly for lawyers untrained in mathematics; arguing intuitively against mathematics seems unprincipled and retrogressive. Moreover, the movement's instrumentalism, and its attention to the limitations of the world's resources and the tradeoffs that these limitations imply, has offered a tremendous service to the law, for which legal economists deserve significant praise.

My central argument in this book, however, is that much of the law-and-economics movement itself is naive, fuzzy, and unprincipled. This assessment may appear harsh, but it is equivalent to the movement's assessment of noneconomic legal analysis, and it is made for the same reasons. Any methodologically limited set of arguments in law is unlikely to capture the full range of concerns that should matter in resolving legal problems; it would be striking if all our personal, political, or even business decisions were made solely on the basis of Chicago-school economics, and it would be equally striking if legal decisions should be made in such a singular fashion. Law is appropriately complex, ever-changing, responsive to countless concerns, and difficult to reduce to singular propositions.[1] An economic model may explain part of the workings of the law, or it may have the capacity to provide a normative justification for a legal rule if certain assumptions hold, but it is normally an incomplete argument.

The point that economics is an incomplete way to analyze law has been made before and, indeed, is commonplace among legal commentators.[2] For example, people are not fully rational, so models that assume that they are do not match the real world. Similarly, achieving knowable measures of efficiency is not the law's only goal; it is easy to identify situations in which a legal rule depends – and should depend – on criteria ordinarily regarded as noneconomic,

---

[1] *Cf.* Melvin A. Eisenberg, The Nature of the Common Law 43, 157–61 (1988).

[2] Among the most piercing and enjoyable early criticisms of the movement is Arthur Allen Leff, *Economic Analysis of Law: Some Realism about Nominalism*, 60 Va. L. Rev. 451 (1974). But it is also important to point out that economists themselves often recognize the incompleteness of models.

Introduction and Background

specifically subordinating conventional economic metrics to another human concern.[3]

My analysis in this book, however, takes a different approach. Instead of arguing that the law-and-economics movement's assumptions make the movement irrelevant from a descriptive or normative perspective, my goal here is to apply analytical techniques, often of a type similar to those that have driven the legal-economics movement forward, in order to show that many leading legal-economic arguments would not reach their goals on their own terms. In that sense, my method here is an "internal" critique. I readily concede that this book's method often *is* "law and economics," broadly conceived; it is just an unorthodox kind of law and economics, one less inclined to reach specific conclusions about legal policy and more inclined to demonstrate the practical limits of modeling and formal argumentation. One way to consider this book's method is to treat it as an epistemically cautious application of economic thinking to law, one that is neutrally unconcerned about promoting economic methodology and instead interested in its accurate, limited assimilation into law.

---

[3] To be clear, I take no position in this book as to whether the broadest welfarist analyses – that is, very general theoretical arguments that seek to include anything that matters to any human's wellbeing (or perhaps to wellbeing overall, even if nonhuman) in their consideration of what to optimize – aim for the wrong goal. For example, I do not reject here Kaplow and Shavell's theoretical argument that social policies should be judged entirely in terms of wellbeing, as long as wellbeing includes anything that matters to anyone or anything. *See* Louis Kaplow & Steven Shavell, Fairness versus Welfare (2002); Louis Kaplow & Steven Shavell, *Fairness versus Welfare: Notes on the Pareto Principle, Preferences, and Distributive Justice*, 32 J. Legal Stud. 331 (2003). My main general response to such arguments is that they are indeterminate and ordinarily not relevant to policymakers in practice, because – at least without empirical information that is impossible to gather and clarification about how to measure, compare, and aggregate "welfare" that has never been forthcoming – such arguments' only response to a policymaker who makes a judgment based on a nonwelfarist concern like "fairness" is "you are using that concern as a proxy for welfarism."

It is worth a reminder that Kaplow and Shavell's argument, though ingenious, is so general as to be indifferent as to what even counts as wellbeing; as they put it, "little of our analysis depends on [a particular] specification of individuals' well-being; as we emphasize in our book, if one favors a different view of well-being, our main arguments imply that policy assessments should be made solely with regard to how policies affect well-being thus construed, with no independent weight given to notions of fairness." Kaplow & Shavell, *supra*, at 333. Moreover, their argument does not depend on (or support) any view as to how the wellbeing of individuals should be aggregated for the purposes of optimization.

The arguments that I consider in this book ordinarily are explicitly or implicitly tied to a more specific sort of optimization. What I treat as "economic" reasoning in this book is ordinarily an applied formal or semiformal model that seeks to justify a particular legal rule.

4 Introduction and Background

In that respect, to be perhaps unfairly glib, it has more in common with Richard Posner's jurisprudence than his earlier scholarship.

Perhaps the best example for this admittedly jocular critique of Richard Posner's early scholarship is his opinion in *Walgreen Co. v. Sara Creek Prop. Co.*[4] A defendant in a breach-of-contract case opposed specific performance and cited the theory of efficient breach to Posner; this theory, as I discuss in Chapter 3, was popularized in significant part by Posner himself. Faced with real-world considerations and acting as a sensitive common-law judge, Posner described the plaintiff's reasoning as "a beguiling argument that contains much truth," then added "but we do not think it should carry the day."[5] Those two phrases almost perfectly summarize my characterization of the law-and-economics movement as a whole.

Posner's opinion is notable for two other reasons that are relevant, just evocatively, in considering the law-and-economics movement's marketing successes among lawyers and legal commentators. First, in reviewing a district judge's discretion under the principles of equity to grant or withhold an injunction, the opinion appears to compare the costs and benefits of injunctions and monetary awards of damages using hard-hitting economic techniques, but on closer inspection the analysis is simply a comparison of some very general advantages and disadvantages of the two types of remedies. In other words, with some limited exceptions, it is more accurate to say that Posner's opinion engages in traditional legal reasoning using economic terminology than that he applies the formal methods of economics to resolve a legal problem. Moreover, the district-court judge had granted an injunction, and Posner was reviewing it only under a very generous abuse-of-discretion standard, so none of the economic analysis was needed to resolve the case.

Second, the opinion contains one of the most awestruck concurrences I have ever seen in a judicial opinion; the concurrence reads simply, "I gladly join in the affirmance reached in Judge Posner's expert analysis."[6] This is not the most deferential minority opinion in the history of the common law. (That distinction probably goes

---

[4] 966 F.2d 273 (7th Cir. 1992).

[5] *Id.* at 275.

[6] *Id.* at 279 (Harrington Wood, Jr., J., concurring).

Introduction and Background 5

to Lord Blackburn in *Foakes v. Beer.*[7] "I had written my reasons for so thinking, but as they were not satisfactory to the other noble and learned Lords who heard the case, I do not now repeat them nor persist in them.") But it is close. My goal in pointing out this concurrence is only to suggest how powerful the skillful use of economic terminology can be in the minds of lawyers and judges, even if it is not necessary to decide a case and even if its innovation is mainly rhetorical. To look at it another way, judicial opinions show virtuosity all the time, but Posner's opinion in *Walgreen* would almost certainly not have received the same concurrence if it had displayed only traditional legal virtuosity.

★ ★ ★

Before proceeding to analytical details, I want to make a few things clear about the arguments that appear throughout this book.

First, it is emphatically not my argument that efficiency is never important; efficiency can be quite important, and as I noted at the start, the law has tended to agree. Traditional legal reasoning has long been concerned, at least implicitly but often even explicitly, with the incentives that legal rules provide and their effects on the world's welfare. My argument is instead that following the policy prescriptions of the orthodox American law-and-economics movement is on balance a poor way – or at least not a demonstrably good way – to achieve efficiency. Efficiency, moreover, is not the law's only goal, does not have a singular definition, and is not always easy to recognize. Processing legal questions as if they are the same sort of questions as those that transportation officials or logistics managers address, with easy-to-identify optimands and easy-to-measure progress, misses a significant part of the analytical debates underlying legal rules.

Second, as I have already suggested, my argument is not that the law-and-economics movement has been worthless. Economic reasoning has shed light on law, can help identify significant features of legal rules or of the facts to which they relate, and will continue to remind us of the important reality that giving one person a benefit often takes something away from someone else. What I think of as

---

[7] [1884] 9 App. Cas. 605.

6   Introduction and Background

naive and fundamentally misleading in the law-and-economics movement is not its attention to these features of legal rules. The movement fails not when it tries to illuminate but when it purports to make
specific, determinative conclusions about legal policy. The difference
is between an observation like "Compared to offering an award of
monetary damages, orders to perform a contract have a cost that not
all legal analyses have identified" (which may be correct and useful)
and one like "Economic reasoning demonstrates that ordering specific
performance is inefficient and that monetary awards are the only efficient legal response" (which is misguided).

I'm not even making the claim that a proper legal rule can never be
determined using primarily economic considerations. Indeed, many
of the best legal-economic analyses – many of which come from outside the so-called Chicago school, though some of which also come
from within it – do this. Much of the best work is not flashy; it does
not claim to be counterintuitive or to present the kind of easy challenge to an imaginary "popular wisdom" made by the Freakonomics-
style books popularly or by the Chicago school academically. Instead,
it tries to integrate broadly economic techniques with sensitivity and
caution into the law.

When studied carefully, however, it becomes hard to see the
Chicago-school law-and-economics movement as anything but a systematic effort to rob the law of its deeper efficiencies and to return only a
mechanical – and usually politically right-wing – understanding of economic policy in its place. At least, that was the effect of the first several
decades of legal economics. More recently, the movement is so broad
and diffuse that it's difficult to say anything specific about it in general,
apart from critiquing individual arguments, which I do throughout most
of this book. The diffusion of the movement is evidence of its influence –
for example, that the use of psychology to analyze actors' responses to
legal rules is often called "behavioral law and economics," when mainly
it is applied psychology, is a testament to the movement's hold over the
minds of legal academics – but also evidence of its analytical weakness:
if "law and economics" can be used to explain or justify any result, then
it is a just-so story, not a productive or scientific technique.

Third, while I think quantitative notions of welfarism are probably problematic for deep philosophical reasons, I don't dwell on those

Introduction and Background

here because they have been covered well elsewhere and because they operate at a somewhat different level of generality from the particular critiques that I emphasize in this book. For example, because of the types of analysis I focus on, I don't rely on critiques of the general coherence of welfarism, though I think there is much that is valuable in those critiques.[8]

In any event, careful study of specific law-and-economics arguments makes it clear that reasoning that is called economic can reach, in ways that are tragically underappreciated, nearly any legal result and that the results often depend on which collection of arbitrary assumptions and perspectives economic models adopt. This book aims to demonstrate this central failing of the law-and-economics movement by analyzing law-and-economics arguments in depth, revealing their hidden assumptions and fault lines, and showing their errors.

My focus here is on private law. That, too, is a limitation of my critique. I make no argument here about the merits of popular legal-economic arguments in such subjects as tax, antitrust, or administrative law; those are different subjects for another time.

The remainder of this chapter provides different types of background that will be useful in understanding the rest of the book's analysis. Section 1.1 briefly elaborates the book's motivation for an internal critique of legal-economic reasoning, and Section 1.2 lays some general groundwork for my analysis by pointing to general, recurring classes of analytical failures.

---

[8] *E.g.*, Joseph William Singer, *Normative Methods for Lawyers*, 56 UCLA L. REV. 899, 918–19 (2009) ("Whatever metric we choose, we then need to assign values to consequences so that we can aggregate and maximize. But we have no natural method for doing this; it is not as if pleasures and pains come in neat packages of 'utils' that have an inherent numerical value. For this reason, law and economics scholars have settled on market measures (dollar amounts) to assign values. But dollar amounts are hardly uncontroversial .... Economists are well aware of the decreasing marginal utility of money, but most law and economics scholars are insufficiently attentive to the ways in which this reality undermines the very measures they use to calculate the effects of alternative legal rules on human welfare."); Mark Kelman, *Hedonic Psychology, Political Theory, and Law: Is Welfarism Possible?*, 52 BUFF. L. REV. 1, 11 (2004) ("[F]ull-blown subjective welfarism is not really possible. Preference utilitarianism both requires and defeats hedonic utilitarianism .... At the same time, there is no variant of hedonic utilitarianism that is either practically realizable (given the incommensurability of both good and bad states) or truly non-perfectionist (given the possibility that self-conception differs depending on the elicitation method we use to discover subjective states).").

8   Introduction and Background

1.1 WHY CRITIQUE LEGAL-ECONOMIC ARGUMENTS ANALYTICALLY?

Many critics of the law-and-economics movement simply dismiss it as irrelevant. Indeed, in the common-law world outside the United States, even mild, largely uncontroversial economic explanations for certain rules are commonly seen as "nonlegal," roughly as Lon Fuller's fictional caricature of a hyperrealist judge intentionally sounds ridiculous to us all when the judge relies on features of the procedural history in a precedential case that he's learned from his "wife's cousin."[9] In all common-law systems, such information is simply legally irrelevant in analyzing the precedent of an authoritative case.

So too, to many commentators, is economic reasoning about such things as the hypothetical incentives imposed by a rule of tort law or the allocative efficiency of a principle of contract damages. The efficiency of a legal rule may be simply beside the point to those who value legal doctrine for its own sake or think it derives exclusively from abstract moral propositions – even if the judges who originally crafted the rule may have been motivated, at least implicitly, by incentives and efficiency. In the late 1800s and early 1900s, the United States' most formalistic legal period, leading commentators tended to reject both moral and instrumental concerns as alien to the legal system. Christopher Columbus Langdell, an architect of both early institutional American legal education and the classical school of American contract law, went so far as to dismiss as "irrelevant" both "the purposes of substantial justice" and "the interests of contracting parties" in analyzing a rule of contract law.[10]

Langdell's doctrinalism still echoes in some of the most formalistic modern American scholarship, and it is not unheard of for a modern legal scholar to treat the law-and-economics movement as irrelevant

---

[9] Lon L. Fuller, *The Case of the Contract Signed on Book Day, in* The Problems of Jurisprudence 81 (temp. ed. 1949) ("I should like to add a fact, however, of which my brothers are probably ignorant. It happens that my wife's cousin was attorney for Pressman in that litigation, and I have learned through him that the case was argued before the Magistrate on grounds that had nothing to do with [the matter understood to be before the court].").

[10] C.C. Langdell, A Summary of the Law of Contracts 21 (2d ed.1880). Langdell's general view of the law still survives, though mostly outside the United States.

1.1 Why Critique Legal-Economic Arguments Analytically? 9

to law on the simple ground that it is instrumental. (In some fields, like American constitutional law, significant strains of commentary and case law remain quite formalistic.) It is difficult to construct a generous interpretation for the type of doctrinalism that treats the law as a self-justifying system rather than one that is justified in terms of morality, instrumental policy, or other social values. At bottom, that type of formalism seems to be little more than a plea to make the law aesthetically pleasing for law professors. Perhaps it is a proxy for particular unstated social or political values. For example, an argument that "rule of law" values require the law not to change may be a fundamentally instrumental argument about the courts' practical ability to manage change, or it may be a fundamentally moral argument about the unfairness of changing a rule that some private parties have relied on. But to avoid circular reasoning, those justifications must be evaluated individually in substantive terms. Pure doctrinalism can never be a sufficient response to moral and instrumental arguments, and practically speaking, the history of common law has shown, time and again, that doctrines that are both unjust and counterproductive are either eroded or overruled.[11]

In the more realistic and adaptive modern American legal tradition, the typical response of the law-and-economics movement's critics is either (1) that economic principles are not the law's primary concern or that they are less important than some other legal goal or (2) that the movement analyzes hypothetical rational actors who do not exist in the real world (or makes equivalently unrealistic assumptions – for example, that everyone knows what the law is and responds accordingly). These two types of criticisms are often valid. As for the first, many legal rules, such as unconscionability in contract law, are justified mainly by moral rather than by economic propositions (unless economic propositions are taken broadly to include anything about which anyone cares in any way, regardless of how the decision is reached or justified). As for the second, the assumptions of many economic models are indeed simply wrong.

It is fair to say, however, that these attacks have been unsuccessful in slowing down the law-and-economics movement, at least within

---

[11] *See* Shawn J. Bayern, *Against Certainty*, 41 HOFSTRA L. REV. 53 (2012); EISENBERG, *supra* note 1, at 117–18, 155–56.

the legal academy. (The movement has always been less successful among practitioners and courts.) The strongest form of the first type of objection – the outright rejection of instrumental reasoning in favor of some other singular goal, like morality – is unrealistic and does not fit with most people's beliefs about the goals of human institutions. Even those outside the Chicago school believe it is normatively appropriate for law to be at least somewhat instrumental. *Fiat justitia ruat caelum* (do justice though the sky may fall) may serve as an important moral reminder when weighing the rights of a criminal defendant against the political convenience of a legally improper determination of guilt, but it takes a particularly committed moral philosopher to apply that motto to defend a rule of contract law that is significantly wasteful for the vast majority of commercial parties upholding modern commercial norms. Even less controversially, in choosing between two morally equivalent alternatives, the law should generally favor the one that produces better consequences, so at the very least instrumental reasoning has a role to play in choosing among legal rules that are otherwise morally permissible. But the point is broader: if there truly were a group of legal scholars who could show convincingly that a particular legal rule would lead, better than all its alternatives, to happiness and human flourishing in the most comprehensive sense – indeed, to the most desirable consequences overall, including all relevant distributional consequences[12] – then practical arguments against that group would diminish, if not fall away entirely.

The second response – that the law-and-economics movement makes unrealistic assumptions – should have been a sufficient objection to the movement's progress because it undermines the claim that following the movement's reasoning will achieve its instrumental goals. It should have been a sufficient objection, but it wasn't. There are several possible reasons for this failure. For one thing, wholesale rejection of the movement's assumptions leaves no room for the counterargument that while the assumptions are imperfect, so is all human activity, and the imperfections may not make a practical difference. In other words, perhaps people are not fully rational but are close enough to rationality

---

[12] Such consequences would include, as Kaplow and Shavell, *supra* note 3, recognize, people's preferences about noninstrumental social propositions, such as morality.

1.1 Why Critique Legal-Economic Arguments Analytically? 11

that the economic models still capture important truths. For another, the objection does little to undermine legal commentators' impression of the movement's scientific progress; as Alexander Pope put it, "men must walk, at least, before they dance,"[13] and a legal economist might suggest that though there have been problems with formal models of human behavior in the past, the models are on balance getting better, as with all scientific progress. Regardless, as a purely descriptive matter, the wholesale rejection of the movement's assumptions has served mainly to divide the legal academy into distinct camps rather than to synthesize or reconcile different strands of arguments.

Still, the rejection of much legal-economic reasoning and its reliance on formal methods is justified. I believe the widespread instinct to reject it is tied at least in part to an intuitive understanding of some of the movement's internal analytical failures – and that those analytical failures are a more important challenge to the law-and-economics movement than a rejection of its consequentialist goals and a potentially more persuasive critique than an outright rejection of its assumptions about human behavior. In other words, my hypothesis is that skeptical reactions to the American law-and-economics movement capture an implicit recognition that legal-economic reasoning fails to persuade us that it can successfully reach its goals even if its assumptions are broadly true. A typical positivistic, amoral argument seems jarring to most common-law commentators precisely because, at least in part, the morality missing from the argument captures considerations that are instrumentally important to human welfare. (Much of my analysis in Chapter 3, on contract law, echoes this observation. Law that undermines parties' sense of fairness is likely to undermine their commercial deals in ways that ought to matter to a consequentialist.) An economist's assertion that a particular rule will produce particular incentives may properly be dismissed because the posited incentives seem implausible or at least have not been convincingly demonstrated, even if we assume for the sake of argument that humans are broadly rational. My principal goal in this book is to develop these intuitions analytically by considering leading legal-economic arguments across private law.

---

[13] ALEXANDER POPE, THE FIRST EPISTLE OF THE FIRST BOOK OF HORACE 7 (1737).

12   Introduction and Background

In short, American legal economics does raise at least a prima facie challenge to classical doctrinal rules. The challenge posed by legal economics to traditional legal reasoning, in other words, is not irrelevant. It needs a response. My suggestion is that the appropriate response is at least in significant part to accept, for the sake of argument, the movement's goals and broad assumptions and then to refute its arguments using analytical techniques and the breadth and fact-sensitivity of common-law methods. This sort of response is surprisingly rare. A refusal by its critics to engage its methods seems to have permitted the movement to blossom, largely unchallenged on the specifics, as one of the chief academic forces in American private law.

1.2 SOME PATTERNS OF ANALYTICAL FAILURES

Before considering economic arguments about legal subjects individually, it will be helpful to identify several general patterns of analytical failure in legal-economic argumentation. This identification will make the scope and nature of my analysis clearer – and also give a taste of the analysis to come – and it will help organize the book's critiques of individual arguments into loose categories. The discussion here is not meant to be exhaustive; it simply lays out some general problematic recurring patterns (or what some in the software industry call "antipatterns")[14] so that it will be easier to recognize them later. Throughout this section, I use sketches of specific arguments as examples, but they are just sketches; the full arguments appear in later chapters.

1.2.1 Ungraceful Degradation

One general failure that my analysis identifies is that many legal-economic arguments do not degrade gracefully. Almost by definition, models of the world do not capture everything about the world; they instead focus on particular variables as a way to describe reality in a

---

[14] *E.g.*, WILLIAM J. BROWN ET AL., ANTIPATTERNS: REFACTORING SOFTWARE, ARCHITECTURES, AND PROJECTS IN CRISIS (1998).

1.2 Some Patterns of Analytical Failures 13

useful, manageable way. Successful models function much like the *ideal gas law* in physics: they state general patterns and relationships that, while not literally accurate, closely predict actual conditions and relationships. Reality may depart from the model's predictions by a few percentage points, but the model still can be helpful for instruction, prediction, and understanding precisely because it is simpler than reality.

There is no formal test for whether a model is a good fit with reality or not; as the computer scientist Alan Perlis once wrote, "One can't proceed from the informal to the formal by formal means."[15] This alone is an important recognition, because legal-economic argumentation cannot itself compel a legal result; there always remains the possibility that mathematically formal argumentation fails to model reality, and that possibility must be evaluated using informal – for example, traditionally legal – techniques.

As I noted earlier, my goal in this book is not to attack legal-economic argumentation merely by questioning its various assumptions, like the assumption that humans are rational or that they are selfish. That said, several of my critiques will interact with that sort of questioning because, as an analytical matter, many important economic models collapse entirely if the assumptions are even slightly undermined. As a rough statement of principle, I would have little objection in this book to an argument that made several assumptions about human nature that, when shown to be untrue, led a formal model slightly astray. An economic argument about a legal rule that gets something right 98 percent or even 85 percent of the time, or that predicts quantities that are 2 percent or even 15 percent away from reality, may well be a successful argument for my purposes in this book. The analytical problem I identify is instead that, for the purposes of various arguments I critique here, the possibility that human beings are not perfect (or that some other assumption is violated) destroys the underlying models entirely, rendering them unable to interact usefully with the world in any way. With this defect, they still may be helpful teaching tools – particularly if the goal is to teach economics – but they cannot even begin to dictate legal policy, even if our goals are entirely instrumental. A more precise

---

[15] Alan Perlis, *Epigrams in Programming*, ACM SIGPLAN NOTICES, Sept. 1982, at 12.

14   Introduction and Background

description of this problem is that an argument that suffers from it has two defects: (1) faulty assumptions and (2) an almost complete intolerance to even small violations of those assumptions. My arguments in this book are more concerned with the latter problem than the former one.

To make the discussion more concrete, it may be helpful to provide a sketch of some examples of this problem. As perhaps the most practically significant, a leading economic justification of the negligence standard of tort law – that is, of the principle that tort liability requires a demonstration that someone has acted wrongfully, as compared to the competing principle of strict liability under which an actor may be liable even without behaving badly – depends on a formal model that uses the threat of liability to control multiple actors' decisions about what precautions to take. The notion, simply put, is that a negligence standard will encourage multiple actors at the same time to take precautions against accidents when it is efficient for them to do so. The model assumes that all actors are rational and that one actor can rely on the presumed rational precautions that the other actors will take because everyone will be acting thoughtfully in their own interests. For example, I may not need to look both ways before crossing the street because drivers will have an incentive to stop at stoplights. Once the rational-actor constraint is violated even slightly, however, the model falls apart entirely. If there's even a 1 percent chance that drivers will not stop at stoplights, I would be foolish not to look both ways before crossing the street. So the model's predictive utility falls apart in the real world. I discuss this argument more in Chapter 2, which covers tort law in detail.

As another example of this problem, Richard Posner and Andrew Rosenfield argued in a foundational article in 1977 that people who make contracts, if they are rational, will assign the risks of various events to the parties best able to handle them (by taking precautions, or by insuring, against them).[16] For instance, a rational buyer and a seller of grain probably will assign the risk of the grain's destruction by fire to the seller while the grain is in the seller's warehouse,

---

[16] Richard A. Posner & Andrew M. Rosenfield, *Impossibility and Related Doctrines in Contract Law: An Economic Analysis*, 6 J. LEGAL STUD. 83 (1977).

1.2 Some Patterns of Analytical Failures   15

because the seller can more readily prevent a fire in that warehouse than the buyer. The seller might prefer to force this and all other risks onto the buyer, all else equal, but because the buyer and the seller can negotiate the contract price, the two parties together will prefer to make the contract more efficient; this will increase the contractual surplus – the collective gains from the contract – which the parties can then allocate between themselves based on bargaining power. As a result, Posner and Rosenfield argue that contract law should make a similar allocation of risks when parties themselves have failed to do so explicitly, effectively filling in contractual gaps in the way that they assume parties would have done because the parties were rational and self-interested.

The argument fails to recognize, however, that not all contracts are negotiated in a perfect world in which parties can maximize the surplus of individual contracts. Economists would be among the first to point out, for example, that a company that employs agents to negotiate their contracts may impose standard rules on the agents in order to reduce agency costs – that is, the overall costs of monitoring agents and suffering losses because of disloyal or careless agents. These rules may prevent agents from negotiating optimal individual contracts. The result is that Posner and Rosenfield's argument, to the extent it aims to predict what contracting parties would have done, threatens to get the result exactly wrong by assuming that the parties were looking to maximize the surplus of an individual contract. Once we can no longer assume the perfect efficiency of that individual contract, following Posner and Rosenfield's argument runs the risk of tampering with that contract in ways that the parties would not at all have intended. Chapter 3, which covers the economics of contract law, discusses this argument more thoroughly.

In both these cases, an argument works (at least on its own terms) if the model is perfect, but it fails to have *any* explanatory or justificatory force if the model is even slightly imperfect. Once we introduce the notion of agency costs in the contracting example, we can no longer make the assumptions that Posner and Rosenfield make about the parties' behavior. It's not just that Posner and Rosenfield might be slightly wrong; it's that their prediction becomes non-predictive once an additional variable is added.

16 Introduction and Background

1.2.2 Conflicting Economic Forces and Problems of Scope

Posner and Rosenfield's argument about contractual gap-filling is also an example of a different pattern of analytical failure for economic arguments that results from the simple recognition that economic forces can conflict. Taking these forces one at a time does not produce efficient or even determinate results. In other words, Posner and Rosenfield have made a choice about what micro-effect to optimize before their argument starts, but as Perlis's warning about formal modeling suggests, we cannot consider whether their choice to focus on the joint surplus of indivual contracts, rather than agency costs, is justified without comparing the two. Of course, an economic model can try to incorporate multiple variables at once, but because it can't include everything, a question will still remain as to why some factors are worth considering and others are not, and a model cannot itself explain why it excludes certain features of the world. Moreover, a methodology that seems tractable with one or two variables is often more clearly futile with even three or four variables, much less the several dozen that might be necessary to come even close to reality.

The problem with the arbitrary scope of Posner and Rosenfield's legal-economic argument, then, is that it may make sense on its own terms but it is difficult to integrate into a broader analysis of efficiency without using a noneconomic method. Once we recognize that we can't assume each individual contract is meant to maximize the joint wealth of the contractual parties in a manner limited to the individual transaction in question, there is no formal basis on which to assume that any specific assignment of risks matches the preferences of the parties (even if the model itself degraded more gracefully). To determine those preferences, we would need to look at the whole situation – something that Posner and Rosenfield specifically don't want us to do.[17]

1.2.3 The Useless or Redundant Incentive

Often a legal-economic argument (1) identifies a desirable result, and (2) connects the result to a legal rule that could achieve it, but (3)

---

[17] *E.g., id.* at 87 (criticizing those who believe that "no general theory is possible" in this area).

1.2 Some Patterns of Analytical Failures

fails to consider whether the proposed legal rule is needed to reach the result in the first place. In this pattern, arguments confuse necessary with sufficient conditions. They often do so because of the background context that their formal modeling ignores.

As an example, consider rules concerning mandatory disclosure in contract law – that is, the law governing when one party needs to disclose privately held material information to the other party (for example, an important hidden defect in a good or the fact that the seller's real estate contains valuable mineral deposits known to the buyer). The leading American legal-economic analysis of contract disclosure dates to work by Anthony Kronman.[18] Dean Kronman's argument differentiated between information that was acquired accidentally and information that was acquired as a product of investment. In short, his argument was that contracting parties should be under a duty to disclose accidentally acquired information – something overheard on a subway, for example – but should be able to profit if they have invested in information. A typical example of investment in information is flying a radar-equipped airplane over land in order to determine whether natural resources are available beneath the land.

Kronman argued that the principal motivation for a rule permitting nondisclosure is to encourage productive information to be developed or discovered. But he and the legal economists who expanded his argument[19] did not recognize that while such a rule may be *sufficient* to encourage investment in productive information, it is not *necessary*. There are other ways to achieve the same results. For example, while requiring disclosure of private information about the value of land might remove the incentive for natural-resource prospectors to fly over the land to determine its value and then buy the land cheaply, it doesn't discourage farmers from hiring a prospecting service to do so, nor does it discourage a prospector from contracting with farmers (in advance of a flyover) for an option to purchase their land if they

---

[18] Anthony T. Kronman, *Mistake, Disclosure, Information, and the Law of Contracts*, 7 J. LEGAL STUD. 1 (1978).

[19] *E.g.*, ROBERT COOTER & THOMAS ULEN, LAW & ECONOMICS 270–75 (3d ed. 2000); Steven Shavell, *Acquisition and Disclosure of Information Prior to Sale*, 25 RAND J. ECON. 20 (1994); MICHAEL J. TREBILCOCK, THE LIMITS OF FREEDOM OF CONTRACT 117–18 (1993).

18   Introduction and Background

find oil. Indeed, this latter possibility is in effect what ordinarily occurs in practice in most US states in the form of the purchase and sale of oil-and-gas or mineral leases.[20]

To generalize somewhat, economic analysis may proceed by identifying a particular incentive that the law might create and then analyzing the effects of that incentive. But there is often no attempt to weigh that incentive against others, to determine whether the incentive will do any good or will simply be redundant with other incentives, and so on. Legal rules do not operate in vacuums, and attention to just one strand of incentives tends to be unpersuasive to those setting legal policy.

Analyzing one type of incentive (in this example, the incentive to invest in productive information) may be helpful but cannot be dispositive. There are clearly other considerations, even if our only motivations in fashioning a novel legal regime are instrumental. One is, as I have pointed out earlier, the necessity of a particular intervention in view of other ways of achieving the same goals of a particular model. Another involves entirely separate efficiencies. For example – sticking with the topic of disclosure requirements in contract law – if the law encourages prospective buyers rather than sellers of homes to hire independent inspectors, the law may promote needless duplication of effort. I discuss arguments about the mandatory disclosure of privately held information between contracting parties in more detail in Chapter 3.

1.2.4 The Neglect of Alternatives

Legal-economic arguments often rest on the premise that if an activity (versus the absence of the activity, considered in isolation) produces wealth, the law should promote that activity. This is like saying that being a manufacturer produces wealth, so we should encourage college graduates to become manufacturers. The argument is fatally incomplete because even if an activity is productive in this sense, other activities may be more productive. Formally, this is a problem

---

[20] *See* Melvin A. Eisenberg, *Disclosure in Contract Law*, 91 CAL. L. REV 1645, 1688 n.93 (2003).

1.2 Some Patterns of Analytical Failures 19

of equivocation, or slippage in the meanings of words like "efficient" or "productive."

American legal economists may have the instinct to minimize the importance of this problem by assuming that all productive activity can occur, so that it will do no harm to encourage any activity that produces wealth compared to the activity's absence. But making that assumption effectively imports deeper assumptions about the perfection of macroeconomic factors (such as capital and labor markets) into microeconomic analyses (about, for example, the efficiency of a rule of tort or contract law). Once we recognize that macroeconomic assumptions do not hold because the macroeconomy is not perfect, we need to recognize the possibility that some activities, though wealth-creating in isolation, may crowd out activities that are even more productive. For example, while it might be good (rather than bad) for society if college graduates become manufacturers, it might be even more productive if they become scientists or doctors. That an activity is better than its absence is not a sufficient reason to promote it; we have to consider what might be better. Voltaire is paraphrased as having said, "The best is the enemy of the good," but the converse from our perspective is more important: the good may be the enemy of the better.

I consider in detail in Chapter 2 arguments that have this problem because those arguments make up a significant part of the economic understanding of tort law. The essential recognition is that even if an activity is good for society compared to its absence, private actors may have too much of an incentive to engage in that activity compared to alternatives that are *more* productive for society if the actors are driven primarily by their personal, rather than society's overall, gain. Arguments of this type also have some implications for contract law in Chapter 3. For example, economists often oppose legal rules that would prevent private contracts or their enforcement – unconscionability, rent control, minimum wages, and so on. At bottom, these arguments rest on the notion that we should not refuse to enforce private bargain contracts, because private bargain contracts are productive. The premise is generally true, but the conclusion does not follow: perhaps many contracts that we think of as unconscionable are problematic because they crowd out better types of contracts

20 Introduction and Background

from the marketplace. Everyone who puts resources into the payday-lending business is implicitly abstaining from doing something else with those resources. Without considering alternative uses of those resources in an imperfect macroeconomy, we cannot automatically rule payday lending as efficient overall just because both parties to a transaction want it to occur.

To be clear, I have not intended to offer a specific efficiency-based argument against payday lending, just a demonstration that such an argument, with for example the right empirical data, would be possible despite the abstract theory. Economics 101 does not always translate to real-world policy.[21]

1.2.5 The Terror of Costs and Externalities

The flip side of the neglect of alternatives is an argument that proceeds along the following lines: (1) a cost or externality exists; (2) therefore, the law must prevent that cost or internalize that externality.[22] One well-known argument that suffers from this type of problem is Tom Merrill and Henry Smith's defense of the *numerus clausus* principle, which would restrict the number of forms of property ownership that the law allows because the creation of novel property interests can increase information costs for third parties. For example, Merrill and Smith do not want to allow property law to recognize the right to use a wristwatch only on Mondays because, if

---

[21] *See* JAMES KWAK, ECONOMISM: BAD ECONOMICS AND THE RISE OF INEQUALITY (2017).

[22] In this book, I adopt Shavell's definition of an externality: "One party's action will be said to have an *external effect* – or to create an *externality* – if it influences, or may influence with a probability, the well-being of another person, in comparison to some standard of reference." STEVEN SHAVELL, FOUNDATIONS OF ECONOMIC ANALYSIS OF LAW 77 n.2 (2004). The concept is often misunderstood because commentators are frequently unclear whether their notion of the concept places it logically antecedent to, rather than subsequent to, a standard of reference. Shavell again puts it nicely: "[I]f in the reference situation I am quiet, then my act of making a noise would be said to create a detrimental external effect, whereas if in the reference situation I am noisy, then my being noisy would not be said to create an external effect .... Whether we tend to call an externality harmful or beneficial depends on what we are likely to assume, if only implicitly, about the standard of reference." *Id.* at 79. For a rich discussion of related questions, see Joseph Singer, *How Property Norms Construct the Externalities of Ownership, in* PROPERTY AND COMMUNITY 57 (Gregory S. Alexander & Eduardo Peñalver eds., 2009).

1.2 Some Patterns of Analytical Failures 21

it does, everyone would need to check whether an individual wristwatch is encumbered by that property right before buying it. (Owners of wristwatches clearly can license others to use their watches only on Mondays by means of contract law, but the question is whether property law should recognize that right so that it will be transferred with ownership of the watch.)

It is possible that unusual forms of property can increase the information costs that some parties face; indeed, as a definitional matter, it is certain. The size of the effect in the real world, however, may not be significant, or (as Merrill and Smith recognize) it may not outweigh the benefits of novel forms of property ownership. Probably more importantly from a practical and legal perspective, the costs that Merrill and Smith identify may already be subsumed, in context, by other costs that relevant actors already face and that the legal system already recognizes. For example, in the case of numerus clausus, while buyers of wristwatches may conceptually have more to investigate when buying a watch if the law recognizes the right to use watches only on Mondays as a new form of property ownership, in context a buyer already runs the risk that a seller may not even own the watch in the first place – a much greater risk in both probability and magnitude, and one that the law already deals with in sensible ways. To put it differently, the additional marginal risk from unusual possessory interests by which a wristwatch may or may not be encumbered is almost certain to be insignificant compared to the background risk that the seller doesn't even own the watch. I discuss this particular argument in more detail in Chapter 4, which covers property law.

1.2.6 An Emphasis on the Counterintuitive

Sometimes, as Dan Farber pointed out in the 1980s, economic argumentation fails just because it is trying too hard to be impressive or counterintuitive.[23] As a result, it sometimes obscures rather than enlightens. This problem has only grown since the 1980s. Several years

---

[23] Daniel A. Farber, *The Case Against Brilliance*, 70 Minn. L. Rev. 917 (1985).

ago, a prominent American legal journal published a paper defending the efficiency of trial by battle.[24]

One theme that ties together the various analytical patterns I have identified in this section is that, in evaluating legal-economic arguments, it is important not to be misled by an argument's technical precision about an isolated effect. The main work of the law involves integrating such effects into workable rules that accommodate factual context, the institutional capacities of courts, and private parties' abilities to adapt in surprising and unexpected ways. This is precisely what orthodox law and economics fails to do; this is why, in the end, legal-economic argumentation essentially consists of isolated legal arguments that contain some truth but, like traditional legal arguments, need to be evaluated in context against alternatives. Just as reading the last provision in a statute may undermine what seemed to be a correct interpretive conclusion until that point, adding one more variable – one more factual detail, or even the possibility of one – can entirely reverse the proper conclusions from a formal economic argument.

Differently, but relatedly, legal economics has been motivated not just by methodological innovation but also by what seems to be an intense desire to popularize the methods of economists; a reader of most of the leading early works of the movement can't escape the conclusion that its proponents were engaged in a zealous and tendentious attempt to show that economic reasoning could be relevant to law and that they could reach any result or justify any legal rule by means of economic reasoning. Perhaps this type of evangelism is understandable as a psychological matter given the skepticism of legal audiences. Such an eager application of economics is a just-so story, however, and it cannot easily direct legal policy, even if it might (appropriately or not) be influential in shaping how commentators talk about the law.

1.2.7 What to Optimize?

Finally, there is a frustrating myopia within the legal-economic project that results from the choice to optimize features of the world

---

[24] Peter T. Leeson, *Trial by Battle*, 3 J. LEGAL ANALYSIS 341 (2011) ("In a feudal world where high transaction costs confounded the Coase theorem, I argue that trial by battle allocated disputed property rights efficiently.").

1.2 Some Patterns of Analytical Failures 23

that are relatively easy to model. For a true utilitarian, nothing rules out an entirely different method from an entirely different starting point. For example, one approach could focus on education as the driver of human intellectual progress, another could focus on technological innovation, and yet another could emphasize the importance of addressing changes to the natural climate in order to ensure long-term human prosperity. Of course, many arguments and models aim precisely at these goals, but practically speaking the individual models themselves can't mediate among the different goals. Any particular consideration in one model might swamp those in other models, but to determine this we need (again, just as a practical matter) to look outside the models. So, for example, perhaps the numerus clausus principle prevents something that would be useful for addressing environmental concerns, like a conservation easement; perhaps a simple static-efficiency analysis of allocation under tort law neglects the desirable (or undesirable) effects of too little or too much liability on the rapid technological progress of self-driving cars.

In short, legal economists' clear directive to optimize "human welfare" is not backed up by particular tools that allow us to do so, at least not in terms as broadly as they would recognize is necessary if the economic project can be justified in the first place. The feeling one gets is as if one has been asked to make sure the horses in the stable are achieving their full potential, but the tools one is given for achieving that goal are nothing but some grain and a cattle prod. Nothing in theory forecloses the development of better tools, but the enthusiasm for legal analysis grounded in economic theory should be tempered by the limitations of today's economic theory.

Bob Cooter, a leading American legal economist, introduces the tension between different possible approaches to optimization very nicely in a relatively recent article:

> After years of parish work, a Catholic priest sat up in bed one morning and thought, "Maybe the Pope is wrong and Buddha is right." After years of teaching and writing about economic efficiency and the law, I sat up in bed one morning and thought, "Maybe efficiency is wrong and innovation is right." The effects on human welfare from inventing the tractor far exceed the effects from more efficient allocation

of horses. Innovation causes compound growth that swamps static inefficiency like a tsunami swamps a scow.[25]

That type of recognition, and a hundred other considerations, are needed to make legal decisions properly. That is what lawyers – at least, those lawyers not bound to formalism – were aiming to do before the Chicago-style law-and-economics movement came along.

---

[25] Robert Cooter, *The Falcon's Gyre: Legal Foundations of Economic Innovation and Growth* (2013), www.law.berkeley.edu/library/resources/cooter.pdf [https://perma.cc/7BWK-DLU7].

2 TORT LAW

Legal scholars often treat tort law as the crown jewel of the law-and-economics movement. "The law of accidents was one of the first bodies of private law successfully analyzed using formal economic models,"[1] a leading law-and-economics textbook confidently declares. Even commentators who are critical of legal economics commonly suggest that tort law has succumbed to fairly straightforward economic modeling.[2] Exactly the opposite is true.

The conventional wisdom that tort law is particularly amenable to simple economic analysis should seem surprising even at first glance. Does anyone focus their attention on tort law when crossing the street, riding a bicycle, or even driving a car? Are incentives from the rules articulated in court opinions about tort law – even if, counterfactually, they weren't complicated and inconsistent as a doctrinal matter – likely to be understood by most people and then implemented reliably?

And tort law as an academic and practical subject, as organized in the treatises and as applied by courts and practitioners, doesn't seem on the surface to have an affinity to economic methods – and it certainly doesn't seem like the subject that would be *most* amenable to those methods. For example, those who study and practice corporate law benefit more obviously and directly from financial and economic expertise, and contract law concerns the voluntary economic dealings of parties, a feature of human behavior that economists emphasize and often study.

---

[1] ROBERT COOTER & THOMAS ULEN, LAW & ECONOMICS 324 (5th ed. 2008).

[2] *E.g.*, Leo Katz, *A Look at Tort Law with Criminal Law Blinders*, 76 B.U. L. REV. 307, 308 (1996) (resisting a solely economic view in criminal law but referring to "law and economics' admittedly remarkable success at explaining tort law").

26 Tort Law

Most of the purported success of the law-and-economics movement in analyzing tort law comes from its apparent ability to cast the fundamental legal standard of negligence in economic terms. This success, however, is an illusion. On one hand, the movement's analysis of negligence isn't even really economic in most relevant respects. While this point may amount only to a dispute over definitions, it is important to recognize that a lot of what passes for economic reasoning in law has very little to do with economics and has much more to do with what is regarded as conventional legal analysis. Indeed, on reflection it seems like a lot of the illusory progress that the law-and-economics movement has made in tort law comes from the fact that Judge Learned Hand, in the famous *Carroll Towing* opinion, happened to express a fairly conventional negligence decision using an algebraic structure! On the other hand, as an analytical matter the movement almost entirely fails to justify the negligence standard, which we might regard as the core architectural feature of at least one of the most significant parts of tort law.

This chapter begins with a discussion of that fundamental negligence standard – the basic questions of whether tort liability should depend on bad behavior and, if so, what counts as bad behavior. This discussion is lengthy because the negligence standard is so fundamental and because the errors that the movement makes in this regard are important for understanding several of this book's remaining arguments. The rest of the chapter addresses legal tort doctrines more focused than the general negligence standard.

At the outset, several general observations may be helpful. First, despite the broad claims of success in this area by legal economists and the movement's influence on teaching tort law (and, for example, on the American Law Institute's *Restatement of the Law (Third) of Torts: Liability for Physical and Emotional Harm*), general economic analysis has in fact barely been influential in the way American courts analyze negligence.[3] Second, perhaps the most obvious explanation of this practical failure is the simple observation, as suggested earlier, that in most cases of potential personal injuries, the fundamental premises

---

[3] *See* Richard W. Wright, *Hand, Posner, and the Myth of the "Hand Formula,"* 4 THEORETICAL INQ. L. 145 (2003).

2.1 Negligence and Strict Liability

of the economic analysis of tort law simply don't apply. Drivers don't respond, except in loosely attenuated ways, to the incentives that tort law provides; fear of increased insurance premiums may prevent some dangerous driving, but significantly more influential is simply most people's instinct or desire not to die or be seriously injured in a car crash. Retailers might mop up messes from their floors because they care in part about slip-and-fall tort liability, or at least about increased liability-insurance costs, but messes on the floor also deter customers and are unpleasant for employees. City or school administrators might worry that an unsafe seesaw in a playground might lead to lawsuits, but they also probably don't like the idea of hurting children even apart from any financial incentives they face, and they probably care as much or more about a public or political outcry from parents than they do about their employer's (or their employer's insurer's) potential financial liability.

As with the rest of the arguments in this book, though, my main goal is not to make the general point that economic arguments adopt straightforwardly false assumptions – here, the notion that actors directly respond to tort law's incentives or that they are driven primarily by a desire to avoid legal judgments rather than by physical self-preservation, moral concerns, or political pressure. Instead, the rest of the arguments in this chapter raise analytical critiques that assume, just for the sake of the argument, that all or at least most of these assumptions may hold. That said, the next section's argument is a hybrid of these approaches, as explained generally in that section: it responds to a leading argument (or perhaps more accurately an argumentative framework) that fails to degrade gracefully when its assumptions are even slightly incorrect.

2.1 NEGLIGENCE AND STRICT LIABILITY

The most significant fundamental question in tort law is whether legal liability for causing harms should depend on bad behavior (a principle known as *negligence*) or whether actors may be liable even if they have done everything right (a principle known as *strict liability*). For the purpose of this section's discussion, I focus on physical injuries and property damage, but the conceptual problem generalizes to any kind of harm.

2.1.1 Basic Economic Features of Negligence and Strict Liability

An example that has become conventional in tort law, as a result of its use by Ronald Coase,[4] involves a railroad that passes by a field and potentially causes damage to the field because of sparks from its engine. I borrow Robert Cooter's formulation of the example for ease of exposition because I will later take up Professor Cooter's arguments (among others) at length:

> Suppose that Xavier operates a railroad train that emits sparks that sometimes set fire to Yvonne's cornfield. Xavier can reduce the harm to the corn by installing spark arresters, by running the trains more slowly, or by running fewer trains. In a like manner, Yvonne can reduce the harm by planting her corn farther from the tracks, by planting cabbage instead of corn, or by leaving the fields fallow.[5]

In this example, there is potential harm that results, at least in some senses,[6] from the interaction between Xavier and Yvonne's business activities. A rule of *no liability* would make Yvonne, the owner of the cornfield, bear the entire cost of the harmful interaction by preventing her from recovering any money from Xavier in the event of damage to her cornfields. A rule of *strict liability*, by contrast, would make Xavier bear the entire cost of the interaction by requiring that he pay Yvonne for any harm she incurs as a result of the railroad's sparks. A rule of *negligence*, in contrast to both other rules, would make Xavier responsible for paying Yvonne only if some social judgment disapproves of Xavier's actions in running his railroad next to Yvonne's cornfields in a way that potentially hurts Yvonne.

A chief feature of the economic analysis of tort law is the economic conception of negligence rules – that is, the reduction of such rules to

---

[4] R.H. Coase, *The Problem of Social Cost*, 3 J.L. & ECON. 1, 29–31 (1960).

[5] Robert Cooter, *Unity in Tort, Contract, and Property: The Model of Precaution*, 73 CAL. L. REV. 1, 4 (1985).

[6] According to what Mark Kelman has called "the most basic Coasean insight," no cases of tortious harm occur without both parties in some sense causing the harm because, at a minimum, the harm can't occur without both of their existence. Mark Kelman, *The Necessary Myth of Objective Causation Judgments in Liberal Political Theory*, 63 CHI.-KENT L. REV. 579, 579 (1987) ("[G]iven that ... injury cannot have occurred unless the plaintiff ... *existed*, ... it will *never* be the case that injury could occur without the plaintiff, such that the defendant is entirely *causally* responsible.").

2.1 Negligence and Strict Liability

a cost-benefit test. This particular formulation, whose popularity is commonly traced to an opinion by Learned Hand,[7] *United States v. Carroll Towing*,[8] would decide Xavier's liability by analyzing the costs and benefits of the precautions he might have taken (in the example, "installing spark arresters, ... running the trains more slowly, or ... running fewer trains").[9] As an example, if the potential sparks from the railroad are estimated to cause fires that lead to $4,000 worth of expected damage to Yvonne's cornfield, Xavier would be liable if *any* of the precautions he might take are expected to cost less than $4,000. If not, he won't be liable.[10]

Analyzed from society's perspective (rather than either Xavier's or Yvonne's private perspectives), economists point out that we want Xavier to take precautions only if their social cost (their total cost to society) is less than their social benefit (their total benefit to society). That is, even though it seems harsh to say so, there is some sense in which we *want* Yvonne's cornfield to burn down if it is too expensive to prevent fires. Of course, in an ideal world we wouldn't want to see Yvonne suffer this harm, but given the real-world choice between cornfield fires and the precautions necessary to prevent them, for reasons of efficiency we prefer whichever is cheaper.[11] Or, as Richard Posner, one of the leading proponents of this efficiency-oriented view, puts it:

---

[7] *E.g.*, Richard A. Posner, *A Theory of Negligence*, 1 J. LEGAL STUD. 29, 32 (1972) ("The essential clue [to the economic analysis of tort law] is provided by Judge Learned Hand's famous formulation of the negligence standard....").

[8] 159 F.2d 169 (2d Cir. 1947).

[9] Cooter, *supra* note 5, at 4.

[10] There are several significant problems with even this simple formulation of the negligence standard. See Section 2.1.5 for a more complete discussion.

[11] Nothing, certainly, mandates that we analyze this scenario only from the perspective of efficiency. For instance, we might think it is unfair to let Xavier cause fires for which he doesn't have to pay. But the instrumental economic view does capture an important insight, which is that Xavier and Yvonne are in some sense symmetric: if the law made Xavier pay for his fires' harm to Yvonne, then Yvonne's choice to grow cornfields would have caused harm to Xavier. And it may not be fair, always, to require Xavier to suffer this harm.

In any event, because my purpose here is to show that the economic accounts of negligence fail on roughly their own terms, I do not dwell here on the noneconomic problems with viewing all legal rules too instrumentally.

30   Tort Law

> If the cost of safety measures or of curtailment – whichever cost is lower – exceeds the benefit in accident avoidance to be gained by incurring that cost, society would be better off, in economic terms, to forgo accident prevention.[12]

Consider how no-liability, strict-liability, and negligence rules fare under this view of efficiency. If Xavier is *never* liable for fires regardless of how much damage they cause, and if he is entirely selfish and entirely profit-oriented, he will have insufficient incentives to take precautions against fire. For instance, it could cost him only $40 to install spark arresters, but he might not want to incur this expense even if fires are expected to cause many thousands of dollars of harm to Yvonne's fields. There may of course be many reasons why Xavier, if he were a real person, would in practice bear a small expense even if the law doesn't require him to do so. He might, for example, have internalized moral norms, be afraid of feeling guilty for hurting Yvonne, empathize with Yvonne or have positive feelings for her, be concerned about adverse publicity, fear retaliatory action by Yvonne, or even consume corn personally and worry that the price of corn will rise if he repeatedly burns down Yvonne's fields. But if he is both selfish and interested only in maximizing his business profits as modeled in the example, it is accurate to say that he won't have proper incentives to take efficient precautions against potentially catastrophic losses.

It may be useful to pause briefly in order to recognize that, in trying to convey the model's conclusions, I have already blurred non-economic reasons with economic reasons that are simply excluded by the particular model. Legal economists intend to exclude the possibility that actors have internalized moral norms or experience empathy with potential victims; if they consider those factors, then they are just describing humans in all their richness and, I believe they would admit, cannot make much progress with their analytical methods. They might try to model morality or empathy as a cost and resort to vague notions that everything humans do must in some sense enhance their "utility," economically conceived, but that is nothing more than a tautological just-so story; it amounts to the proposition that humans act in the ways they act, and if we accept that we might as well abandon most of the

---

[12] Posner, *supra* note 7, at 32.

2.1 Negligence and Strict Liability

stronger conclusions of the law-and-economics movement altogether. But the legal economists do *not* intend to exclude, for all time, many of the other factors I listed that might cause Xavier to take what the model under discussion would treat as inefficient precautions: concerns about retaliation from Yvonne, an interest in the price of corn, adverse publicity, and so on. These are all economic features of the situation themselves that economists would like to think they could model but are excluding in order, as I believe they see it, to make incremental progress in a larger project of producing better and more comprehensive models. In other words, any honest economist would need to admit that we can't derive solid legal conclusions from a single model alone; the economists are emphasizing a *tendency*, all else equal, or an isolated effect, or else they are taking one feature at a time in order to understand it better. That is, after all, how the "hard" sciences have progressed. The problem is that the analogy to hard science fails because there is little or no opportunity for empirical refinement; at some level all are doing by discussing Xavier and Yvonne is specifying an abstract truth about abstract parties in a very limited situation. There is in fact no reason to exclude the other economic factors I have listed, or even more: the concern that fires to a cornfield will spread to the tracks and destroy them; concerns about air pollution from the fires; the worry that passengers or staff on the trains will be alarmed by causing fires or object to doing so; and so on. Nothing suggests any of these economic factors are less important than the ones the economists are focusing on at any particular moment.[13]

---

[13] In a different context and with a different purpose, Alexander Pope summarized well in his *Essay on Criticism* a pattern that I think applies to the law-and-economics movement in view of what those in the movement regarded as its early successes:

> Fired at first sight with what the Muse imparts,
> In fearless youth we tempt the heights of Arts;
> [...]
> So pleased at first the towering Alps we try,
> Mount o'er the vales, and seem to tread the sky;
> The eternal snows appear already past,
> And the first clouds and mountains seem the last;
> But those attained, we tremble to survey
> The growing labours of the lengthened way;
> The increasing prospect tires our wandering eyes,
> Hills peep o'er hills, and Alps on Alps arise!

In any event, returning to the simple model, which assumes Xavier is both rational and that he cares about only one particular economic effect, consider next a rule of *negligence*, under which Xavier is made to pay for the costs of fires only if he is judged to be negligent or unreasonable. The main innovation of the early economic analysis of negligence rules was that they depend on whether Xavier took efficient precautions:[14] Xavier is called negligent (or unreasonable) if he didn't take socially efficient precautions, and he's called nonnegligent (or reasonable) otherwise. For example, if spark arresters could have prevented $4,000 fires at a cost of $40, and if Xavier does not install spark arresters, he is said to be negligent for not doing so. But if the spark arresters (and all the other precautions) cost more than $4,000, he is not negligent for failing to take precautions. I will say more about the Hand formula from the *Carroll Towing* case later, but for now it is sufficient to understand it simply as a semiformal expression that Xavier is negligent if and only if he fails to take cost-justified precautions. If Xavier is made to pay only when he is negligent, then he may have an incentive to take efficient precautions.

Recall that from the perspective of social efficiency, we want Xavier to take efficient precautions and do not want him to take inefficient ones. Because a negligence rule appears to give Xavier incentives to take efficient precautions and not to take inefficient ones, the early economic analysts of law presented it as an efficient rule. For instance, as Posner wrote:

> If ... the benefits in accident avoidance exceed the costs of prevention, society is better off if those costs are incurred and the accident averted, and so [injurers are] made liable, in the expectation that self-interest will lead [them] to adopt the precautions in order to avoid a greater cost in tort judgments.[15]

From the way the early legal economists presented negligence rules, it was possible to infer that their instrumental analysis supported those rules and only those rules (versus rules of no liability or strict liability). For instance, early in the economic analysis of law, Posner wrote as follows:

---

[14] *See* Posner, *supra* note 7, at 32.
[15] *Id.* at 33.

2.1 Negligence and Strict Liability

> A rule making [an] enterprise liable for the accidents that occur [when precautions are more expensive than accidents] cannot be justified on the ground that it will induce the enterprise to increase the safety of its operations.[16]

That is, Posner seems to be saying that negligence rules are sufficient to ensure that potential injurers like Xavier behave efficiently, and as a result rules like strict liability are unnecessary.

But even early on, economic analysts of law recognized that negligence rules and strict-liability rules provided similar incentives to injurers. To see why this is so, recall that a negligence rule gives Xavier an incentive to spend $40, but not $8,000, on spark arresters that prevent $4,000 fires. A strict-liability rule does the same thing, however. Under a rule of strict liability, Xavier will be liable for *all* cornfield fires that his railroads cause, regardless of their costs and the costs of various precautions. So Xavier will have to pay both (1) the costs of any precautions he takes and (2) the costs of the fires. Given that he faces both these costs, he will have incentives to take efficient precautions. For instance, if spark arresters cost $40 but fires cost $4,000, he will need to pay only $40 if he installs the spark arresters but $4,000 if he does not. And if spark arresters cost $8,000 but fires still cost $4,000, he will need to pay $8,000 if he installs the spark arresters but only $4,000 otherwise. As a result, he has incentives to take precautions only when they are efficient.

In other words, it is indeed true that a rule of strict liability (compared to negligence) "cannot be justified on the ground that it will induce [injurers] to increase the safety of [their] operations."[17] But it is *also* true that negligence itself cannot be justified in that way (compared to strict liability). The two rules are just as good at providing efficient incentives to injurers, at least when they are applied to the schematic representation of injuries with which we have been dealing.

The early legal economists recognized this symmetry. Posner saw it clearly as early as 1973, when he wrote: "Economic theory provides no basis, in general, for preferring strict liability to negligence, or negligence to strict liability, provided that some version of a contributory

---

[16] *Id.*
[17] *Id.*

negligence defense is recognized."[18] This was true, as Posner also recognized fairly early, even after considering the effects of negligence rules and strict-liability rules on the costs of adjudication.[19]

Accordingly, the early economic analysis of law appears to justify the proposition that *either* strict-liability or negligence rules are better than rules of no liability. Of course, this proposition is uncontroversial; few were seriously arguing in the 1960s and 1970s for a complete absence of tort liability (or for some other standard far less than negligence liability) – although it is worth pointing out that in fact many areas of tort law do exempt injurers from liability on grounds that, as we will see, economists have defended in other terms.[20] But we can perhaps read the early economic analysis generously to spell out clear efficiency-related reasons for why we should have some tort liability at all.

Beyond this basic observation, however, that early analysis offered less than commentators sometimes suppose. Posner and others believed,[21] and generally still believe,[22] that this early form of economic analysis of tort law demands, from the point of view of social efficiency, that we conceive of the negligence standard in terms of the Hand formula. To make this point clear, it is important to distinguish two possible normative conclusions from the kind of economic analysis I have discussed in this section so far.

First, the analysis purports to address the choice between no liability, negligence, and strict liability. As I have noted, the analysis is correct, at least on its own terms, if it means to suggest that rules of negligence *or* strict liability are superior to a complete absence of tort liability (at least to the extent that the tort regime aims to govern the conduct of injurers).

---

[18] Richard A. Posner, *Strict Liability: A Comment*, 2 J. LEGAL STUD. 205, 221 (1973).

[19] RICHARD A. POSNER, ECONOMIC ANALYSIS OF LAW 442 (2d ed. 1977) ("No clear-cut prediction of the impact on the aggregate costs of the procedural system of substituting strict for negligence liability emerges from our analysis.").

[20] Some commentators have suggested that historically, tort law imposed liability less often than it does today because of the prevalence of "no duty" rules and other roadblocks to recovery. *See, e.g.*, Robert L. Rabin, *The Historical Development of the Fault Principle: A Reinterpretation*, 15 GA. L. REV. 925 (1981).

[21] *See* Posner, *supra* note 7, at 32 (referring to the Hand Formula as "one of the few attempts to give content" to the negligence standard).

[22] *See generally* RICHARD A. POSNER, ECONOMIC ANALYSIS OF LAW 167–71 (7th ed. 2007).

2.1 Negligence and Strict Liability 35

Second, the analysis purports to give *form* to negligence rules by observing that under the Hand formula, negligence rules give injurers incentives to take efficient precaution. But this purported conclusion is only partially correct. It is true (under the economic model's logic) that a standard of negligence that requires *less* than the Hand formula would be inefficient, at least in the schematic situations we have considered involving Xavier and Yvonne. For example, if spark arresters cost $3,000, fires cost $4,000, and the legal standard for negligence liability calls Xavier reasonable (or nonnegligent) based on an arbitrary decision that nobody need install spark arresters on railroads, then Xavier will not have incentives to install (efficient) spark arresters. To put it differently, such a legal standard would be insufficient because it falls below the standard of the Hand formula.

But a legal standard that exceeded, or perhaps even just tended to exceed, the Hand formula could well be efficient. If spark arresters cost $5,000 and fires cost $4,000, but the legal standard for negligence liability calls Xavier reasonable only if he spends $5,000 or more on spark arresters, then he would still prefer to pay for the fires than for the (inefficient) spark arresters. More generally, a negligence standard based on broad social judgments (rather than narrower cost-benefit tests) can give injurers efficient incentives if those social judgments tend to require more precaution than a more limited cost-benefit test would suggest, thereby imposing a standard that is in some sense between negligence and strict liability. For instance, consider a social judgment that it's wrong, without a significant overriding justification, to cause preventable fires through industrial activity.[23] Based on that judgment and the numeric figures I used earlier, a tort regime that holds Xavier liable for all preventable fires caused by his railroad can be just as efficient – again, in the terms of the economic model we're discussing – as a tort regime based exclusively on an economically conceived negligence rule.[24]

---

[23] *Cf.* Stephen G. Gilles, *Inevitable Accident in Classical English Tort Law*, 43 EMORY L.J. 575 (1994) (suggesting that old English law imposed liability for accidents that could have been prevented, rather than imposing liability only for those that *should* have been prevented).

[24] My point in the text, more strictly, is that it is *possible* for a tort regime with a higher standard than that of a negligence regime to be efficient. Not all such regimes are necessarily efficient, however. Cooter and Ulen, in their textbook, give one reason a legal regime with a standard higher than that of negligence could be inefficient: it could encourage excess precaution when the legal standard is slightly higher than that of the negligence standard,

36   Tort Law

Accordingly, what the early economic analysis of law justified, even if all its assumptions about human behavior were correct and even if it were appropriate to exclude all economic factors outside the analysis's ambit, is less than is often imagined. On its own terms, the early analysis justified only two propositions: (1) that either negligence or strict liability can give injurers efficient incentives and (2) that an efficient negligence standard needs to be *at least* as strict as the Hand formula, but it could well be stricter. In short, the early economic analysis told us why we need a legal standard that is *at least* as strict as negligence liability, but it told us little more than this. Of course, this point was probably not controversial; it is not clear that anyone had seriously been arguing for a modern negligence standard that was significantly weaker than the Hand formula – that is, that would have permitted a defendant in a tort suit to say, "I recognize that I am subject to a negligence standard and that there was a precaution I could have taken relatively easily, but I am not negligent for failing to take it even though my failure caused great harm."

But while the early economic analysis justifies a liability rule that imposes *at least* that standard, it is important to recognize that it would be a mistake to take the early analysis as even slightly suggesting that *no greater* a standard would be efficient. The early economic analysis is compatible with many possible negligence standards, as long as they provide liability when a Hand formula analysis would. (Again, it is worth pointing out that many areas of tort law do indeed have a weaker standard than simple negligence; for example, no-duty rules and heightened duty requirements mean that even wrongdoers who cause harm pay no liability for doing so – and there may well be justifications, including economic justifications, for that state of affairs.)

---

because injurers would prefer to pay for slightly excess precautions rather than to pay for lower precautions plus the expected cost of accidents. *See* COOTER & ULEN, *supra* note 1, at 356. Cooter and Ulen's conclusion appears to be too strong, however. They conclude that "[i]n general, [the] injurer's precaution responds exactly to court errors in setting the legal standard under a negligence regime." *id.* However, if the legal standard of conduct exceeds what they call the "social optimum" standard sufficiently, it will typically be more efficient for injurers to conform to the social optimal standard than to the legal standard.

2.1 Negligence and Strict Liability

2.1.2 The Modern Formal Economic Conceptions of Negligence

In contrast to the early economic analysis discussed so far, the arguments at the center of modern economic discussions of tort law (and therefore a significant part of tort-law discussions in the United States) are substantially more complex. They aim to address a wider range of problems and to provide more specific recommendations concerning when injurers should or shouldn't be liable for the harms they cause.

Robert Cooter and Steven Shavell have rearticulated, in slightly different ways, the leading modern analysis of negligence rules. These rules depend on the recognition that many tort cases potentially demand *bilateral precaution*, which means that both injurers and victims (Xavier and Yvonne) can take steps to reduce the likelihood or severity of accidents. Recall that in Cooter's example, "Xavier can reduce the harm to the corn by installing spark arresters, by running the trains more slowly, or by running fewer trains. In a like manner, Yvonne can reduce the harm by planting her corn farther from the tracks, by planting cabbage instead of corn, or by leaving the fields fallow."[25]

Not all cases involve bilateral precaution, but it is a feature of many cases – more than most students initially suppose when presented with the idea. A pedestrian afraid of being hit by cars can avoid walking on sidewalks; a homeowner afraid of airplanes falling from the sky can live in a location where fewer airplanes pass overhead; and so forth. In saying that a case involves bilateral precaution, there is no inherent moral or normative judgment; for instance, when economists say that

---

[25] Cooter, *supra* note 5, at 4. The economic model that forms the basis of both Cooter's and Shavell's restatements of the reasons that negligence rules are efficient in cases of bilateral precaution appears to originate with John Prather Brown, *Toward an Economic Theory of Liability*, 2 J. LEGAL STUD. 323 (1973). Brown recognized, interestingly, some features of the fragility of his model. For instance, he observed: "The standard of care is critical, for, when it was changed to [a particular alternative formulation], the identity between equilibrium and optimality was destroyed." *id.* at 347. For ease of exposition, and to ensure that I respond to arguments in the forms in which they remain influential, I address my discussion of bilateral precaution in the text to Cooter's and Shavell's more recent formulations.

For further notes on the history of the economic analysis that informs modern academic understanding of tort law, see STEVEN SHAVELL, FOUNDATIONS OF ECONOMIC ANALYSIS OF LAW 192–93 (2004).

38   Tort Law

pedestrians can walk more safely, this does not mean, on its own, that a pedestrian *should* do so or is *at fault* for not doing so.[26] To an economist, normative judgments depend on costs. Accordingly, a pedestrian should, as a general matter, walk more safely if doing so is less expensive, overall, than asking drivers to drive more safely. Whether it is cheaper might, of course, depend on complicated and possibly subjective social calculations.

In this section, I first lay out the modern economic understanding of tort rules by explaining and elaborating Cooter's and Shavell's analysis. This understanding is based on two principles: (1) that negligence rules provide bilateral threats of liability and (2) that activity levels can generally inform liability decisions. Then I respond to the argument that negligence rules provide efficient bilateral threats of liability, demonstrating that the economic models that underlie the leading economic understanding are exceedingly fragile and almost impossible to apply – as I described briefly earlier in Chapter 1. Next, I respond to the argument that activity levels can serve as a principled way to assign the costs of accidents between two innocent parties, showing that modern activity-levels arguments are both narrow and unadministrable. Finally, I address further problems that apply generally to the Hand formula and similar attempts to conceive negligence solely using economic models.

Bilateral Liability Threats

As suggested earlier, the term *bilateral precaution* can refer to two slightly different concepts, and it is important to keep them separate. Consider again the case of Xavier (an injurer) and Yvonne (a victim). In the example we have been using, both Xavier and Yvonne can take precautions against railroad fires, and in that sense the *available* precautions are bilateral. But ordinarily, economic analysis of bilateral-precaution cases assumes that the case has an additional property – namely, that the *optimal* mix of precautions to be taken in a given situation includes

---

[26] British comedian Jimmy Carr has used this distinction as a source of dark humor. Discussing drunk driving, he says: "I think the people that make the drink-driving ads should be forced to make an advert aimed specifically at pedestrians, simply saying, 'Pedestrians: Watch where you're going; some of us have had a drink.'" Jimmy Carr, *Jimmy Carr: Comedian* (2007).

2.1 Negligence and Strict Liability

some measures that Xavier should take and others that Yvonne should take.[27] For example, given the optimal set of precautions that can be taken, some may be in the injurer's exclusive control and others may be in the victim's exclusive control – or perhaps the injurer will be able to take at least one of the optimal precautions more cheaply than the victim, and the victim will be able to take at least one of the optimal precautions more cheaply than the injurer.[28] Throughout this section, when I refer to cases of bilateral precaution, I refer to the second kind of case, rather than just those where bilateral precaution is *possible*.

In bilateral-precaution cases, it is easy to see that rules of either strict liability or no liability will, on economic grounds, come up short. This is because rules of strict liability give incentives for injurers (but not victims) to take precautions, and rules of no liability give incentives for victims (but not injurers) to take precautions. For example, in the case of Xavier the railroader and Yvonne the cornfield owner, a rule of strict liability would place the whole cost of fires on Xavier, leading him to take precautions (spark arresters, slower trains, or fewer trains) against fires if it is efficient for him to do so; by contrast, a rule of no liability would place the whole cost of fires on Yvonne, leading her to take precautions (growing corn further away from the tracks, growing a crop more resistant to fires, or not growing anything) against them if it is efficient for her to do so. But in neither case will *both* Xavier and Yvonne – assuming again that they are purely rational and self-interested, and assuming again that they have no other incentives – take precautions against fires.

The modern formal economic conception of negligence rules in tort law attempts to address this problem. In short, the modern economic understanding of negligence rules is that they provide efficient

---

[27] *See, e.g.,* SHAVELL, *supra* note 25, at 182–83 ("[E]xamples can obviously be constructed in which it is optimal only for injurers to take care or only for victims to take care (or for neither to do so). These possibilities are not the focus [of the bilateral-precaution discussion]."); COOTER & ULEN, *supra* note 1, at 341 ("[W]e consider the case in which *both* the victim and injurer *can* take precaution, and efficiency *requires* both of them to take it. We call this condition the assumption of *bilateral precaution.*").

[28] *See* Cooter, *supra* note 5, at 6 n.16 ("Some efficient precautions may cost less when taken by one party or the other. Precaution is bilateral when at least one such precaution for each party exists.").

40   Tort Law

incentives to *both* parties by making both think that they may be liable
if they don't live up to their efficient standard of care. As Cooter says:

> [T]he paradox [of encouraging both Xavier and Yvonne to behave
> efficiently] can be resolved by adopting fault [i.e., negligence] rules
> that assign responsibility for harm according to the fault of the par-
> ties. To illustrate, a simple negligence rule requires the victim to be
> compensated by the injurer if, and only if, the latter is at fault. Under
> a simple negligence rule, Xavier will satisfy the legal standard in order
> to avoid liability. Thus, if the legal standard corresponds to the effi-
> cient level of precaution, Xavier's precaution will be efficient. Since
> Yvonne knows that she bears residual responsibility, she internalizes
> the costs and benefits of precaution; therefore, her incentives are effi-
> cient. Thus, if the legal standard of fault corresponds to the efficient
> level of care, both parties will take efficient precaution.[29]

Shavell puts it similarly:

> As in the unilateral model, if the courts choose due care to equal the
> socially optimal level [i.e., if negligence is set via the Hand formula],
> then injurers will be led to take due care. Victims too will be induced
> to take the optimal level of care because they will bear their losses
> if injurers take due care. (Drivers will be led to take due care; and
> knowing that they will bear their losses, bicyclists [that the drivers
> might hit] will decide to take appropriate care.)[30]

In other words, a negligence rule appears to encourage injurers to take
whatever precautions are efficient for them to take. But then, because
victims will expect injurers to take these precautions and thus avoid
liability, the victims will fear that they're going to suffer the costs of
accidents themselves. As a result, the victims, too, will take efficient
precautions.

For those without economic training, what economists mean when
they refer to some precautions that victims can take may seem counterintuitive. Why is it a "precaution" for Yvonne, for example, to
avoid growing anything in her fields at all? The answer is that by not
growing corn, she prevents any social waste that comes from investing in corn. A fire to an empty field might well cause no "harm."

---

[29] *Id.* at 6–7.
[30] SHAVELL, *supra* note 25, at 185–86.

2.1 Negligence and Strict Liability 41

By not planting anything in her field, Yvonne is able to remove the possibility that fires caused by trains will cause her to waste money in growing corn that will simply be burned down. Of course, by not planting anything, Yvonne presumably suffers some loss because her field isn't being put to productive use. But to an economist, this loss is exactly the same kind of loss that Xavier himself would suffer by having to install spark arresters (or to run fewer trains). In other words, Xavier and Yvonne interact to cause a social loss. Stripped of all moral dimensions and other kinds of social judgments, both parties simply face potential costs from two sources: (1) planning in advance of an accident in order to reduce the expected harm from it, and (2) either harm from the accident (in Yvonne's case) or a requirement to pay for harm from the accident (in Xavier's case).[31]

An example of the economists' overall argument about negligence rules' effects on bilateral precaution may be helpful here. Suppose that in the case of Xavier and Yvonne, two precautions are said to be optimal: as the cheapest mix of accident-avoidance and harm-avoidance, imagine that it is efficient (1) for Xavier to install spark arresters at a cost of $1,200 and (2) for Yvonne to avoid planting corn within 10 feet of the railroad track and instead to install nonflammable rubber in that space at a cost of $800 (which includes both the cost of the rubber and the cost of the forgone corn). Why would such a mix be optimal? Just for the sake of the hypothetical, suppose that fires are hugely expensive, causing $40,000 worth of damages. Now, suppose also that if Yvonne didn't leave a buffer of 10 feet, Xavier would have

---

[31] Brown's formalization of the case he describes is a clear and helpful aid to the intuitions that underlie economists' understanding of the bilateral tort model:

> Consider a small device, a black box, which is attached to some otherwise useful object such as a railway crossing, an airplane, or a sidewalk. The only function of the device is to emit a bill for a large amount of money from time to time, so we shall call it a liability generator....
>
> On the liability generator are two controls, X and Y.... Increasing either or both increases the probability that the accident will be avoided.... Examples of what will be meant here by controls are built-in safety devices and careful driving in the railway crossing case, defect-free radar and careful flying in the airplane case, and shoveling snow and careful walking in the sidewalk case.

Brown, *supra* note 25, at 324. The description shows the economic symmetries between victims and injurers in a case of bilateral precaution.

42 Tort Law

to install super-safe spark arresters at a cost of $8,000 in order to prevent fires. But suppose, conversely, that if Xavier didn't install any spark arresters, Yvonne would have to leave a buffer of 50 feet, at a cost of $6,000 (as a result of the greater amount of forgone corn), to prevent the huge costs of fires. Given this mix, the particular efficient state of affairs is for both Xavier and Yvonne to spend some money on precautions. This itself is not unrealistic. For example, if drivers never stop for pedestrians, it may be hard to find a time or place to cross a road safely; if pedestrians are constantly in the road, it will be hard for drivers to use the road at all; but if there is a set of rules that coordinates drivers and pedestrians, each group can be better off and achieve their goals at a relatively modest cost in many situations.

According to Cooter and Shavell, under a negligence regime both Xavier and Yvonne can be encouraged to take efficient precautions. This is because, if the legal standards for negligence are set correctly, they believe both Xavier and Yvonne will be afraid of suffering the $40,000 harm from fires if they don't take the relatively cheap – and, more importantly, optimal – precautions available to them. So they both will do so, and together they will create a social surplus (over other scenarios in which money is wasted either on precautions or on fires).

It sounds attractive enough: the negligence rules provide the same sort of coordination, perhaps, as traffic signals do for drivers and pedestrians in my earlier example. And on the surface, the models appear to work out the way that Cooter and Shavell suggest. But beneath the surface, the models face significant technical problems that prevent them from being applied determinatively in at least many kinds of tort cases. I will describe those problems in due course. But first, it will be helpful to explain the other central features of the modern understanding of liability rules in tort law.

Residual Liability

Even if negligence rules could be implemented in a way that encourages efficient bilateral precaution, there remains an incompleteness in the model: what happens when both parties live up to their efficient standard of care? Just as under the early, straightforward economic models, which suggested that both negligence rules and strict-liability

2.1 Negligence and Strict Liability

rules could encourage efficient precaution, the bilateral-precaution model is consistent with assigning the cost of accidents either to injurers or to victims when both act reasonably.

To see why this is so, consider that an ordinary rule of negligence is symmetric with a rule of "strict liability with a defense of contributory negligence."[32] If a rule of simple negligence encourages an injurer to take precautions, and then encourages a victim to take precautions because the injurer avoids liability and leaves the victim holding the bill, then a rule of strict liability combined with contributory negligence can do something very similar, but opposite in one important way. Specifically, it can serve as a threat of liability to both parties, causing both of them to behave efficiently, but then leave the injurer (instead of the victim) responsible for any harms that occur.[33]

So, in our last example, Xavier and Yvonne might both be encouraged to take small precautions. But if a large spark occurs from the railroad and causes a fire anyway, Yvonne will suffer the harm under a negligence rule: both parties met their standard, and Yvonne cannot claim in court that Xavier was negligent. Under a strict-liability regime that incorporates a defense of contributory negligence, by contrast, Xavier will have to pay for Yvonne's harm in such a case.

Given this symmetry, how can we distinguish among the potential rules? Indeed, there aren't just two possible rules. In addition to (1) negligence and (2) strict liability with a defense of contributory negligence, other possibilities that lead to similar results (because they all achieve bilateral liability threats in theory in the same way) are (3) negligence with a defense of contributory negligence and (4) comparative negligence.[34] Perhaps surprisingly, the economic analysis of all these rules – including comparative negligence – is essentially the same, at

---

[32] COOTER & ULEN, *supra* note 1, at 346; *see also* SHAVELL, *supra* note 25, at 184–87.

[33] The liability threats under such a regime work as follows: the victim will take efficient precautions knowing that if they don't, they will be held liable because the injurer will be able to show that the victim was contributorily negligent. But then the injurer will fear liability themselves, because the victim has behaved properly and the rule is one of strict liability. So the injurer will take efficient precautions too. The mechanism by which the incentives operate is simply the mirror image of a negligence regime's.

[34] *See* COOTER & ULEN, *supra* note 1, at 344–47; SHAVELL, *supra* note 25, at 184–89. Both Cooter and Shavell explain how these rules achieve similar bilateral liability threats, which should not be a surprise: the mechanism is essentially the same under all these regimes.

44   Tort Law

least in the basic cases I have outlined here.[35] The supposed incentives
are the same; the only difference is who ends up with the cost of accidents that occur when everyone behaved efficiently (nonnegligently).

Nothing in the analysis of bilateral precautions lets us distinguish,
then, between these various possible tort regimes.[36] A different kind of
analysis needs to serve that role, and in the modern economic understanding of tort law, it comes from an analysis of activity levels.

To be clear, though, we have come all this way, and the economic
models still have not addressed whether a basic rule of negligence is
preferable to a basic rule of strict liability. This is a far cry from the
claims reported at the start of the chapter, like "The law of accidents
was one of the first bodies of private law successfully analyzed using
formal economic models."[37]

Activity Levels

To figure out whether a rule of negligence is more efficient than a rule
of strict liability (with a defense of contributory negligence) – which is
to say, to figure out who should bear the cost of an accident when both
injurers and victims have behaved reasonably (nonnegligently) – economists have turned to an understanding of *activity levels*, as pioneered
by Steven Shavell.[38] The concept is simple, though perhaps unfamiliar
to most lawyers. As Shavell originally put it:

> By definition, under the negligence rule all that an injurer needs to
> avoid the possibility of liability is to make sure to exercise due care
> if he engages in his activity. Consequently *he will not be motivated to
> consider the effect on accident losses of his choice of whether to engage in
> his activity or, more generally, of the level at which to engage in his activ-
> ity*; he will choose his level of activity in accordance only with the
> personal benefits so derived. But surely any increase in his level of

---

[35] For a more complete economic analysis, see Robert D. Cooter & Thomas S. Ulen, *An
Economic Case for Comparative Negligence*, 61 N.Y.U. L. REV. 1067 (1986) (arguing that
comparative negligence is superior to other negligence-based rules only when parties face
particular informational limitations).

[36] *Cf.* COOTER & ULEN, *supra* note 1, at 348 ("[T]he ... model [of bilateral liability threats]
provides a policy reason to prefer a negligence rule whenever precaution is bilateral. The
simple model does not, however, provide a reason for preferring one form of the negligence rule to another.").

[37] COOTER & ULEN, *supra* note 1, at 324.

[38] Steven Shavell, *Strict Liability Versus Negligence*, 9 J. LEGAL STUD. 1 (1980).

2.1 Negligence and Strict Liability 45

activity will typically raise expected accident losses (holding constant the level of care). Thus he will be led to choose too high a level of activity; the negligence rule is not "efficient."[39]

Consider the activity of driving.[40] Under a negligence regime, drivers are encouraged to drive safely (because if they don't, they have a greater risk of being held liable for their dangerousness). If they drive safely – more specifically, if they are confident that they will always be able to drive safely – then they know that they won't be held liable for car accidents. But if their very decision to drive increases the likelihood of accidents – because there is always a nonzero risk of accidents even if drivers behave reasonably, and more cars will be on the road if more people drive, leading to greater congestion – then they will drive *too much*, even while driving safely.

Of course, it is reasonable to wonder why courts would not simply judge drivers negligent if they drive too often, if indeed excessive driving increases the risks of accidents. For instance, a driver out "on a mere whim"[41] could be held liable more readily than an ambulance on an urgent errand, even if both drivers were handling their vehicles with similar care. Or a driver on a trip with virtually no social utility could be judged negligent, when they get into an accident, merely for being out on the road. But courts don't make determinations like these in practice, and in general it would be difficult for them to do so. We'll return to problems concerning the distinction between individual choices and activity levels later in this chapter.

Modern law-and-economics scholars relate an understanding of activity levels to liability judgments in the following way: they argue that, when both the injurer and the victim behave nonnegligently, liability should be assigned to the party whose choices about activity level have a greater chance to reduce accidents efficiently. Thus, for instance, Cooter and Ulen write as follows: "Usually one party's activity level affects accidents more than the other party's activity level. Efficiency requires choosing a liability rule so that the party whose

---

[39] *Id.* at 2.
[40] This example – now standard in the activity-levels literature – is drawn from Shavell. *See id.* at 2–3.
[41] *Id.* at 2.

activity level most affects accidents bears the residual cost of accidental harm."[42] Shavell puts it similarly, although perhaps in a way that accommodates broader considerations: "Strict liability [with a defense of contributory negligence] will result in greater social welfare [than a rule of negligence] if it is more important for society to control injurers' levels of activity than victims.'"[43]

As an example, consider the kinds of "abnormally dangerous" activities described in the *Restatement (Second) of Torts*[44] – activities that give rise to strict liability under prevailing legal doctrine. In destroying buildings with dynamite, it appears (at least on the surface) that those using dynamite influence the likelihood of harm more via their choice of activity level than those who operate stores on nearby streets. To summarize the modern economic approach to tort cases, analyzing this case would work as follows: (1) both store owners and blasters can take precautions against harm from dynamite in a variety of ways, and the case is accordingly one of bilateral precaution; (2) as a result, in terms of basic precautions, any negligence-based rules (including either (a) negligence or (b) strict liability with a defense of contributory negligence) will be optimal; (3) to choose between them, we note that blasters' activity levels influence accident costs more than store owners'; (4) as a result, the efficient rule is strict liability with a defense of contributory negligence.

* * *

Having laid out this modern economic understanding, my goal now is to demonstrate why it comes up short if its goal is to justify or recommend particular legal rules. In the next subsection, I address the problems with the basic bilateral-precaution model, arguing that it insufficiently justifies negligence rules in the first place. In the subsection after that, I demonstrate that even if we assume that negligence rules (including strict liability with a defense of contributory negligence) are efficient, activity-level arguments – at least as understood economically – are of little help in choosing among them. As a result, economics remains of little help in determining when to assign tort liability. Finally, I address a variety of other issues that affect the applicability of the reigning

---

[42] COOTER & ULEN, *supra* note 1, at 349.
[43] SHAVELL, *supra* note 25, at 202.
[44] RESTATEMENT (SECOND) OF TORTS § 520 (1977).

2.1 Negligence and Strict Liability

47

economic models and show that fundamentally noneconomic social judgment, rather than discrete economic cost-benefit tests, would be needed even if the models otherwise worked as economists intend.

2.1.3 The Collapse of the Modern Models

As I have noted, there are two central features of the modern economic understanding of negligence rules: (1) bilateral threats of liability and (2) activity levels as a mechanism to decide who bears residual liability when all parties behave optimally. In this section, I describe several fundamental problems with the first of these pillars.

The Prevailing Economic Model

To do this, it will be necessary to consider a little more deeply, and mathematically, the formal models at issue. For ease of exposition, I will draw in part, at first, from a particularly clear summary of these views by Cooter and address variations of this model later.[45]

Consider, again, the example of Xavier (a railroader) and Yvonne (a cornfield owner). Formally, the total social cost of fires from Xavier's railroad that burn Yvonne's corn is

$$SC = x + y + p(x, y)a$$

In this formula, SC is the total social cost, x is the cost of Xavier's precautions (like installing spark arresters), y is the cost of Yvonne's precautions (like growing less corn), $p(x,y)$ is the likelihood of a fire, and a is the cost if there is a fire.[46]

A few features of this formalization are especially worth noting. First, the cost of accidents when they occur, a, is held constant.[47] This is a reduction, and most reductions threaten the ultimate applicability of formal models; however, this particular reduction is not one I

---

[45] The material in the first part of this section is, accordingly, based on Cooter, *supra* note 5, at 8–11.

[46] *Cf. id.* at 8. I have simplified Cooter's formula somewhat in ways that do not affect the argument. Specifically, for Cooter, $p(x,y)$ is the likelihood that an accident will *not* occur, whereas in my example, $p(x,y)$ is the likelihood that it *will* occur. Accordingly, Cooter uses $(1 - p(x,y))$ to represent the likelihood of an accident.

[47] *Cf. id.* at 8 n.24.

48 Tort Law

need to challenge for the purposes of this section, so I accept it in the remaining discussion.

Second, more importantly, the probability of fire-related accidents is expressed as $p(x,y)$. Here, p is a function – a mapping of some values to others. The important feature of the way that the probability of fires is expressed, here, is that it depends on both x and y – that is, on the precautions that both Xavier and Yvonne take. If the probability were expressed simply as $p(x)$ or $p(y)$, it would depend wholly on Xavier's or Yvonne's precautions, respectively, and the case would therefore be one of unilateral precaution. That the probability is expressed as $p(x,y)$ means the case is potentially one of bilateral precaution. (I say "potentially" because the optimal x or y could still be zero.)

To summarize so far, the total social costs (SC) are the sum of Xavier's precautions, Yvonne's precautions, and the expected costs (the probability times the magnitude) of fires' harms. For the economists who have set forth these models, the goal is simply to reduce SC through tort rules.[48]

Ultimately, social costs in this case depend only on x and y. That is, given particular levels of precaution by Xavier and Yvonne, there is an associated social cost (which consists, again, of the costs of those precautions and the expected harm from fires, which itself just depends on the precautions that Xavier and Yvonne take). To economists, accordingly, the goal is to find rules that give parties incentives to adopt an optimal pair of values for x and y. Call these optimal values x^* and y^*.[49]

Now, consider the private costs that Xavier and Yvonne face individually. These private costs will depend on tort law's liability rules, because Xavier and Yvonne can respond to tort law's incentives. The central conclusion of the economists' models is that negligence rules (including, again, rules of strict liability with a defense of contributory negligence)[50] create efficient incentives for Xavier to adopt x^* as his level of precaution and for Yvonne to adopt y^* as hers.

---

[48] *See id.* ("Efficiency is achieved when social costs are minimized.").

[49] *Cf. id.*

[50] In the remainder of this section, I will use simple negligence rules as an example of the class of rules that includes strict liability with a defense of contributory negligence, negligence with a defense of contributory negligence, and comparative negligence. This is a simplification without any loss of generality; the economists' arguments at stake in this section, and my responses to them, treat all models in the same way.

2.1 Negligence and Strict Liability 49

Consider first Xavier, the potential injurer. Under a negligence rule, Xavier's costs can be separated into two distinct cases: (1) if he pays for enough precaution to satisfy tort law's standard, then his only cost is that of the precaution, because he won't have to pay for any of the costs of fires; (2) if he does *not* pay for enough precaution, then his cost is that of whatever precautions he does pay for, plus the costs of fires, because tort law will hold him liable for the damages from the fire. In the first case, we can express Xavier's costs simply as x. In the second, Xavier's costs are $x + p(x,y)a$.

And in this formulation, we reach the first central stumbling block of the economic model. Because this is a case of bilateral precaution, Xavier's costs in this case depend in part on the precautions that Yvonne adopts (y). This means that, if all we know is x, there is no way to determine Xavier's costs. If we admit that we don't know what Yvonne's costs might be, there is little more we can say about Xavier's costs. Economists, accordingly, specify one more piece of information. They state, as an example, that "Yvonne's precaution is held constant at the efficient level ($y = y^*$)."[51]

This additional assumption, though it may appear minor, severely undermines the model's applicability to real tort cases. But before I explain its problems, it will first help to understand what the assumption allows the formal model to do. By holding Yvonne's costs constant at the optimal level, Xavier's costs can now be expressed solely as a function of his own precaution. Assuming that tort law's negligence standard (as applied to Xavier's behavior) is optimal, Xavier's costs are (1) x if $x \geq x^*$ and (2) $x + q(x)a$ if $x < x^*$, where $q(x)$ simply represents the cost of accidents given Xavier's level of precaution x, assuming Yvonne behaves optimally.

Essentially, Xavier gets to pick between options 1 and 2, based on the level of x he chooses. Because $x + q(x)a$ is greater than x (because $q(x)a$ is positive), Xavier would prefer to pay only x. The way for him to do this is to choose his level of precaution x to equal x^*, the optimal amount of precaution and the legal negligence standard for him.

---

[51] Cooter, *supra* note 5, at 9. Shavell's formulation is similar, although not identical (for reasons I explain *infra*): "injurers will exercise optimal care *given that victims take due care*, because then injurers will be liable for accident losses." SHAVELL, *supra* note 25, at 184–85 (emphasis added).

50   Tort Law

Consider his choice in the following way: if he chooses less precaution than x^*, he will have to pay for accident costs *plus* whatever precaution he takes; if he chooses a level of precaution equal to x^*, he avoids liability and pays only x^*. Therefore, he will (under the model) choose a precaution equal to x^*.[52]

Yvonne's decisions are the mirror image of Xavier's. When considering her costs, the economists tell us to hold Xavier's precautions constant at the optimal level.[53] Then, she can choose either a cost of y or $y + p(x^*,y)$ depending on whether y is less than y^* (the legal standard for *her*, based on what precautions are socially optimal for her to take). For reasons that track the discussion of Xavier's incentives, the economists conclude that Yvonne will adopt the optimal level of precaution, y^*. Accordingly, negligence rules are said to give both Xavier and Yvonne efficient incentives; the economists expect that Xavier will choose x^* and Yvonne will choose y^*, their respective optimal levels of precaution.

Failure of the Model

As I have suggested, however, the model is flawed, or at least limited in its applicability to many kinds of cases. The internal flaws of the model – as opposed to those that highlight the model's incorrect or incomplete assumptions about human behavior – derive from a feature to which I drew attention in the previous section: namely, that Yvonne's behavior is held constant when considering Xavier's and that Xavier's behavior is held constant when considering Yvonne's.

To put this more succinctly, Xavier's optimal behavior depends on Yvonne's, and Yvonne's depends on Xavier's. Or, more formally, x^* depends on y^*, which depends on x^*. This may seem circular, and in a sense it is, but the internal problem with the economic model isn't precisely that it is *logically* circular. Variables can depend on each other, in this sense, without collapsing a mathematical model. Indeed, this kind

---

[52] For a more mathematical elaboration of this point, see Cooter, *supra* note 5, at 9–10. For an even more formal proof of essentially the same conclusion, see generally the original discussion in Brown, *supra* note 25.

[53] *See* Cooter, *supra* note 5, at 10 (premising the conclusions for the victim's case on the assumption "that the injurer is nonnegligent"); SHAVELL, *supra* note 25, at 185 ("The specific reasoning [for victims] is analogous to that in the explanation ... of why injurers will take due care under the negligence rule.").

2.1 Negligence and Strict Liability 51

of codependence between variables underlies much of game theory: in a game, the actions of one party influence the actions of another, which in turn can influence the actions of the first, until an equilibrium is reached.[54]

The central problem comes instead from what the mirror-image dependence demands in this particular model's case. The only way to determine what the legal standard for Xavier (x^*) should be is to know what the legal standard for Yvonne (y^*) should be, and vice versa. Accordingly, before we can set the particular negligence rules that govern *either* Xavier or Yvonne, we have to know what the optimal behavior is for *both* of them. That knowledge must come as a package, and if the economic model is to work, we must use it to set the standards for both parties.

More precisely, for the economic model even to get off the ground, we need to imagine that Xavier and Yvonne can determine such optima ex ante and also that they expect that a court analyzing the situation ex post will be able to infer the same optima. If Xavier and Yvonne can't determine the optima themselves, they have no way to plan their behavior accordingly. And if they don't expect courts to be able to determine the proper standards ex post, then being purely rational and selfish, they will have no reason to plan their behavior in view of the correct legal standards.[55]

The central difficulty with the formal model of bilateral precaution arises from the impracticality of knowing in advance, with perfect accuracy, what the optimal costs and benefits are for parties like Xavier

---

[54] For a short introduction to game theory and the analysis of equilibria, see COOTER & ULEN, *supra* note 1, at 32–42.

[55] Shavell clearly outlines this requirement for his argument: "to ascertain the optimal level of due care for just one party, a court must generally determine (if only implicitly) the optimal level of care for the other as well, because the optimal level of care for one party will in principle depend on the other's cost of, and possibilities for, reducing risk." SHAVELL, *supra* note 25, at 188. "This latter point," Shavell admits, "makes the comparison of liability rules with respect to their ease of application different from what it might at first seem to be." *Id.* Shavell also recognizes that "courts must generally consider the entire tableau of costs and effectiveness of care for the two parties to determine optimal care for either." *Id.* at 188 n.17. One way of understanding my central argument in the text about the model's fragility is that this "entire tableau of costs and effectiveness" need not, in any situation, exhibit any regularity or predictability. Minor changes to it (based on, for instance, small changes in what courts expect injurers and victims to do) can radically change courts' beliefs about which precautions are optimal.

52   Tort Law

and Yvonne. Economists, to be sure, do not think parties or courts (or regulators) have access to this kind of perfect knowledge or that parties in Xavier and Yvonne's positions will have access to perfect information about one another.[56] But if the model is to be applied to tort cases in practice, the legal economists' arguments implicitly depend on the belief that the model nonetheless provides a useful idealization of the world and that minor variations from the model's assumptions will only slightly degrade the model's normative power.[57]

That may be true of some models, but it is not true of this one – at least not at the level of generality at which formal deductions about law operate. Recall that the reason a situation involves bilateral precaution in the first place is that the injurer and the victim face different costs in the precautions they might take.[58] (Otherwise, the case could more easily be treated as one of unilateral precaution, in which a single party takes all the care needed to reduce the costs of accidents to an optimal level.) Because of the way parties' precautions may interact, a small change in the precautions Xavier actually takes can mandate a very large change in the precautions Yvonne should efficiently take, and vice versa.[59] As an example, Yvonne's optimal behavior (from both her perspective and an overall social one) might look very different depending on whether Xavier does or doesn't install spark arresters on his railroads, even if those spark arresters are very cheap.

As a result, the central internal problem with the prevailing formal models of negligence is that they are untenably *fragile*: they do not withstand minor modifications to the parties' behavior. To say this differently, the models are premised on a theoretical perfection, and the slightest variation from this perfection can make their equilibrium collapse entirely, rather than degrade gracefully. Instead of providing

---

[56] *See, e.g.,* Brown, *supra* note 25, at 343–47 (analyzing, as a variation on the economic model that came to underlie economists' modern understanding of tort law, the effects of informational limitations for injurers and victims).

[57] *Cf.* COOTER & ULEN, *supra* note 1, at 347 (suggesting, with specific reference to the bilateral-liability-threat model of tort law, that "[i]t is usually best to build theory from clean results and then handle any messy results as exceptions").

[58] *See supra* notes 27–28 and accompanying text.

[59] More formally, a small change in x can require a large change in y^*, and a small change in y can require a large change in x^*.

2.1 Negligence and Strict Liability

an approximation of the real world, they threaten to provide virtually nothing in the real world.

For example, even if we can narrow down x^* to a relatively small range (say, a rough projected expenditure on a few different kinds of spark arresters), this may not be sufficient to determine what y^* is. In the general case, we need *full* information about x^* in order to specify y^*, and vice versa. There is little opportunity to reach a second-best result: admitting that we aren't sure of x^* means we can't be sure of y^*, and nothing in the economic model guarantees that this uncertainty won't spiral out of control, so we are no longer even roughly sure of x^*.[60] Even a very good prediction based on aggregate or generally constant behavior is insufficient to ensure that the model reaches what economists call a convergent – that is, a stable – result. Slight changes to one party's precaution can have unpredictable effects on those that the other parties should take.

To be clear, I am not arguing that the model cannot work in any case, no matter how stylized; my criticism is that the model cannot be applied to the general case and that it therefore cannot justify negligence rules as a general matter. In the general case, even when an injurer can estimate victims' precaution reasonably well and a victim can represent injurers' precaution reasonably well, the model cannot tell us what to do.

Moreover, even if we assume that injurers, victims, and courts have perfect information about what precautions would be socially optimal given the expected probability and harm from accidents, there are additional reasons that the model's fragility is triggered as soon as it is applied to most real cases.

For one thing, even if an individual party is perfectly rational and has perfect information, they must accommodate the possibility – even in just a probabilistic sense – that other parties will not behave perfectly rationally or have perfect information. In other words, even if both parties turn out to be perfectly rational and fully informed, they each

---

[60] Of course, it is unfair to expect an economic model to provide stronger conclusions than are justified by the information available to us in the real world. My objection to the model is not that it cannot yield an optimal result given suboptimal information. Rather, my argument is that the model cannot work at all in the general case, in the way it was intended, without perfect information.

54   **Tort Law**

would have to account for the possibility that other people aren't. As soon as they account for this, their behavior changes entirely: Xavier and Yvonne cannot each assume that the other will take optimal precautions, and as a result the model unravels again.

As a more formal example, consider a simple game in which a group of people are asked to choose numbers from 0 to 100.[61] The group's numbers will be averaged. The winner of the game is the member of the group who chose a number closest to half the group's average. In a game populated only by fully rational players, the optimal choice would be 0.[62] But in practice, even a fully rational agent would not choose 0, because they would expect error or irrationality in other people's choices.[63] In other words, it is fully rational to expect irrationality or lack of information in others, at least probabilistically.

The problem that this observation poses for the bilateral-liability-threat model is that it cannot in practice be efficient to dictate efficient legal standards, x^* and y^*, based on the presumption that both parties will expect the other to behave perfectly. Xavier and Yvonne cannot (and should not) plan their behavior in view of that assumption. But once we recognize this, the model unravels; again, without shared knowledge of the optimal pair of values for x^* and y^*, neither can be set in the general case. We can try to guess what precautions Xavier will in fact choose and set the legal standard for Yvonne accordingly; then, we can try to guess what Yvonne will in fact choose, based on this standard, and set the standard for Xavier accordingly. But then this change in the standard will alter Xavier's behavior, which in turn will alter Yvonne's behavior, and nothing guarantees that an efficient equilibrium will result in the general case.

There is another, perhaps simpler, way to express this problem and related ones: we can analyze the situation from the perspective of

---

[61] This example, called a "p-beauty contest game," is drawn from HERVE MOULIN, GAME THEORY FOR THE SOCIAL SCIENCES (2d ed. 1982); *see also* Avinash Dixit, *Restoring Fun to Game Theory*, 36 J. ECON. EDUC. 205 (2005) (discussing this game from a pedagogical perspective).

[62] If all players in the group chose 100, the best choice would have been 50. Members of the group, knowing this, could all choose 50. But then, all players could figure out that 50 would be the average, so they would want to choose 25, and so on.

[63] For experimental results of this game in practice, see Rosemarie Nagel, *Unraveling in Guessing Games: An Experimental Study*, 85 AM. ECON. REV. 1313 (1995) (demonstrating that people do not behave as if they assume everyone else were perfectly rational).

2.1 Negligence and Strict Liability

the parties, rather than the policymakers setting x^* and y^*. For example, Cooter is rightly concerned, throughout much of his analysis of legal rules, with what he calls the "paradox of compensation"[64] – the notion that when efficiency requires "double responsibility at the margin"[65] from multiple parties, there is no single efficient legal rule that provides the right incentives to everyone. This was, in short, the problem we saw with rules of strict liability and no liability earlier: strict liability might give injurers efficient incentives, but it leaves victims free to take no precautions at all, at least in theory, because all their harms are compensated by injurers. Rules providing for no liability do the reverse: they give victims incentives to take precautions because victims bear the costs of harm, but injurers are free to do as they please. In defending the bilateral-liability-threat model of negligence rules, economists have offered it as a solution to this "paradox" of compensation.

But the problem is that a mere *threat* of liability cannot solve this paradox. Even a fully rational Xavier, or Yvonne, will know under a negligence regime that there is some chance they will avoid liability and some chance they will not. For instance, suppose that the legal standard sets x^* (Xavier's efficient precautions) to \$80, which might correspond to a requirement to install spark arresters. The economic model that justifies negligence rules suggests that Xavier will choose \$80 as his level of precaution because he fears liability if he doesn't.[66] But this liability is not certain under all negligence rules, even if perfect enforcement of the law is assumed. For instance, under a rule of negligence with a defense of contributory negligence (unlike a rule of pure strict liability), Xavier knows that there is some chance that Yvonne will not meet her standard of liability (y^*). As a result, it may not be efficient for Xavier to spend \$80 on precautions in all cases, even if he is fully rational.[67] Instead, he may spend less under some conditions because he may expect that he will sometimes be able to

---

[64] Cooter, *supra* note 5, at 3–4.

[65] *Id.* at 4.

[66] *See id.* at 9–10; SHAVELL, *supra* note 25, at 184–85.

[67] This result is well understood in the economic literature. *See, e.g.,* John E. Calfee & Richard Craswell, *Some Effects of Uncertainty on Compliance with Legal Standards*, 70 VA. L. REV. 965 (1984).

avoid liability altogether (because of Yvonne's own negligence).[68] But given this possibility, then – as before – the y^* that courts have chosen for Yvonne may not be socially optimal in a second-best sense, which in turn means that the x^* that courts have chosen for Xavier may not be optimal in that sense, and so on. The model threatens to unravel, again, because of the slightest perturbation.

To be clear, we cannot solve this problem in the model's coherence by assuming that parties will depart only slightly from their optimal precautions. Slight departures by one party can have extremely large effects on the optimal precautions for the other party. At least, the economic model doesn't guarantee otherwise, and it is easy to imagine many real-world cases where slight departures will have outsized effects. For example, in a world where pedestrians start crossing the street slightly earlier after a stoplight than they currently do, drivers' behavior at stoplights may need to change sharply. A slightly improved fire barrier might make fire sprinklers wasteful for a building. Slightly different hurricane shutters or a slightly different roof-to-wall attachment for a house can change whether it is safe for the occupants to stay in the house during an impending windstorm of a particular projected strength. As the real world presents itself, tiny changes in precautions can make significant differences.

Moreover, given also the probabilistic nature of the harms in question – that is, fires in Xavier and Yvonne's case are not certain but

---

[68] In other words, there is no reason to assume that Xavier will assume that the probability of Yvonne's compliance with her legal standard (y^*) is equal to 1. To elaborate the discussion in the text, consider that the formal economic model guarantees that Xavier's total cost when he chooses $x < x^*$ will be at least as great as his cost when he chooses $x \geq x^*$, because if the total social costs of accidents were lowest at a point smaller than x^* (given a constant y^*), then x^* itself ought to be lowered to that point. But nothing guarantees that Xavier's *expected* costs, in view of the probability of Yvonne's compliance with her legal standard y^*, are not lower when $x < x^*$. These expected costs are essentially a weighted average between x and $(x + p(x,y)a)$ when $x < x^*$ (weighted by Xavier's estimated probability of Yvonne's compliance), and such an average might be smaller than x^*.

Of course, if both parties assume the other will make calculations of this kind, the analysis becomes even more complicated. The particular expected results depend on a variety of case-specific features and cannot be derived in the abstract, and there is no reason to assume it will result in an efficient equilibrium in the general case.

This situation shares some features with a continuous iterated prisoner's dilemma. For an interesting analysis of that phenomenon from a biological perspective, see generally Stephen Le & Robert Boyd, *Evolutionary Dynamics of the Continuous Iterated Prisoner's Dilemma*, 245 J. Theoretical Biology 258 (2007).

2.1 Negligence and Strict Liability

merely possible – the construction of purportedly optimal standards is even more difficult. As Shavell notes, the economic models in question are meant specifically to address probabilistic harms.[69] But this means that x^* and y^* may change slightly as a result of new information that comes to light; for instance, if the likelihood of a train-related fire for the next year is estimated to be 1 in 200,000 on March 22, the likelihood may go down to 1 in 240,000 as the result of greater-than-expected ambient humidity (which makes fires less likely) in late March. This kind of minor perturbation in probabilities wouldn't pose a significant problem for a robust model, but given the kinds of fragility in the model that I have described, it is impossible to be confident that a stable justification for purportedly efficient standards (that is, for specific values of x^* and y^*) will exist in many cases. If nothing else, the economic model's dependency on full knowledge of both parties' efficient precautions makes it less likely that either side's efficient precautions can be specified in any given case.

In short, while some idealizations – including economic ones – can serve as useful approximations of the world from which we can later veer, the bilateral-liability-threat model underlying modern economists' view of tort law is untenably fragile if its goal is to justify application of negligence standards to real cases. An idealization cannot justify specific policy propositions in law when the slightest change in information or behavior threatens chaotic results.[70] Far from explaining the central feature of Anglo-American tort law, the purported economic justification of the negligence standard provides very little justification for the rule in practice.

Alternative Formulations of the Model

My observations and analysis in the prior section addressed a *continuous* version of the model – that is, one that allows precautions to vary to any

---

[69] SHAVELL, *supra* note 25, at 177 ("We will assume that accidents and consequent liability arise probabilistically.").

[70] I mean "chaotic" in both a lay sense and a technical sense. For more information on chaos theory, which characterizes (among other things) the way in which small changes in the inputs to a system can cause wild swings in its output, see Robert Bishop, *Chaos*, in STANFORD ENCYCLOPEDIA OF PHILOSOPHY (2008, rev. 2015), plato.stanford.edu/entries/chaos/ [https://perma.cc/C8AV-YJRK].

58 Tort Law

possible levels, so that a level of precaution might be set to $74.82, or $100.64, and so on. Strictly speaking, dollar values are not continuous because they do not extend beyond two decimal places (to cover cents). But because the value of a cent is so small, familiar statements of value in dollars and cents are for many practical purposes treated as continuous.

We might alternatively formulate the bilateral-liability-threat model as discrete rather than continuous, which is to say that we might imagine (say) four particular on-or-off precautions that the parties might take. For instance, in a particular situation, we might observe that Xavier has a choice between two spark arresters, one that costs $80 and reduces the likelihood of fires by 50 percent, and one that costs $240 and reduces the likelihood of fires by 90 percent. If these are Xavier's only options, his precaution is said to be *discrete* (or *discontinuous*) rather than *continuous*.[71]

In his comprehensive book on law and economics, Shavell's statement of the purported economic basis of tort law is framed in largely discrete terms. For instance, though his argument tracks the one I have already laid out, and though it is formalized in the same way,[72] his particular example involves three possible levels of precaution: "none," "moderate," and "high."[73]

The reason that the difference between discrete and continuous models may be important here is that discreteness, versus continuousness, may save a model from its own fragility. In other words, if Xavier has only three levels of precaution available to him, then minor perturbations in probabilities as he understands them, or in his expectations of Yvonne's conduct, are less likely to be significant enough to cause him to change from an efficient option to a distinct, inefficient one.

While it is possible that the discreteness of available precautions will allow an efficient equilibrium to emerge in some cases, there are several reasons that the flaws of the continuous model are still likely to apply to real cases. For one thing, the danger of unraveling is still present under discrete models; the best hope for those models is just

---

[71] *Cf.* COOTER & ULEN, *supra* note 1, at 247 ("Notice that buckling a seat belt is a discontinuous choice (yes–no). For discontinuous precaution, the relative efficiency of different rules depends upon particular facts.").

[72] *See* SHAVELL, *supra* note 25, at 179.

[73] *Id.*

2.1 Negligence and Strict Liability

that it may be smaller than for continuous models. For another, the real world ordinarily offers many options, rather than just two or three. Drivers setting air-conditioning levels in their cars might have only a few levels to choose from (off, low, high, and so on), but in choosing the speed of their cars they face possibilities that are continuous rather than discrete. Pedestrians have enough options in choosing their speed, location, and how often they look at traffic for us to imagine, plausibly, that they face essentially a continuous range of choices about the amount of precaution they take. Railroaders usually won't have only a simple choice among spark arresters but an array of choices in both the *kind* of precautions they choose (spark arresters versus alternative track design versus alternative track location) and the *level* of precautions they choose (perhaps facing a smorgasbord of 80 different spark arresters they might purchase from a variety of suppliers). The same is true of many other decisions, like what kind of seatbelts an automobile manufacturer should install, what sort of fence to use to surround a swimming pool, how a car's anti-collision software is configured, and so forth.

In any event, the legal economists recognize that the success or failure of the formal economic model at stake here depends on the adequacy of the continuous model, rather than a discrete analogue of it, because it is the continuous model that expresses in a general form the conclusions that result from formal proof. As Cooter and Ulen write, "In general, discontinuous variables and cost functions yield messy results about optima, whereas continuous variables and cost functions yield clean results. It is usually best to build theory from clean results and then handle any messy results as exceptions." If the bilateral-liability-threat model depends on "messy results" in specific cases, that would, if nothing else, sharply limit its force as a general explanation of tort law's negligence standard; the analysis would start in each case to resemble a more fact-intensive, noneconomic analysis than a theoretically deductive economic one.

2.1.4 The Limits of Activity Levels

The other pillar of the modern economic analysis of tort law is the view that residual liability – that is, decisions about whether the injurer or the victim should bear the costs of accidents when both have behaved innocently (nonnegligently) – should be determined based on an analysis of activity levels. Specifically, the leading economists' argument is that residual liability should depend either on "[w]hether injurers' levels of activity are more important to control than victims'"[74] or on which party's "activity level most affects accidents."[75]

The problem with this view is that, while an understanding of activity levels sheds significant insight into the formal economic analysis of tort law, it ordinarily cannot serve as a basis for decisions in real cases. The main reason for this is that the activity-levels arguments are normally impossible to administer.

At the outset, it is important to consider whether economists have even attempted to offer a clear operational role for activity levels in determining tort rules. Consider, for example, the explanation in Shavell's law-and-economics book for how activity levels should matter in tort law:

> Whether injurers' levels of activity are more important to control than victims' will depend on the context. As discussed before, when an activity of injurers (walking dogs of a vicious breed) creates substantial risks despite their exercise of due care, the activity will be desirable to control. This point is not fundamentally altered if account is taken of the activities of victims that expose them to risk. Especially if the victims' activities are just the activities or ordinary life (walking about, going to work), we would not want the activities constrained in favor of injurers' more dangerous activities. Conversely, when an activity of injurers (playing baseball) is not very dangerous if appropriate care is taken, the importance of controlling the activity will not be great; instead, we may see some advantage in reducing certain activities of victims that subject them to particular risks (such as pushing a baby in a stroller across a baseball field while a game is in progress).[76]

Though motivated by efficiency, this formulation is essentially noneconomic in nature, as if economic analysis has led us to a point where other considerations ought to reign or where the costs and benefits are too complicated for present-day economics to study. If this is the case, there is little more to say except to note my agreement, for my

---

[74] *Id.* at 202.
[75] COOTER & ULEN, *supra* note 1, at 349.
[76] SHAVELL, *supra* note 25, at 202.

2.1 Negligence and Strict Liability 61

goal here is to show that formal economics is insufficient on its own to determine optimal legal rules.

To put this differently, Shavell's explanation, read broadly, is a sensitive balancing test – so sensitive that it appears to allow noneconomic considerations, or at least considerations very hard to quantify through narrow economic analysis, to influence tort rules. It is not clear, ultimately, that Shavell disagrees with me that formal economic analysis on this point is not especially helpful. It is almost as if Shavell has shown that formal reasoning brings us to something that in formal terms might almost be considered a singularity (in the mathematical sense, in which a formal parameter is undefined or beyond analytical treatment): a need for informal human judgment! Again, if that is true, Shavell and I have simply reached the same result by different paths; this is what I meant in Chapter 1 by saying that I admit I am in some sense *doing* "law and economics," but it is not the sort of law and economics that produces purportedly determinative results by means of formal analysis.

The formulation in Cooter and Ulen's textbook, though more specific than Shavell's, appears to be incomplete, at least on a narrow reading. They describe the role of activity levels as follows:

> Usually one party's activity level affects accidents more than the other party's activity level. Efficiency requires choosing a liability rule so that the party whose activity level most affects accidents bears the residual costs of accidental harm.[77]

But, of course, looking only at which party's activity level more directly causes *accidents* violates the general economic observation that the law needs to be sensitive not just to the costs of activities but also to their benefits. Extra driving might indeed affect the level of accidents more than extra pedestrian activity on sidewalks, but it is at least possible that the benefit drivers get from extra driving is worth this extra cost. On economic terms alone, Cooter and Ulen's conclusion should likely be read more broadly and interpreted to assign liability in ways that reduce the total costs of precaution (including limited activity) plus the total expected costs of accidents. In other words, it is not the party whose activity most increases the likelihood of accidents that

---

[77] COOTER & ULEN, *supra* note 1, at 349.

62 Tort Law

needs to bear residual liability but the party who can restrict activity in ways that reduce social costs optimally.

Even on this broader reading of Cooter and Ulen's (and perhaps Shavell's) conclusion, however, activity-levels arguments would face serious problems as soon as courts or other parties tried to apply them. As I noted when I introduced activity levels,[78] there is in principle little difference between choices about levels of care and choices about levels of activity, except that courts judge the former but tend not to judge the latter. But there are several reasons, in fact, that it makes sense for courts to avoid making judgments related to activity levels, and these reasons apply regardless of whether it is courts or other policymakers (or commentators) who set or defend particular legal rules.

To begin with, as Shavell's formulation of the role of activity levels seems to recognize,[79] there are many cases in which *more activity* does not lead to *more accidents*, as long as the activity is conducted safely. Does more walking on the sidewalk necessarily lead to more accidents between cars and pedestrians, assuming the pedestrians are all safe? It seems unlikely, or at least any effect will be extremely small: safe pedestrians keep to the sidewalk (and crosswalks), look for oncoming traffic, and in general don't get hit by cars unless those cars veer off the road. Now, it *is* possible that increased pedestrian activity increases the likelihood that people will get hit by cars even if the pedestrians are careful, because there might be some cases in which cars veer onto sidewalks but avoid accidents only because those sidewalks were empty. In other words, there might be cases in which empty sidewalks result in harmless veering by cars, whereas full sidewalks result in serious accidents. But in practice, this situation is unlikely to matter: there is enough physical space in the world, and on most sidewalks, that it is implausible that there is even a measurable increase in the likelihood of an accident between a car and a pedestrian just because an additional pedestrian has chosen to use the sidewalk.

Many cases are like this on both sides. Despite frequent assumptions that faultless accidents are commonplace, it is not, in fact, even clear that many car accidents result from mere activity, when all the

[78] *See* text accompanying *supra* note 41.

[79] SHAVELL, *supra* note 25, at 203 (referring to activity that "is not very dangerous if appropriate care is taken").

2.1 Negligence and Strict Liability 63

activities involved (driving, the construction of cars, the construction of roads, the operation of the software in cars, and so on) are safe. Ordinarily in a car accident there is some culprit, perhaps unidentified, who was at least careless: machinery fails because of a defect, a driver was driving unsafely given road conditions, a tire was under- or over-inflated, some driver-assist software went awry, or something else was done incorrectly. Perhaps some car accidents are truly unavoidable even when everyone involved has behaved reasonably safely, but it is not clear that there are many such accidents or that their possibility should dictate tort policy.

A separate problem is that the force of activity-levels arguments depends in part on the proposition that parties expect to be able to avoid liability when they act safely. But in many cases, this proposition assumes too much: many people who engage in potentially dangerous activities do not *know* that they are able to maintain a high level of safety, and in fact many know otherwise. For example, drivers cannot ensure that they are not going to be careless.[80] If nothing else, people's general knowledge that they cannot avoid carelessness mitigates the force of activity-levels arguments.

But perhaps the most significant problem with applying activity levels to real tort cases is that reasoning in view of activity levels requires classificatory judgments that are nearly impossible to make in a principled fashion. For one thing, there are many situations in which injurers and victims are similarly situated or, in fact, engaged in the same activity (or an activity that might as well be the same). For instance, what would an understanding of activity levels suggest for accidents between two automobiles? Both drivers chose to drive. What about airplane crashes, as between the airline and its passengers? Both the airline and the airplane passengers chose to take the particular flight that crashed.[81]

---

[80] *See* Mark Grady, *Res Ipsa Loquitur and Compliance Error*, 142 U. PA. L. REV. 887, 900 (1994) ("It is impossible to drive a car for any period of time without missing a required precaution"); MARC FRANKLIN ET AL., TORT LAW & ALTERNATIVES 46 (8th ed. 2006) (discussing Grady's article).

[81] *Cf.* Robert Cooter & Ariel Porat, *Liability Externalities and Mandatory Choices: Should Doctors Pay Less?*, 1 J. TORT L. (2006) (observing the same thing, in a related context, about doctors and patients), doi.org/10.2202/1932-9148.1040.

64   Tort Law

Even when parties are situated differently in noticeable ways, there is generally not a principled economic method to determine whose activity level makes more of a difference (including both its costs and its benefits) and is therefore more worth regulating. What of accidents between cars and pedestrians where both were behaving reasonably safely? If such cases indeed occur frequently enough to worry about, whose activity makes more of a difference, accounting for both costs and benefits, and responds better to incentives? On what basis could a court decide?

Even Shavell's examples of cases that are meant to be clear raise many of these problems. When considering "walking dogs of a vicious breed," for example, it is important to ask whether this activity really is dangerous "despite [the] exercise of due care."[82] And, though pushing a baby in a stroller through the middle of a baseball game is obviously an activity that should be minimized (and indeed not one that would appear to reflect the exercise of due care in a way that even triggers activity-levels arguments, because the activity can be judged unsafe on its own), what should we do about baseball stadiums and the people who live (or build houses) behind them, such that baseballs might break their windows? The levels of activity of both injurers and victims in cases like this appear to be symmetric, and recognizing activity levels does not break the symmetry.

Dynamite cases, and other activities where "a commercial actor has come to the type of location where [some] sort of dangerous thing is not normally done,"[83] reflect perhaps the strongest case for activity-levels arguments, in view of the administrative problems I have just discussed. In these cases, there is perhaps a clear social understanding that an accident can be attributed to the level of one party's, rather than another party's, activities. Still, even these cases involve something of a noneconomic value judgment. For one thing, in theory, victims can still choose where to live in a way that minimizes the costs to them of activities like dynamite blasting, and the proper formal comparison of costs and benefits on their own seems hard to derive without empirical data. What seems to matter in cases of abnormally dangerous activities is that one party did something unexpected or unusual, *changing* a baseline

---

[82] SHAVELL, *supra* note 25, at 203.

[83] Stephen D. Sugarman, *Rethinking Tort Doctrine: Visions of a Restatement (Fourth) of Torts*, 50 UCLA L. REV. 585, 608 (2002).

2.1 Negligence and Strict Liability

level of activity that was occurring in an area and thereby violating social expectations.[84] But an analysis that depends on considerations like that is much broader and factually richer than a formal economic one.

2.1.5 Limits in Applying the Hand Formula

The Hand formula itself occasionally suffers from classificatory problems similar to those faced by activity-levels arguments.[85] These are best conceived as problems of time-framing, though I mean something different by this than many other discussions of time-framing in this context.[86]

To see these problems, consider again the example of Xavier and Yvonne, the railroader and the cornfield owner. In this example, which we borrowed from Cooter, Xavier was said to have three precautions available to him: installing spark arresters, running trains more slowly, and running fewer trains.

Running fewer trains sounds like an activity-levels concern, in that it would be hard to judge from a single instance whether Xavier had run inefficiently many trains. Consider, for instance, an accident that occurred on May 13, 2006, at 12:10 a.m. It makes little sense to ask whether Xavier was running too many trains at that particular point in time; the question is not "What should Xavier have done at time T, the moment the accident occurred?" because the decision to run more or fewer trains goes beyond that particular time. More precisely, there are multiple time intervals that include time T, and there is no clear way to choose among them. What does it mean to say that Xavier should have run fewer trains? Fewer trains on May 13, 2006? In May 2006? In all of 2006 up to that point? Or over a broader period? What if Xavier had planned to run fewer trains later in the year, after the fateful accident happened (unfortunately) to arise? Could he convince a court that this plan was genuine, or would he have an inefficient incentive under an economically informed negligence rule to reschedule his trains evenly throughout the year (even if this weren't otherwise optimal) in order

---

[84] *See id.*
[85] See the previous section.
[86] *Cf.* Douglas Husak & Brian P. McLaughlin, *Time-Frames, Voluntary Acts, and Strict Liability*, 12 LAW & PHIL. 95 (1993) (discussing "time-framing" problems raised by Mark Kelman and Larry Alexander that concern how individual acts are to be judged).

66   Tort Law

to be confident that he could demonstrate that he ran fewer trains? Because courts cannot easily answer these questions, running trains is classified as an activity-levels problem, not as one about which courts can judge care or precaution directly.[87]

Unfortunately for tests like the Hand formula, however, the same kind of reasoning applies to questions that are not so readily seen as activity-levels problems. For instance, what does it mean that on May 13, 2006, Xavier didn't use spark arresters on his trains? Perhaps he had decided that, given the expected wear on spark arresters and the expected cost of fires, it was optimal to use them some but not all of the time.[88] Over what period are we to evaluate that question? In some sense, every question about precaution under the Hand formula can be reframed as a potentially intractable activity-levels problem.[89]

The Hand formula also, as it is commonly stated, hides vast complexity under a simple veneer. Law students for generations have learned the hand formula as comparing B, the cost (or "burden") of precautions that prevent accidents, against PL, the product of the probability (P) and magnitude (L) of loss from accidents. This is commonly expressed (arbitrarily) as an inequality: conduct is said to be negligent if a precaution is untaken under circumstances where

$$B < PL$$

But it is an arbitrary result of Judge Hand's particular formulation in *Carroll Towing* that the common presentation of the formula (1) makes only one side probabilistic and (2) treats the possible losses as singular rather than composite. A fuller treatment of the formula would need at least to expand it to a determination of whether *expected burdens* are greater than *all expected losses from accidents*, or something like

---

[87] Note that decisions about activity levels suffer from a similar problem: in addressing which party's activity more directly affected accidents, or whatever else, questions of time framing may be decisive.

[88] *Cf.* Grady, *supra* note 80 (distinguishing the adoption of standards of precaution with *compliance* to those standards, and observing that "[i]n most activities, courts require perfect compliance; in others they do not").

[89] Shavell admits that there are other, somewhat similar concerns about the Hand formula. For instance, "there may be dimensions of injurers' care (such as the frequency with which drivers look in their rearview mirrors) that courts would not take into account in the determination of negligence because of difficulties in assessing them." SHAVELL, *supra* note 25, at 189.

2.2 The Neglect of Alternatives

$$qB < p_1 L_1 + p_2 L_2 + p_3 L_3 + \ldots$$

This is not itself fatal conceptually, but it suggests how difficult it would be to administer a legal standard based on this formula in practice. Expected costs of precautions, as seen forward in time from the perspective of a reasonable actor, are nontrivial to produce, judge, and verify; accounting for all the possible harms is also not easy.

The widespread use of the Hand formula in legal pedagogy probably arose from its ability to standardize and simplify, but in any workable form it does neither. It is at best an evocative recognition – nothing more – of the fact that reasonable people take sensible precautions in view of the costs and benefits of those precautions. It is hard to imagine a jury sensibly applying a properly expanded version of the formula.

2.2 THE NEGLECT OF ALTERNATIVES AND THE INABILITY TO ISOLATE MICROECONOMIC FEATURES OF PROBLEMS FROM BROADER ECONOMIC CONCERNS

A different problem – part of a general pattern I described in Chapter 1 that I call the "neglect of alternatives" – applies to the general analysis of negligence and strict liability in tort law. The problem is fundamentally one of equivocation in the meaning of efficiency. That is, efficiency has multiple meanings, and it is easy to slide between them accidentally.

2.2.1 Background

Consider, as an example, an argument like the following: (1) banking creates wealth; that is, it is socially productive;[90] (2) therefore, on grounds of efficiency, we ought to encourage college students to become bankers.

---

[90] Of course, the global economy of the last fifteen years has put this proposition into some doubt. *See generally* Simon Johnson & James Kwak, 13 Bankers: The Wall Street Takeover and the Next Financial Meltdown (2010) (chronicling the 2007–2008 financial crisis); *see also The Cost of Repair*, The Economist, Oct. 9, 2010 ("Paul Volcker, a former Fed chairman, has caustically called the ATM cash dispenser the only worthwhile financial innovation of recent decades, a sentiment widely shared by venture

68   **Tort Law**

Of course, this argument needs a few modifications before it can even get off the ground. For one thing, we might not want to encourage college students to become bankers if the administrative costs of doing so were substantial. If it cost billions of dollars to wage a marketing campaign to encourage college students to become bankers, it would be inefficient to do so if the expected gains from encouraging more people to become bankers were more modest. Similarly, the argument assumes that encouraging college students to become bankers will increase the likelihood that they will in fact become bankers – rather than, say, increasing the chances that they will rebel against a heavy-handed advertising campaign and choose an alternative path, becoming instead musicians who write songs about the evils of banking.

But there is a further flaw in the argument, and that flaw is the important one for our purposes: encouraging someone to become a full-time banker necessarily discourages them from pursuing other full-time work. Even assuming (contrary to fact) that all modern banking is necessarily a productive activity, other activities might still be *more* productive.[91] Accordingly, it would be a mistake – even on grounds of efficiency alone – to say that just because something is wealth-producing, or "socially productive" in the narrow sense that the argument has in mind, it should be encouraged.[92]

In other words, the conclusion of the hypothetical argument we're considering is not just that students should become bankers; it is that

---

capitalists and non-financial businesses."). But the extent to which it is in fact true is not relevant to the argument's use as an example.

[91] President Obama appears to have been motivated by this recognition when he said, in an interview on the Tonight Show in early 2009:

> [W]hat we need is steady growth; we need young people, instead of – a smart kid coming out of school, instead of wanting to be an investment banker, we need them to decide they want to be an engineer, they want to be a scientist, they want to be a doctor or a teacher. And if we're rewarding those kinds of things that actually contribute to making things and making people's lives better, that's going to put our economy on solid footing. We won't have this kind of bubble-and-bust economy that we've gotten so caught up in for the last several years.

Executive Office of the President, *Interview of the President by Jay Leno on the Tonight Show*, Mar. 19, 2009.

[92] Of course, we could define the terms "productive" or "wealth-producing" in ways that are absolute rather than relative – that is, we could chose not to describe banking as "productive" unless it were the *most* productive possible career for whatever person or people are in question. But my point is that in much legal-economic analysis, the terms are used more narrowly in ways that cause economic arguments to be insufficient to justify their conclusions.

2.2 The Neglect of Alternatives

students should become bankers *instead of choosing some alternative career.* When the argument is put that way, its incompleteness is clear because the opportunity costs of encouraging people to become bankers are highlighted: those we're encouraging to become bankers might have become scientists, law professors, professional athletes, successful humorists, unsuccessful humorists, or any number of other types of professionals (or nonprofessionals) who might produce, or destroy, more or less wealth than bankers.

The same considerations apply, with perhaps surprising regularity, to many kinds of law-and-economics arguments. The general problem is that an activity may be "efficient," "productive," or "wealth-producing" in the narrow sense that it is better for it to occur than for it not to occur. Thus, for example, we might be asked whether it is efficient for a railroad to run (versus not to run) given the social value of the transportation it provides and the likelihood it will crash and cause injuries to passengers. In analyzing the efficiency of a railroad, we don't need to stop with those particular costs and benefits; indeed, we might, and often do,[93] consider a multitude of others: the harms that arise from the pollution caused by its engine, the indirect effects on the price of goods and the market for employment resulting from a more effective system of transport, the likelihood that sparks from the train will cause fires that affect nearby agricultural fields,[94] the effects on nearby residences of noise from the train, and so on. Even so, the analysis would necessarily be incomplete unless it incorporates one further consideration, too often neglected in these sorts of discussions: the activities prevented when capital, credit, labor, and other economic "production factors" are used to build and manage a railroad rather than to engage in entirely unrelated activities (such as organizing and operating sports teams, law schools, science labs, and so forth).

Suppose we try to analyze the efficiency of the railroad from the perspective of tort law's Hand formula, which would determine that the railroad is efficient if its costs outweigh its benefits. That is, a

---

[93] *E.g.*, Robert Cooter & Ariel Porat, *Does Risk to Oneself Increase the Care Owed to Others? Law and Economics in Conflict*, 29 J. LEGAL STUD. 19 (2000) (considering, additionally, risks of harm to injurers themselves).

[94] *Cf.* Coase, *supra* note 4, at 29–31 (using a similar, now-famous example); *see also* section 2.1.

70 Tort Law

standard conclusion of law and economics is that if the railroad's operation generates $100,000 in social benefits (often manifested simply as private profits to the operator of the railroad) but causes $95,000 in unavoidable harms externalized to others (for example, because the railroad's unavoidable sparks burn down nearby cornfields or because its unavoidable crashes cause property damage), then the railroad's operation is "efficient" and should be encouraged – or at least not discouraged. That is, the railroad, taken on its own, is said to produce wealth; it's better on instrumental economic grounds for the railroad to exist and to operate than for it not to exist or not to operate. Putting aside noneconomic concerns (such as those related to fairness and the distribution of wealth) and assuming the figures of $100,000 in gains and $95,000 in losses are accurate and complete, we'd prefer that the railroad run than that it not run.[95] Of course, to be clear, I'm assuming that the $95,000 in harms can't be prevented by means of a simple and cheap precaution; this is what I mean when I call the harms "unavoidable."[96]

Compared to other ways of making $100,000, however, the railroad may be far worse for society than its alternatives. We'd easily prefer someone to make $100,000 in a way that causes only $2,000 of harm to others (or, of course, ideally no such harm) than in a way that causes $95,000 of harm to others, even putting aside fairness and considering grounds of allocative efficiency alone. That is, even though the operator of the railroad might earn $100,000, the railroad is worth

---

[95] The activity may be undesirable, of course, for any number of other reasons, including concerns about fairness, rights, virtue, autonomy, and the overall social distribution of wealth. I do not mean to minimize these concerns, which may be important in explaining and justifying legal doctrines. But again, my argument proceeds by showing that even on economic grounds alone, many of the conclusions of the law-and-economics movement cannot be justified.

[96] If the harms totaling $95,000 could be prevented by means of a $5 precaution taken by the railroad – for example, if the $95,000 in harm reflects fires that sparks from the railroad cause, and these sparks could be prevented if the railroad installs a $5 spark-arrestor – then clearly the operation of the railroad is unreasonable, even in purely economic terms. I am treating the $95,000 in harms as a cost that can be avoided only if the railroad stops operating; that is, by hypothesis, the cheapest precaution that can prevent the $95,000 in expected harms, in my example, is the cessation of the railroad's operation. Because this would have a cost of $100,000 (in forgone benefits to the operator of the railroad), the Hand formula would deem the railroad's operation as cost-justified and therefore reasonable (nonnegligent).

2.2 The Neglect of Alternatives 71

only a net \$5,000 to society because of the harms that it causes. But another activity that earns its proprietor \$100,000 may be worth far more than \$5,000 overall – indeed, up to \$100,000 if it externalizes no harms.

Asking only whether a railroad is better than no railroad may miss the point. The railroad may well be more efficient than its *absence* but significantly less efficient than its *alternatives*. Often, however, legal-economic modeling – such as the Hand formula – focuses (sometimes just implicitly) on the comparison between an activity and its absence, rather than the comparison between an activity and its alternatives.

The same problem can be described in terms of opportunism. In the case of a railroader who earns \$100,000 but causes \$95,000 in harms to others, the wrongdoers earn more – potentially much more – than their overall contribution to society. The railroader, if rational and selfish, will choose \$100,000 in profit over an activity that earns them \$90,000 but causes no social harms. In other words, when an activity allows a private profit disproportionate to its social value, parties who are selfish and rational will have too much incentive to engage in it and not enough incentive to engage in more productive activities.[97]

Though the general form of the concern that I have described arises occasionally in legal-economic literature,[98] legal economists overall are not sufficiently concerned with the problem. One reason is perhaps that the problem does not arise – that is, it is impossible as a matter of

---

[97] It is important to stress, again, that both the "less productive" and the "more productive" activities are *efficient* in the sense that when considered in isolation, it is better (on grounds of efficiency alone) for them to occur than for them not to occur. The problem is not that wealth-destroying activity may occur in isolation; it is that wealth-promoting activity may occur with excessive frequency compared to activities that create even *more* wealth. Again, this is not an issue if activities' costs and benefits are evaluated with metrics that accommodate their alternatives – if, for instance, we consider opportunity costs in activities' valuations, as we might begin to do when fully considering the costs of capital and other production factors as transaction costs. My point again, however, is that models like the Hand formula fail to do this appropriately.

[98] If seen as a problem of opportunism, my critiques share features with those by other commentators concerned, ordinarily in somewhat more focused contexts, with the opportunism associated with wealth-transfer rather than the social productivity associated with wealth-production. *See, e.g.,* Anthony T. Kronman, *Mistake, Disclosure, Information, and the Law of Contracts,* 7 J. LEGAL STUD. 1 (1978) (proposing a rule concerning disclosure of potentially valuable information in contract law that aims to encourage investment in productive rather than redistributive information-gathering); Ronald H. Coase, *Blackmail,* 74 VA. L. REV. 655, 674 (1988) ("Blackmail involves the

72   Tort Law

theoretical economics – if several deep assumptions are made about
the perfection of certain kinds of markets. If all "efficient" activity can
occur because funding can flow to it through credit markets and capital markets, and if there is a functionally unlimited supply of materials
and labor, then we might not worry that some "efficient" activity can
occur because it doesn't interfere with other "efficient" activity. But as
market crashes, credit crunches, and supply-chain problems all show
us, not all activity that is "efficient" in this sense can occur, and the
law can cause significant distortions by permitting actors to externalize costs.

2.2.2 Application to Tort Law

The economic study of torts has tended to limit its focus[99] to the optimization of allocative efficiency through incentives for injurers and
victims to take precaution. In doing so, it has neglected the broader
effects of tort rules on social costs.

Consider the ordinary case of what I call *allocative negligence* – that
is, negligence that directly creates an allocative inefficiency, in terms
of the costs of precaution and the costs of accidents. For example,
suppose Xavier has the opportunity to install $80 spark arresters to
prevent $4,000 accidents and chooses not to do so. If the law sup-
ported his choice, there could be a clear misallocation of resources:
spark arresters ought to be installed, but Xavier has no incentive to
install them.[100]

---

expenditure of resources in the collection of information which, on payment of blackmail, will be suppressed. It would be better if this information were not collected and
the resources were used to produce something of value."); DAVID D. FRIEDMAN, PRICE
THEORY: AN INTERMEDIATE TEXT 152 (1990) ("The analysis of rent seeking suggests
that, at least under some circumstances, monopoly profit is not a transfer to the firm
from its customers but a net loss. The higher the monopoly profit, the more resources
the firm will burn up ... in the process of getting it. If so, perhaps the best solution to the
problem posed by monopoly is not regulation but taxation ....").

[99] *E.g.*, RICHARD A. POSNER, ECONOMIC ANALYSIS OF LAW 69–70 (1st ed. 1972) (giving
the classic allocative-efficiency argument for negligence rules).

[100] Of course, in a world without transaction costs, Xavier and Yvonne might bargain over
the installation of spark arresters. *See generally* Coase, *supra* note 94 (demonstrating that
with no transaction costs, assignments of rights in nuisance law does not affect allocative
efficiency).

2.2 The Neglect of Alternatives

But in casting problems this way, focusing on the particular relationship between injurers and victims, economic tort analysts often ignore a potential problem. I call this the problem of *redistributional negligence* – that is, distorted incentives (still ultimately allocative in nature) that arise from tort regimes that give some parties the opportunity to engage in activity that is largely or even primarily redistributive. Of course, such opportunities for opportunistic redistribution may also be unfair, but for the purposes of this section the important point is that the standard economic tort analysis will promote inefficient activities in a world in which not all efficient activities can occur.

To say this somewhat differently, selfish rational actors who can choose between a variety of productive activities will not choose the one that is socially most productive. Instead, they will choose the one that earns *them* the most. However, some activities are more profitable to actors because they externalize costs onto others, not because they are more productive overall. With sufficient capacity to redistribute wealth through externalities, sanctioned by law, activities can function as capitalistic black holes, drawing in resources and effort even if they would be more productively applied elsewhere.

For example, return to the example of Xavier and Yvonne from the previous section. It is common to see this kind of two-party example in economic analyses of tort law. But consider the following variation of the situation, which both (1) makes new particular costs and benefits clear and (2) looks beyond the two activities in question (railroading and cornfield growing):

Xavier has recently graduated from business school. He has little chance to obtain credit, but he has an inheritance that he can use to invest in the business of his choice. His skills and experience make two choices salient: he can set up either a railroad company or a hotel. Both choices would consume his entire inheritance and require his full-time attention. Given all the costs and benefits associated with the opportunity to set up a hotel, Xavier's calculation of the expected value[101]

---

[101] Ordinarily, particularly as a business-school graduate, Xavier would engage in a net-present-value calculation that would consider the lifetime of the opportunity, the discount rate of income streams over that lifetime, and similar considerations. I put aside those details to keep the discussion in the text simple; they have no bearing on questions relevant to my discussion.

74   Tort Law

from that opportunity is $20,000.[102] To compute the expected value of the railroading opportunity, Xavier considers the following information he has learned: running the railroad would be worth $40,000 to him, but the expected costs of fires from the railroad to Yvonne's adjacent cornfields are $37,000. Accordingly, the railroading opportunity is worth only $3,000 to Xavier if tort law makes him liable for these fires; if not, the opportunity is worth $40,000. Given the figures in this example, the tort regime directly influences Xavier's decision between his two business opportunities. Under a strict-liability regime, Xavier will choose the hotel because the railroad – though profitable – needs a large part of its value set aside to pay for the harms it causes. Under a negligence regime, however, Xavier can ignore these harms because his $40,000 value exceeds the $37,000 cost to the cornfield and is thus deemed "reasonable."[103] In that case, we expect that he will choose the railroad over the hotel, even though it is less socially valuable, because it gives him an opportunity to redistribute more wealth to himself through the externalities he causes.[104]

An analysis of activities limited to whether a railroader or a corn grower's activity "most affects accidents"[105] (or similar formulations) as between those two parties misses an important feature of the situation in our example: from the perspective of allocative efficiency, assuming we have a choice between railroading and no railroading, we *want* railroading. It creates more value than the fires it causes. But we may want other things more, and if capital and other resources are limited, we want a tort system that discourages relevant parties from

---

[102] We can take this as an opaque figure, although it would be possible to specify details about the costs and benefits of the hotel opportunity and to assess the liabilities that Xavier could face as the owner-operator of a hotel. For the purposes of the example, however, I assume (just for simplicity) that the hotel gives rise to no significant liability or cost externalization, whereas the railroad does. This assumption does not change the force of the argument in the text.

[103] Assuming, again, that he is strictly rational and selfish, does not fear negative publicity, and so on.

[104] Cooter and Porat call this situation a "liability externality" and agree generally that legal rules "should discourage activities with negative liability externalities." Cooter & Porat, *supra* note 81, at 1.

[105] COOTER & ULEN, *supra* note 1, at 349.

2.2 The Neglect of Alternatives

making decisions based on how much of other people's wealth they can redistribute to themselves by externalizing costs onto others.[106]

Of course, if every wealth-producing business opportunity can be pursued – for instance, if factor markets are perfectly efficient and other significant transaction costs are minimal – then we may not care whether Xavier becomes a hotel operator or a railroad operator. In a world with no transaction costs and unlimited resources, whichever opportunity he forgoes (with its attendant wealth-producing and externalizing effects) will be taken up by someone else anyway. But as long as resources are not infinite and there are significant inefficiencies in the ability to nimbly pursue new business opportunities (because of resource limitations, borrowing costs, capital-market inefficiencies, and so on), social efficiency requires such opportunities to be priced as correctly as possible. To say this differently, it is not enough to say that we want to limit activities to levels at which they are still wealth-producing; it may also be vital to overall allocative efficiency for activities to be appropriately priced.

Note that this recognition, alone, doesn't solve the central problem that faces tort law because it does not specify precisely what it means for activities to be priced appropriately. As commentators have long recognized,[107] there is a symmetry between injurers and victims: strict liability for railroaders, though it prevents railroaders from engaging in redistributive, cost-externalizing activity, might mean that corn growers have too much of an incentive to engage in corn growing compared to other activities. But for tort law's solutions to this problem to be efficient, they cannot conceptualistically restrict their scope to the costs of accidents and precautions; they need instead to face all social costs and benefits squarely.

---

[106] Otherwise, the amount of harm that an actor can choose to externalize through an activity is limited only by the personal benefit that the actor can document from the activity.

To say this differently, economists who promote negligence rules for reasons only of allocative efficiency would subject tort victims to Nozick's "utility monsters," who derive so much value from some activities that others must suffer, on utilitarian grounds, in order to satisfy their appetites. *See* ROBERT NOZICK, ANARCHY, STATE, AND UTOPIA 41 (1974). If utility monsters are rewarded, however, then an allocatively inefficient result obtains: there is too much incentive to become like them and not enough to engage in other activity.

[107] *See, e.g.*, POSNER, *supra* note 19, at 138–40 (making the point, among others, that strict liability gives injurers but not victims efficient incentives to research new precautions, and vice versa).

To summarize, analysis *internal* to a particular activity, or to the interaction between one activity and another, may well be insufficient to decide even the efficiency (much less the broader social appropriateness) of tort regimes that govern that activity. It may well be necessary to look at the "entire tableau"[108] (to borrow Shavell's phrase) of social costs and benefits – not just for the individual activities in question but for those activities as compared with other activities – in order to decide who should pay for which costs. Each activity, and its costs and benefits, are only part of a broader economic landscape.

Of course, Shavell is ultimately right – if we interpret him broadly enough – that our focus in deciding between strict liability and negligence depends on which activity is "more important to control."[109] But there is no reason to suppose that the question can be decided by the kind of activity-levels arguments that economists have marshaled so far. Instead, deciding between strict liability and negligence seems to demand a significantly broader judgment about which activities should bear the costs of accidents and which should not. Abstract and formal methodologies, unsurprisingly, have little aid to offer those seeking to make that kind of judgment. In any event, it would be a mistake – even on grounds of efficiency alone – to focus only on incentives to take precautions in deciding questions of tort liability, because the prices of activities can have broader incentive effects in society.

2.3 LEAST-COST-AVOIDER ARGUMENTS

A different, largely unrelated theme that recurs in the law-and-economics literature, especially in tort law, is the notion of the *least-cost avoider*, the party who can take precautions or insure against an accident at the lowest cost.[110] The least-cost-avoider principle seems like a clean

---

[108] SHAVELL, *supra* note 25, at 188 n.17.

[109] *Id.* at 202.

[110] The concept is ordinarily associated with Guido Calabresi. *See* GUIDO CALABRESI, THE COSTS OF ACCIDENTS: A LEGAL AND ECONOMIC ANALYSIS (1970); Guido Calabresi & Jon T. Hirschoff, *Toward a Test for Strict Liability in Torts*, 81 YALE L.J. 1055, 1060 (1972); *see also* Stephen G. Gilles, *Negligence, Strict Liability, and the Cheapest Cost-Avoider*, 78 VA. L. REV. 1291 (1992) (offering a more recent broad defense of the least-cost-avoider principle).

2.3 Least-Cost-Avoider Arguments

way to break the conceptual symmetry between injurer and victim that we have discussed. For example, as between an injurer and a victim, we can simply try to assign liability to the party who could have most cheaply avoided the accident. If the injurer would need to stop their activity entirely to avoid the accident and the victim can avoid being injured by engaging in a $2 precaution, the rule would force the victim to bear the costs of the injury.

On the surface, the least-cost-avoider principle seems sensible enough, but it provides a perverse long-term incentive to avoid *becoming* the least-cost avoider in order to take advantage, opportunistically, of the ability to externalize costs under the principle. The principle might work in theory if courts could evaluate all motivations over all time periods and detect this sort of abuse or opportunism. Because they cannot, the principle yields a perverse incentive to engage in activities that cause a redistribution of wealth; the activities particularly encouraged are those that prevent a party from becoming the least-cost avoider in contexts where the party expects liability to be significant. We might call such actors *least-cost-avoider avoiders*.

The least-cost-avoider principle arises often in law-and-economics literature. For example, it has been applied to legal rules concerning offer and acceptance, and damages for reliance, in contract law;[111] civil-procedural rules concerning sanctions for frivolous claims;[112] and even tax law.[113] In all these contexts, the potential problem is the same: favoring one who has high costs encourages people to avoid being in a situation where their costs are low, even if having low costs is better for society.

It also can be a very difficult principle to administer. And it can be impossible to square with other, more specific kinds of economic analysis.

---

[111] Avery Katz, *When Should an Offer Stick? The Economics of Promissory Estoppel in Preliminary Negotiations*, 105 YALE L.J. 1249 (1996).

[112] James E. Ward IV, Note, *Rule 11 and Factually Frivolous Claims – The Goal of Cost Minimization and the Client's Duty to Investigate*, 44 VAND. L. REV. 1165 (1991).

[113] Kyle D. Logue & Joel Slemrod, *Of Coase, Calabresi, and Optimal Tax Liability*, 63 TAX L. REV. 797 (2010).

2.4 MORE FOCUSED QUESTIONS OF TORT LAW

The tension between negligence rules and strict-liability rules is foundational to tort, but it does not come close to exhausting all questions of tort doctrine. Economics has had surprisingly little to say about some other areas of tort law, which should not be the case if tort law really had easily succumbed to economic analysis.

Consider the basic cause of action for negligence. One element of that cause of action is whether the defendant owed a duty to the plaintiff in the first place. The term "duty" is misleading in this context and would probably better be replaced; under modern law it is simply an opportunity for courts to determine that they should not impose a remedy in certain classes of cases. For example, the current Restatement notes modern law's general duty of ordinary care to avoid causing "a physical harm" to others[114] but adds: "In exceptional cases, when an articulated countervailing principle or policy warrants denying or limiting liability in a particular class of cases, a court may decide that the defendant has no duty or that the ordinary duty of reasonable care requires modification."[115]

Many of the legal law-and-economics books barely mention duty – or more particularly the possibility of what we might think of as "no duty" exceptions.[116] There overall has been surprisingly little treatment of the subject.[117] Keith Hylton, one of the few people to address it, has attempted to explain several "no duty" rules and even to provide an economic typology for them. He would classify the rules into at least two categories: (1) those that subsidize desirable behavior that has positive externalities on others and (2) those that function as "property rules."[118] But, with respect, this exploratory attempt is not a persuasive vindication of the role of economic reasoning in tort law.

---

[114] RESTATEMENT (THIRD) OF TORTS: LIABILITY FOR PHYSICAL AND EMOTIONAL HARM § 7(a) (2010).

[115] *Id.* § 7(b).

[116] *See* Stephen D. Sugarman, *Why No Duty?*, 61 DEPAUL L. REV. 669 (2012).

[117] *See* Keith N. Hylton, *Duty in Tort Law: An Economic Approach*, 75 FORDHAM L. REV. 1501, 1501 & n.1 (2006) ("Theories of tort law have focused on the breach and causation components of negligence, saying little if anything about duty.").

[118] *Id.* at 1502.

2.4 More Focused Questions of Tort Law

The second of Professor Hylton's categories is the easier to dispatch; it is unpersuasive because the underlying rules themselves are hard to defend in the first place. By "property rules," Hylton refers to rules that permit people to exercise dominion over their property; by tying no-duty rules to property law, Hylton aims to defend rules that say that property owners owe no duty to trespassers on their property. In its general form, this rule is almost certainly undesirable, as evidenced by its many inconsistent doctrinal exceptions[119] and its common-law erosion.[120]

No-duty rules as subsidies make logical sense, but the cases and doctrines do not fit well into that pattern. For example, Hylton lists no-duty rules for athletes and litigators, but there is little need to subsidize conduct in those spheres if it is valuable; they are certainly not impoverished fields that lack markets to supply needed service. The role of no-duty rules in these areas is likely complex and not easily reduced to a simple economic proposition; for example, as Stephen Sugarman proposes, "professional sports have privately developed mechanisms for dealing with the social goals said to be advanced by tort law, and they are the method for dealing with careless conduct that injures athletes."[121] Hylton's justification for the general proposition that there is no duty to rescue – probably the most doctrinally and theoretically significant of the no-duty rules – appears to be largely noneconomic in nature because it depends on broad theoretical concepts like "nonreciprocal exchange of risk,"[122] ideas that have been offered by others as justifications not grounded in formal economics.[123] As Hylton puts

---

[119] *See* RESTATEMENT (SECOND) OF TORTS §§ 333–344 (1965). On inconsistent doctrinal exceptions and their role in analyzing and predicting changes to common law, see MELVIN A. EISENBERG, THE NATURE OF THE COMMON LAW 105–27 (1988).

[120] *E.g.*, Rowland v. Christian, 443 P.2d 561, 568 (Cal. 1968) ("A man's life or limb does not become less worthy of protection by the law nor a loss less worthy of compensation under the law because he has come upon the land of another without permission or with permission but without a business purpose. Reasonable people do not ordinarily vary their conduct depending upon such matters, and to focus upon the status of the injured party as a trespasser, licensee, or invitee in order to determine the question whether the landowner has a duty of care, is contrary to our modern social mores and humanitarian values. The common law rules obscure rather than illuminate the proper considerations which should govern determination of the question of duty.").

[121] Sugarman, *supra* note 116, at 673.

[122] Hylton, *supra* note 117, at 1517.

[123] *E.g.*, George P. Fletcher, *Fairness and Utility in Tort Theory*, 85 HARV. L. REV 537 (1972).

80   Tort Law

it: "Tort law, however, avoids taxing activities in the absence of an imbalance between externalized costs and benefits or a nonreciprocal exchange of risk."[124] As a doctrinal matter, this is not clearly true; for example, two drivers of bicycles on a path can each be liable for negligence to the other, though they are operating in reciprocal ways and facing coordinate risks. And, more to the point, a careless pedestrian can be liable to a bicyclist if both have the right to use a shared path.

More generally, if the bilateral-precaution model for analyzing negligence and strict liability were correct, it would not depend on reciprocity or its absence; nothing in the model requires prior activity or distinguishes "activity" from "inactivity" in the subtle ways that an explanation of tort doctrine would require. It is difficult to believe that "duty" fits sensibly into any economic model. As a thought experiment – just a hypothetical test case – does anyone seriously believe that a theoretical economist, working only with the state of the law in the early 1900s, could with economics alone have predicted (1) the start of the common-law erosion of segmented categories of "duty" owed to different types of entrants onto land or (2) the adoption of a new category of "flagrant trespasser"?[125]

As for the element of causation, the movement never seriously engaged with it. Posner and Landes treated the topic briefly in the early 1980s,[126] and there have been occasional attempts to frame causal concepts and doctrines in purportedly economic terms, but not with analysis that was ever influential – or that even, arguably, related closely to tort law in the first place.[127] In general, much of the economic analysis of causation reduces to a general introductory discussion of the institutional design of the civil legal system, recast in slightly economic terms; for example, here is a significant part of Posner and Landes's treatment of the basic causation rule in tort as compared to a rule of proportionate liability:

---

[124] Hylton, *supra* note 117, at 1517.

[125] *Compare* RESTATEMENT (SECOND) OF TORTS §§ 333–344 (1965) (laying out the older, segmented categories with many complicated exceptions) *with* RESTATEMENT (THIRD) OF TORTS: LIABILITY FOR PHYSICAL AND EMOTIONAL HARM § 52 (2012) (defining a special category for "flagrant trespassers").

[126] William M. Landes & Richard A. Posner, *Causation in Tort Law: An Economic Approach,* 12 J. LEGAL STUD. 109 (1983).

[127] *Cf.* Jules L. Coleman, *The Structure of Tort Law,* 97 YALE L.J. 1233, 1250–52 (1988) (reviewing Posner and Shavell's volumes).

2.4 More Focused Questions of Tort Law 81

> If we ignore the costs of administering the tort system and the role of victims as enforcers of tort law, the optimal solution would be to allow every cancer victim in the area in which the radiation was emitted to claim his damages – discounted, however, by the probability that he would not have gotten cancer if the emission had not occurred.... But as the victims became more numerous, and as the difference in conditional probabilities becomes smaller, the damages recoverable by each under this approach would fall and the administrative costs of litigation would rise. The class action offers a possible though imperfect device for avoiding some of these cost and incentive problems.[128]

The law-and-economics movement's shortcomings are similar in the other areas of tort law. For example, if the standard economic explanations are correct for physical injury, why do they not apply to "pure" emotional or economic harms? It is hard to see anything but a mismatch between the theoretical explanations and the actual doctrine.

Even as to damages, which, being monetary, might seem to be more readily susceptible to economic analysis, economic reasoning comes up short. For example, it is simply impossible to capture the harm associated with loss of life (including loss of all the potential descendants of a victim who could have produced children) in any manner approaching anything that a utilitarian would accept; tort law provides the grossest sort of approximations in this and other areas of nonpecuniary harm. No objective observer would look at the tort system and think it leads to anything approaching an efficient level of deterrence on its own.

Areas beyond negligence – the so-called intentional torts – are similarly elusive for theoretical economists. It is possible to describe the dignitary harms that intentional torts protect as subjective losses in utility that the law has chosen to notice, but could any economist predict, from abstract formal reasoning alone, that a legal system would impose liability for short false imprisonment but not for serious customer-service errors that cause anxiety and significant loss of customers' time? Could they derive the rule that intentional infliction of

---

[128] Landes & Posner, *supra* note 126, at 124.

82   Tort Law

emotional distress requires "outrageous" conduct? That an important doctrinal line for battery is drawn at physical contact, but that many physical contacts are judged to be either inoffensive or covered by implicit consent?

With all these shortcomings, it seems impossible to maintain the claim that "[t]he law of accidents was one of the first bodies of private law successfully analyzed using formal economic models."[129]

2.5 CONCLUSION

Economic reasoning, in the end, seems quite poor at either explaining or justifying tort law. And that conclusion comes even if we don't dwell on the broader, less analytical mismatch between models and real life – for example, the recognition that in large classes of careless accidents there's no specific decision about precautions that anyone took that caused the unusual behavior that led to the accident, that actions that contribute to background levels of safety are exceedingly hard to judge, that individual people's incentives in dangerous situations have little to do with tort law, that corporations' decisions (which may be more readily influenced by tort law) are hard to discover and require a rich understanding of organizations in order to analyze successfully.

Moreover, nobody could be expected to process the information necessary to conform their behavior to all of tort law's rules in the context of, say, riding a bicycle or mopping a floor. So we rely on very broad customary, statutory, and other rules, like speed limits and common sense – and of course reasonable-person standards. The economists, therefore, want to say that "common sense" is motivated mainly by allocative efficiency. But this would be striking when common sense (say, practices involving how often to mop the floors of supermarkets) has many motivations other than the costs of precautions and the benefits of safety.

As with this understanding of reasonableness or common sense, there is a kind of sleight of hand where whenever a decision important to tort law is made, the analysis jumps to some noneconomic analysis

---

[129] COOTER & ULEN, *supra* note 1, at 324.

2.5 Conclusion

(or at least an analysis that cannot easily be reduced to models) – as, for example, in Shavell's conclusion that the ultimate decision between strict liability and negligence depends on whether it is "more important for society to control injurers' levels of activity than victims.'"[130]

It is not as if economics has had nothing to add to tort law, however. Shavell's activity-levels model is an example of an economic idea that provides significant insight. The problems come from too much zeal and too much faith from the outset in the range and capabilities of formal analysis. As I noted in passing earlier, the economist whose model became the foundation for the bilateral-precaution model of the legal economists understood its limitations,[131] and in general the problem is not in economic thought itself but in its overly enthusiastic application.

---

[130] SHAVELL, *supra* note 25, at 202.
[131] See *supra* note 25.

3   CONTRACT LAW

From the perspective of economic analysis, contract law is different from other fields of law. Economic prescriptions in other areas tend to be exclusively about incentives; all the economic discussion of tort law's rules, for example, is aimed to give potential injurers and victims incentives to take cost-effective precautions against injuries. Analysis of contract law can rest on incentives as well, but there is another feature of contract law that complicates the general analysis: at least in the case of bargain contracts, parties have reached their own deal. Economic analysis of contracts is therefore often caught up in the odd and difficult activity of trying to predict what rational private parties will do in order to develop rules that will match those predictions – the idea being that contract law should simply, from an economic perspective, function to supply terms that rational parties would have chosen, because rational parties know best.[1] This has led to a particular recurring pattern of dysfunction in which legal economists develop a model, use the model to predict what purportedly rational parties would do, and then conclude that a rule that imitates those rational parties would be efficient; the reason this pattern is dysfunctional is that if the model is even slightly off from reality, it threatens to get the deals of many, most, or all parties exactly wrong and thereby to lead to dramatic inefficiency. It will be useful to keep this pattern of dysfunction in mind in considering the arguments in this chapter.

---

[1] *E.g.,* Richard A. Posner & Andrew M. Rosenfield, *Impossibility and Related Doctrines in Contract Law: An Economic Analysis*, 6 J. LEGAL STUD. 83, 89 (1977) ("Since the object of most voluntary exchanges is to increase value or efficiency, contracting parties may be assumed to desire a set of contract terms that will maximize the value of the exchange.").

Contract Law

The essential economic justification for enforcing private bargain contracts is that private parties tend to be in the best position to judge the best uses of their own resources, so we should ordinarily let them make binding commitments about those resources. This notion, conceived modestly and subtly – parties *tend to* be in the best position, so *ordinarily* contracts should be enforced in the way parties would have expected them to be – is sound. Sometimes it is unfortunately mistaken for a naive libertarian notion and converted to a much grander set of statements without nuance: courts should simply enforce parties' deals and otherwise get out of the way; there should never be *mandatory* rules (that restrict enforcement or shape contracts) as opposed to *default* rules (which fill gaps); and, for more elusive reasons I discuss later in this chapter, contract interpretation enforcement should proceed formalistically and without human judgment. In the real world, however, contract law is not such a blunt instrument, so proponents of this kind of more naive analysis either need to recognize they are proposing radical legal reform or admit that contract law is difficult for them to explain.

Instead of walking through contract law in the traditional order (starting with consideration or formation, for example), the chapter proceeds roughly in order of importance of the various topics to the economic analysis of law. It starts with a discussion of the theory of efficient breach, which is a foundational and monumentally incorrect pillar of the economic analysis of contract law, and then generalizes slightly to consider economic treatments of contract damages. It proceeds to questions of contract interpretation, which happen to inform discussion of such other topics as formation and excuse[2] and which is probably the most commonly litigated question in contract cases.[3]

---

[2] *See, e.g.*, Shawn Bayern, *Offer and Acceptance in Modern Contract Law: A Needless Concept*, 103 Cal. L. Rev. 67 (2015) (arguing that questions of contract formation are fundamentally interpretive questions); Melvin Aron Eisenberg, *Expression Rules in Contract Law and Problems of Offer and Acceptance*, 82 Cal. L. Rev. 1127 (1994) (presenting the interpretive basis for many individual rules governing contract formation); Melvin A. Eisenberg, *Impossibility, Impracticability, and Frustration*, 1 J. Legal Analysis 207, 211 (2009) [hereinafter Eisenberg, "Impossibility"] (discussing a legal test for unexpected-circumstances cases that has a conceptual grounding in an interpretive question); George S. Geis, *Empirically Assessing* Hadley v. Baxendale, 32 Fla. St. U. L. Rev. 897, 952 (2005) ("Contract interpretation raises some of the same questions as *Hadley* ....").

[3] *See* Steven J. Burton, Elements of Contract Interpretation 1 (2008) ("Issues of contract interpretation are important in American law. They probably are the most

86   Contract Law

After those two foundational questions, the chapter takes up more particular questions of contract law – unconscionability, excuse, disclosure, and so on.

The chapter's general message is that though economic reasoning certainly provides insights into contract law – in many cases, insights far more valuable than those of the conceptualistic and circular reasoning that lay behind the contract law of the early 1900s – modern law-and-economics reasoning about contract law is severely flawed. Chicago-style economic reasoning runs through all areas of modern contract scholarship and tends to reach conclusions that are not just unjust but also less efficient than the more nuanced and sensitive contract doctrines that they would replace. For example, as the next section shows, a keystone of economic argumentation about contract law is that breach of contract is often efficient and that law should encourage it, but in fact the "theory of efficient breach" would lead to rules of contract law that are profoundly inefficient in multiple respects.

3.1 THE THEORY OF EFFICIENT BREACH

Perhaps the biggest misstep in all economic reasoning in private law is what has come to be called the *theory of efficient breach*. I think of it as the biggest misstep for two reasons. First, it is almost entirely wrong. Second, it has achieved quite a significant following; it is taught uncritically in many or most first-year Contracts courses in the United States, and lawyers tend to accept it at face value as one of the cold analytical truths about contract law.

---

frequently litigated issues on the civil side of the judicial docket. They are central to the settlement of a larger number of contract disputes ...."); Alan Schwartz & Robert E. Scott, *Contract Interpretation Redux*, 119 Yale L.J. 926, 926 & n.3 (2010) (summarizing sources). Similar patterns apply to a variety of more specialized cases, like online contracting and government contracting. *See* Ty Tasker & Daryn Pakcyk, *Cyber-Surfing on the High Seas of Legalese: Law and Technology of Internet Agreements*, 18 Alb. L.J. Sci. & Tech. 79, 88 (2008) ("With regard to the scope of issues involved in online contracting, the most frequent focus of litigation has been on laws related to the element of assent, followed by frequent arguments over unconscionability, public policy, and contract interpretation."); W. Stanfield Johnson, *Interpreting Government Contracts: Plain Meaning Precludes Extrinsic Evidence and Controls at the Federal Circuit*, 34 Pub. Cont. L.J. 635, 636 (2005).

3.1 The Theory of Efficient Breach

Even so, I don't want to overstate its importance or success. Courts have never seriously adopted the rule, which (for reasons we will see) would require that they eliminate specific performance as an available remedy for breach of contract. When given an opportunity to apply the theory of efficient breach – which for now we can take simply to be the proposition that parties *should* breach their contracts if it appears to them privately that it would be profitable to do so – the law tends to hold otherwise across a wide range of questions and legal disciplines.

For example, despite half a century of discussion of the theory of efficient breach, the economic tort of "intentional interference with contract" indisputably remains a part of tort law. That tort imposes liability for intentionally and improperly inducing a breach of contract; as the Dobbs treatise puts it, the "basic kind of intentional interference with the promisor's contracted-for performance is actionable almost everywhere upon proof of intended and improper interference with a known enforceable contract, and at least a partial breach or other disruption of the contract that results in economic harm."[4] Section 16 of the ALI's recent *Restatement (Third) of Torts: Liability for Economic Harms* lays out the tort; the core element remains intentionally "caus[ing] a breach of the plaintiff's contract or disruption of its performance."[5]

The courts' lack of concern with the theory of efficient breach, even in the face of lawyerly awareness of that theory, is nicely captured in this lively exchange between Ward Farnsworth, the reporter for that Restatement, and a questioner on the floor of the American Law Institute's annual meeting during which the membership considered and approved that project:

> Judge A. James Robertson II (CA): So I have a comment on the way § 16 works with respect to someone that's causing a breach in a situation where it would be efficient for the party to the contract to breach it for economic reasons. So under contract law, a person can breach a contract and pay the expectation damages of it. In the case where you have that happening, it's good for the economic system.

---

[4] Dan B. Dobbs et al., The Law of Torts § 631 (2d ed., updated through July 2022) (internal citations omitted).
[5] Restatement (Third) of Torts: Liability for Economic Harm § 16 (2020).

So in the case where you have, for example, a supply contract, and there is an alternate supply that's much cheaper, it makes sense for the party to breach it. The problem is the person that usually knows about that inefficiency is the person that wants to get the contract.

So as I read the way you've put this Restatement together, there would be liability for such a person, even though it would be in the best interest to have the contract basically breached. So you'd go through and you'd find that there was a contract, a person breached it, and then you'd go find under (c) the defendant engaged in the purpose of the defendant acted for the purpose of appropriating the benefits of the contract ....

Dean Farnsworth: Just for my own clarity, what is it you wish it would say?

Judge Robertson: I think you should have a privilege. I think there should be a privilege for someone that causes a breach and has a good-faith belief that the party breaching the contract will be able to pay expectation damages.

Dean Farnsworth: Do you have cases saying that?

Judge Robertson: I don't have a case.

Dean Farnsworth: Neither do I. *(Laughter)*

I understand. I don't mean to be flip. I understand your reasoning, and in many ways, I'm sympathetic with it. I was not able to find adequate support in the case law. I'm happy to keep looking at it.

I'm not dismissive at all at raising a serious economic point. But I don't know that the point you're making is well supported in the cases, as you might have imagined.[6]

Similarly, the *Restatement (Third) of Restitution and Unjust Enrichment* endorses a remedy of disgorgement of profits against a promisor in "deliberate breach" of a contract:

> If a deliberate breach of contract results in profit to the defaulting promisor and the available damage remedy affords inadequate protection to the promisee's contractual entitlement, the promisee has a claim to restitution of the profit realized by the promisor as a result of the breach. Restitution by the rule of this section is an alternative to a remedy in damages.[7]

---

[6] 95 A.L.I. Proc. 11–12 (2018).

[7] Restatement (Third) of Restitution & Unjust Enrichment § 39(1) (2011).

3.1 The Theory of Efficient Breach

89

The Restatement elaborates that "breach of contract results in profit" if "it results in gains to the defendant (net of potential liability in damages) greater than the defendant would have realized from performance of the contract."[8] In other words, as we will see in more detail in a moment, it squarely rejects the theory of efficient breach.

It is possible that the theory has made some inroads or at least has been consistent with other doctrinal developments. For example, under traditional legal ethics and the Model Code of Professional Responsibility from the 1960s, it may have been improper for lawyers to advise clients to breach a contract intentionally,[9] whereas under the Model Rules of Professional Conduct from the 1980s such counsel is generally permissible.[10]

We will see, though, that even when squarely presented with the question, Richard Posner as a judge has rejected the theory. I can also report hearing at least one leading economist apologize for it in public, admitting that the early proponents of the Chicago school were too zealous in their presentation of the theory; that admission hasn't, however, diminished the force of the theory in law-school classrooms around the country.

Richard Posner, a leading proponent of the theory, has outlined it as follows:[11]

> [I]n some cases a party is tempted to break his contract simply because his profits from breach would exceed his profit from completing performance. He will do so if the profit would also exceed the expected profit to the other party from completion of the contract, and hence the damages from breach. So in this case awarding damages will not deter a breach of contract. It should not. It is an efficient breach.[12]

Posner illustrates the theory with the following example:

---

[8] *Id.* § 39(3).

[9] *See* CHARLES WOLFRAM, MODERN LEGAL ETHICS 704 (1986).

[10] *Id.* at 229, 704; MODEL RULES OF PROF'L CONDUCT RR. 1.2(d), 4.4; *see also* RESTATEMENT (THIRD) OF THE LAW GOVERNING LAWYERS § 57 cmt. g (2000).

[11] For a discussion of the changes in Posner's formulation of the theory over the years, and also of the origins of the theory, see Melvin A. Eisenberg, *Actual and Virtual Specific Performance, the Theory of Efficient Breach, and the Indifference Principle in Contract Law,* 93 CAL. L. REV. 975, 997 (2005)

[12] RICHARD POSNER, ECONOMIC ANALYSIS OF LAW 131 (9th ed. 2014).

90 Contract Law

> Suppose I sign a contract to deliver 100,000 custom-ground widgets at 10¢ apiece to A for use in his boiler factory. After I have delivered 10,000, B comes to me, explains that he desperately needs 25,000 custom-ground widgets at once since otherwise he will be forced to close his pianola factory at great cost, and offers me 15¢ apiece for them. I sell him the widgets and as a result do not complete timely delivery to A, causing him to lose $1,000 in profits. Having obtained an additional profit of $1,250 on the sale to B, I am better off even after reimbursing A for his loss, and B is also better off. The breach is therefore Pareto superior.[13]

The normative consequence of the theory is that, if it were correct, any remedy for breach of contract more forceful than expectation damages – such as specific performance or disgorgement – should not be available. If specific performance is available, the seller in Posner's example will not be permitted to breach; they will be ordered to perform, making the putative gains from breach unavailable. If some monetary remedy greater than expectation damages is available, that remedy would prevent some, though not necessarily all, supposedly efficient breaches.

The most foundational flaws in the theory – and thus the bases of an economic defense of specific performance's availability – are in fact relatively easy to describe once they are exposed.[14]

First, just because B is willing to bid more than A after A signs a contract does not mean that B values the goods more highly than A; A may simply have cut a better deal or negotiated at a better time. In Posner's example, B's offer of 15¢ does *not* in fact imply that B values the goods more than A does; all we know is that B is willing to offer a higher price now than A once accepted. Without contacting A and engaging in some new mechanism to discover the price A would be willing to pay now, the seller has no basis to determine whether A or B values the goods more highly.

---

[13] *Id.*

[14] Many have detailed these types of arguments elsewhere over the years; the best analysis and presentation of them is in Eisenberg, *supra* note 11, at 997–1016; *see also* Shawn J. Bayern & Melvin A. Eisenberg, *The Expectation Measure and Its Discontents*, 2013 MICH. ST. L. REV. 1, 25–26. The discussion of the theory's flaws in the text is heavily influenced by Mel Eisenberg's analysis.

3.1 The Theory of Efficient Breach 91

As an aside, much of what people seem to have in mind when they talk of the theory of efficient breach isn't breach of contract but amicable renegotiation of terms. If the seller reapproaches A and explains the situation, A may well be happy to accept contract damages or even to adjust the price A is willing to pay to suit new or unexpected circumstances in the market. That is not breach; that is just contract modification. If the seller in Posner's example breaches, they thereby are simultaneously forcing a new state of affairs on A and guessing the costs of A's damages. Parties who do this often get it spectacularly wrong.[15]

Second, as even Posner admits, breach is not the only way B (the user who putatively places a higher value on the goods) can get the goods; B could also buy them from A. Posner claims that it will be cheaper (in terms of transaction costs) for the original seller to sell to B, but this is little more than an arbitrary supposition, and it seems particularly unlikely in view of the extremely large transaction costs of the litigation that would result from breach. To say this differently, the goal of the theory of efficient breach is to get the goods in question to the user who values them most, but even if B is that party, the theory is unnecessary to get the goods in question to B. Because of this problem, the theory of efficient breach is reduced to tenuous arguments about the likely differences in transaction costs among generalized parties: the seller is already in the business of selling goods, so they (compared to A) are in a better position to sell the goods to B. That is tendentious speculation, however, and all the more unconvincing if it necessitates litigation. Again, the theory of efficient breach seems to think everything will be amicable and easily calculated in advance.

Third, A's damages will not necessarily measure A's costs for all the reasons that contract damages may fall short of the full damages that would make promisees subjectively indifferent between performance and breach. Some of these reasons are structural rules, like those concerning limits on damages that are unforeseeable or uncertain; those that make some damages, like the wasted time of individuals, simply uncognizable under law; and those that, under the rule of US jurisdictions, deny compensation of winning plaintiffs' legal fees. Some are just factual and probabilistic: if the seller breaches, A will need to find

---

[15] *See, e.g.*, Egerer v. CSR W., L.L.C., 67 P.3d 1128 (Wash. App. 2003).

92   Contract Law

a lawyer, sue in a timely way, marshal the right evidence, and convince a factfinder.

For those three foundational reasons, the theory of efficient breach shouldn't even get off the ground – at least in cases like the one Posner applies it to.[16] But there are also subtler reasons that the theory fails. One relates to the same "neglect of alternatives" argument that I introduced in Chapter 1 and developed in Chapter 2.

Conceived in view of that analytical pattern, the theory of efficient breach is likely to give parties too much of an incentive to be in lines of business that face unstable preferences and sudden, unpredictable needs. That would not necessarily be a problem if all efficient activity can occur, but because it cannot, artificially favoring actors or industries that can't or don't plan for increased costs is an unhelpful economic distortion.

As a judge on the Seventh Circuit rather than an academic champion of the Chicago school, Posner recognized, at least once, the inefficiency of the efficient-breach theory. In *Walgreen Co. v. Sara Creek Prop. Co.*,[17] discussed briefly in Chapter 1, the owner of a mall promised one of its tenants (Walgreen) that it would not lease space in the same mall to another pharmacy. When it sought to do so, Walgreen sought specific performance against the landlord. The district court issued an injunction. On appeal to the Seventh Circuit, Posner needed to determine whether to uphold the injunction or not. Because of US appellate standards, Posner's panel was faced with the relatively narrow question of whether the district court had abused its discretion in issuing an injunction – a standard very rarely met by an appellant. But Posner chose to defend the injunction affirmatively and thus to reject the theory of efficient breach. He described the landlord's argument as follows:

> Sara Creek [the landlord] reminds us that damages are the norm in breach of contract as in other cases. Many breaches, it points out, are "efficient," in the sense that they allow resources to be moved into a more valuable use. Perhaps this is one – the value of Phar-Mor's [the second pharmacy's] occupancy of the ... premises may exceed the cost to Walgreen of facing increased competition. If so,

---

[16] *See* Eisenberg, *supra* note 11, for a discussion of the rule in other factual "paradigms."
[17] 966 F.2d 273 (7th Cir. 1992).

3.1 The Theory of Efficient Breach

society will be better off if Walgreen is paid its damages, equal to that cost, and Phar-Mor is allowed to move in rather than being kept out by an injunction. That is why injunctions are not granted as a matter of course, but only when the plaintiff's damages remedy is inadequate. Walgreen's is not, Sara Creek argues; the projection of business losses due to increased competition is a routine exercise in calculation. Damages representing either the present value of lost future profits or (what should be the equivalent) the diminution in the value of the leasehold have either been awarded or deemed the proper remedy in a number of reported cases for breach of an exclusivity clause in a shopping-center lease. Why, Sara Creek asks, should they not be adequate here?

Sara Creek makes a beguiling argument that contains much truth, but we do not think it should carry the day. For if, as just noted, damages have been awarded in some cases of breach of an exclusivity clause in a shopping-center lease, injunctions have been issued in others. The choice between remedies requires a balancing of the costs and benefits of the alternatives.[18]

The same logic, nearly word for word, could be applied to Posner's academic example about pianolas, widgets, and boiler factories. It is not economically significant that the resource in question is a lease (or a promise not to use part of a lease) rather than a good. If damages are sufficient to move resources to their highest-value uses, they should have been sufficient here. They weren't sufficient because the theory of efficient breach is incorrect.

To be clear, in saying that, I'm not arguing that no breach is ever efficient; that was never the question. The question is whether the theory of efficient breach should have any consequence for contract doctrine. As Posner seems to agree, it should not "carry the day," it is neither an explanation of nor a successful normative argument about contract doctrine. A "balancing of the costs and benefits of the alternatives" – specific performance and damages – is in fact the traditional, noneconomic rule brought down from equity; traditional lawyers speak of "reasons" or "weights" or "advantages" or whether damages are "sufficient," whereas economists speak of "costs" and "benefits," but the mode of reasoning is the same. Moreover, in Posner's analysis, none

---

[18] Walgreen Co. v. Sara Creek Prop. Co., 966 F.2d 273, 274–75 (7th Cir. 1992) (internal citations omitted).

94   Contract Law

of the "costs" or "benefits" – features of the situation like the difficulty
of computing damages, how accurate they're likely to be, and whether
the parties are likely to be able to negotiate out of an injunction if it's in
their common interest to do so – are capable of precise measurement;
they are broad factors casually sized up with human judgment. They
are merely being spoken of, not applied, in economic terms.

3.2 OTHER REMEDIAL MATTERS

As I noted in the last section, the theory of efficient breach is really
an argument about contract remedies. If it is correct, there should be
no specific performance or disgorgement; if it is incorrect, then it has
nothing to say about those remedies. Given that damages in particular concern money and that contract law is central to any modern
economy, it is surprising in retrospect how little progress economic
reasoning has made in making definite descriptive or normative pro-
nouncements about damages.

To be sure, some of the economic reasoning is extremely intelligent
and thoughtful. But it is hard to connect most of even the best research
to legal doctrine. Richard Craswell's treatment of damages, which
Mel Eisenberg and I took up in a 2013 article called *The Expectation
Measure and Its Discontents*,[19] is exemplary both of virtuosity and of
the difficulties in using straightforward economic theories to try to
explain damages. My goal here isn't to rehash all that analysis, but it
will be instructive to show how often Craswell's own models demonstrate that, based on particular features, the efficient damages in contract law might be anywhere – around the level of expectation damages
or much higher or lower. For example, Craswell notes

- that in view of the need for optimal damages to give incentives about
  precaution to potential wrongdoers, "the most efficient measure of
  damages could be either higher or lower than the level that might
  otherwise be deemed compensatory";[20]

---

[19] 2013 MICH. ST. L. REV. 1.

[20] Richard Craswell, *Instrumental Theories of Compensation: A Survey*, 40 SAN DIEGO L.
REV. 1135, 1162 (2003).

3.2 Other Remedial Matters

- that in view of the need for optimal damages to influence contracting parties' precontractual investigation of risks, "the optimal damage measure (in terms of its effect on the incentives to investigate) could be either above or below expectation damages, with the exact measure depending on the exact costs and benefits of further investigation";[21]
- that in view of incentives for plaintiffs to bring lawsuits, "the efficient damages could be either higher or lower (higher or lower, that is, than whatever measure of damages would otherwise be most efficient)";[22]
- that "even if we limit our attention" to only two factors, deterrence of breach and enforcement of contract claims, "the most efficient measure of damages could be either higher or lower than an exactly compensatory measure";[23]
- that "efficient outcomes under a property rule could be achieved with much larger measures of damages, including injunctive relief (backed by fines for contempt) or even criminal sanctions."[24]

In other words, in view of economic considerations, damages might be anywhere. To be clear, this is not a criticism of Craswell's work on this subject; it is true that in view of the various economic considerations he describes, the efficient level of damages might well be anything. In other words, economic analysis is as indeterminate as any other open-ended analysis that looks at a variety of considerations in order to find strands that might influence an optimal damages measure. Closely related to this observation, as Professor Eisenberg and I also pointed out, many proposed alternatives that would aim or purport to micro-optimize particular features of contract damages would be impossible for courts to administer, either because they would be impossible for anyone to administer or because they play to the weaknesses rather than the strengths of courts.

Much as the formal discussion of activity levels in tort law, as discussed in Chapter 2, end up in a sort of mathematical "singularity" where human judgment seems to be required, contract damages may

---

[21] *Id.* at 1164.
[22] *Id.* at 1169–70.
[23] *Id.* at 1171.
[24] *Id.* at 1144.

not easily be susceptible to any unified form of economic analysis. The possible damage measures to be evaluated and defended in economic terms are always chosen against a baseline that is selected for some other reason: "efficient precautions," for example, to prevent "harms" as conceived against a particular baseline that is not defensible in purely economic terms.

In the end, it is surprising how little economic analysis there is either to explain or to justify the basic practices of contract law's remedial regime. As I have explained elsewhere in analyzing contract formation,[25] in many cases – particularly those where the law imposes expectation damages shortly after a contract is made – the most convincing economic justification for damages may be very similar to the most convincing moral one: that it is simply unfair to allow parties to make a deal and then continue to speculate at the other party's expense. It is not surprising that fairness and efficiency are closely linked – again, despite the Chicago school's desire to separate them – because contract parties act against a background of norms and expectations that are informed, at least in part, by beliefs about what is moral and what is fair. Hyper-rational or reductive concepts of allocative efficiency, on that view, miss the point.

3.2.1 The "New Business" Rule

There is a rule in contract law, known as the "new-business rule," that has largely eroded. The rule seems almost bizarre from the perspective of the modern world in which startups can be so successful: it is that a breach of contract that prevents a new business from starting up leads to no damages because the new business has no way of establishing its lost profits as sufficiently "certain."

The rule is not very important in modern contract law. But Victor Goldberg has defended it in an interesting way that merits a response. His justification for the rule is as follows:

> The relevant question should not be whether the project would make money but whether it would make more money than the next best alternative. The investment might have turned out to be wildly

---

[25] Bayern, *supra* note 2, at 95–96.

3.2 Other Remedial Matters 97

successful or a dismal failure, but there is no a priori reason to believe that the expected rate of return would exceed the going market rate. After the breach the promisee still has the money that it would otherwise have invested in the project and it would be free to do anything it wants with those funds. The expected value of the specific project would be the same as the market rate, so the promisee's loss would be zero. I need not qualify this by comparing the riskiness of the particular project with the market rate since the opportunity cost of the funds takes the relative riskiness into account. For this class of cases the per se rule – no compensation – makes sense.[26]

This argument operates to dictate facts to litigants – facts in their individual cases – on the basis of economic theory. In other words, the essence of the argument is "you have no damages because, statistically, someone in your position has no damages."

I highlight this not to suggest the new-business rule is significant in modern law but because it is important to resist the tendency, very common in law and economics and elsewhere in the social sciences (and perhaps in current thought generally), to treat everything as a statistical aggregation rather than an individual sample. Individual litigants are more than the random variables that characterize their economic success as a theoretical matter; there's no harm in arguing about what those random variables are for the benefit of the factfinder, but there is still a factual determination to be made about what profits an individual litigant would have lost as the result of a particular breach of contract.

By contrast, Professor Goldberg's argument is that someone's loss, under conditions of uncertainty, is their expected loss – and the expected loss is derived not empirically (for example, by sampling similar parties) but by economic theory that rests on the notion that parties earn the normal rate of return. But individual parties earn supranormal profits all the time – contrary to what would occur in abstract theory – and should have the opportunity to prove them in court if the legal question is what damages they have suffered in response to a particular breach. Statistics are not fate. Moreover, like Schwartz and Scott's argument about interpretation, discussed later in this chapter, Goldberg's argument also assumes, based on theoretical reasoning, that there is a particular known

---

[26] Victor Goldberg, Rethinking the Law of Contract Damages 231 (2019).

98   Contract Law

probability distribution about an individual case when there in fact isn't; his "expected value of the specific project" is a construct derived only from abstract theory about the sound functioning of the overall macro-economy (thus preventing supranormal profits).

Goldberg's argument is also peculiar because it does not aim to assign the *average* appropriate damages to a group of plaintiffs (which could, at least in theory, provide proper incentives to defendants in the aggregate) but instead collapses their damages to $0 based on the notion that the average supranormal profits in the relevant class of plaintiffs is $0. In the example he presents, there is a plaintiff who loses the opportunity to earn profits in a "new business" but has, by hypoth-esis, the opportunity to invest the same funds in an alternative busi-ness. For the sake of argument, imagine the range of potential profits from the lost original business as something like a bell curve. Even supposing the plaintiffs at or below the mean in fact have no dam-ages (because, taking into account their opportunity to mitigate their damages by making an alternative investment, they have lost nothing from breach), the plaintiffs experiencing a loss higher than the mean do probably have damages. The average damages suffered by the class of plaintiffs Goldberg has in mind is, then, not zero. In other words, Goldberg focuses on the average *overall profits* for plaintiffs in a rel-evant class, not the average *loss* for plaintiffs in a relevant class, and that focus would get the average damages measure wrong. If a breach sometimes causes harm and sometimes doesn't, the proper response even in the aggregate is not to deny liability.

Goldberg's analysis is insightful in drawing attention to the oppor-tunity for plaintiffs in new-business cases to mitigate their losses by making alternative investments. This is a valuable contribution to our understanding of new-business cases. But as applied to real facts, this feature of the argument assumes that there is too little friction between operating one venture and operating another. It is the rare entrepre-neur who has contracted for a particular opportunity, sees that oppor-tunity go away because of breach of contract, and then can shift gears immediately into something equally profitable. That sort of mitigation is not theoretically impossible, but if it's happened in any particular case, the law does and should make the defendant prove that the plain-tiff mitigated their damages (or could have done so).

3.3 CONTRACT INTERPRETATION

Contract interpretation is probably at once the trickiest, the most important, and the most litigated question in contract law. One of the most significant fault lines in debates about interpretation is whether agreements between two parties are to be interpreted based on some formal or textual reduction of their agreement – usually a written or electronic record, "signed" in some way – or whether courts should try to figure out what the parties' actual agreement was. Though the terms are a bit reductive, the first of these positions is often called *textualism* and the second is called *contextualism*.

When considering debates about textualism and contextualism in contract law, it is important to say at the outset that the policies in contract law may well be very different from those in public law. Substantial political effort over the last fifty years has promoted textualism in statutory interpretation (and forms of textualism in constitutional interpretation) for various reasons, probably including the pursuit of various political goals and the desire to constrain the discretion of federal judges (although whether textualism does in fact constrain judges is doubtful). Regardless of the merits of that political effort, there is no reason in logic, efficiency, or morality for it to have much bearing on the interpretation of contracts. Nonetheless, for unclear and probably poor reasons, contract textualism is often seen as a "conservative" position and contextualism as a more "liberal" position.

One of the striking patterns in the economic analysis of contract textualism and contract contextualism is that the leading Chicago-school economic arguments have generally been strongly in favor of textualism, though for wildly different reasons (and with wildly different assumptions) over time. It is as if legal economists are sure that a hard-edged textualist interpretive regime must be efficient, even though they have not settled on why that must be the case.

The first round of analysis was fairly general: the economic justification of textualism was that it made legal entitlements more certain and therefore lowered transaction costs for contracting parties. So, for example, Robert Scott wrote in 2000: "A rigorous application of the common-law plain meaning and parol evidence rules would preserve

100   Contract Law

the value of predictable interpretation and encourage parties to take precautions in selecting terms with well-defined meanings."[27]

This early type of argument was replaced, starting in 2003, with a much more elaborate model that depended on preferences of contracting parties themselves, derived theoretically. Interestingly, the model works in exactly the opposite way to the earlier economically minded formalism: it recognizes that textualism makes rights *less* predictable for contracting parties (because textualism curtails nuanced, contextual decision making) but justifies that decreased precision in terms of textualism's ability to reduce litigation costs. More recently, empirical studies – normally beyond this book's scope but tied so closely to the arguments about what interpretive regimes contract parties will supposedly prefer that I don't want to ignore them completely – have weighed in. The rest of this section considers these arguments in turn.

3.3.1 Theoretical Derivations about Rational Contracting Parties: Contract Theory, Risk-Neutrality, and Textualism

In an extremely influential article,[28] Alan Schwartz and Robert Scott in 2003 introduced a theoretical economic argument that rational parties – and thus, according to them, business firms – prefer textualism. I take their argument to be the leading modern statement of the law-and-economics movement's theoretically derived textualism.[29] The argument is subtle. After summarizing the argument that Schwartz and Scott have made in their original article and elsewhere,[30] this subsection lays out several critiques of it.

Schwartz and Scott's approach to interpretive questions in contract law is deductive and theoretical; that is, their method to determine the best set of interpretive rules is to deduce an answer based on the necessary behavior of rational parties, as modeled by formal economics.

---

[27] Robert E. Scott, *The Case for Formalism in Relational Contract*, 94 Nw. U. L. Rev. 847, 848 (2000).

[28] Alan Schwartz & Robert E. Scott, *Contract Theory and the Limits of Contract Law*, 113 Yale L.J. 541 (2003). As of late 2022, according to Google Scholar the individual article had been cited 1,240 times.

[29] *See* Shawn J. Bayern, *Rational Ignorance, Rational Closed-Mindedness, and Modern Economic Formalism*, 97 Cal. L. Rev. 943 (2009) for further discussion.

[30] *See* Schwartz & Scott, *supra* note 3.

3.3 Contract Interpretation

They do briefly survey empirical evidence that they believe supports their position,[31] but their argument fundamentally is an attempt to demonstrate on theoretical grounds that rational parties, particularly business firms involving five or more people, are (1) necessarily risk-neutral and (2) as a result of that risk-neutrality, prefer a textualist mode of interpretation.[32] My most significant disagreements with Schwartz and Scott are that I deny that business firms are necessarily risk-neutral and that risk-neutral firms necessarily prefer textualism.

To understand the debate, it will be helpful to elaborate Schwartz and Scott's deductive model in some detail. The essential insight of their model is that a risk-neutral party will be a contract textualist because admitting evidence about the intent of the contracting parties increases the costs of litigation without changing the expected value of an unbiased court's interpretive result.[33] This conclusion depends on a model of interpretive results as (1) reducible to scalar values that (2) have a mean value that is invariant to the amount of evidence used during the interpretive process.[34] Moreover, their model of the difference between textualism and contextualism – which I accept for the purposes of this discussion – is also essentially scalar; the different interpretive modes simply allow a court to use a larger or smaller "evidentiary base"[35] to carry out its interpretive process. On one end of the spectrum, a court might flip a coin (using no evidence at all). On the other, a court might use all relevant evidence that the parties submit. Schwartz and Scott's argument for textualism is an argument for what they call the "minimum evidentiary base," which includes specifically "the parties' contract, a narrative concerning whether the parties performed

---

[31] *Id.* at 955–57.

[32] *E.g., id.* at 952–56.

[33] Schwartz & Scott, *supra* note 28, at 574–77 ("Thus, courts that interpret contracts as typical parties prefer would be indifferent to variance as well, and sensitive only to the costs of administering their evidentiary standard."). I of course mean "expected value" in the literal technical sense as defined in the analysis of random variables. *See generally* CHRISTIAAN HUYGENS, DE RATIOCINIIS IN LUDO ALEÆ (1657) (introducing the basic notion underlying the modern understanding of random variables).

[34] Schwartz & Scott, *supra* note 28, at 575–76 ("In other words, the court is as likely to make an interpretation that is more favorable to the buyer (less favorable to the seller) than the correct answer as the court is likely to make a less favorable interpretation. Judicial errors therefore cancel, in expectation.").

[35] *Id.* at 575.

102   Contract Law

the obligations that the contract appears to require, a standard English language dictionary, and the interpreter's experience and understanding of the world."[36] In other words, their argument is that any more evidence than that "minimum evidentiary base" – such as testimony or documentary evidence about the parties' intent, their prior deals, and industry custom – may well make interpretive outcomes more precise, but rational parties would (if asked at the time they made their contract) decline to permit its use in interpreting the contract because they don't care about the precision of the result; because they are risk-neutral, they care only about the average result from an unbiased court.

To be clear, while this sort of modeling is artificial and not particularly appealing to me – it is not how contracting parties or courts think about contract interpretation – I don't need in this subsection to reject the very use of it. It is possible to make intuitive sense of reductive models. For example, an agreement between two parties might be vague as to any number of factual matters, like the level of quality of a particular supplied good, the degree to which the seller has promised to fix it if it breaks, or the amount of time it will take to ship the goods to their destination. Though each of these matters of possible disagreement is potentially rich in context and hard to reduce to a spot on a one-dimensional numeric scale, it is not wholly counterintuitive to imagine such a scale. Different points on the scale represent different legal results; one point might be more favorable to one party and correspondingly less favorable to the other. We might say that the scale can never fully capture the richness of the underlying dispute – at least for many types of disputes – and that may be true. If so, it is a further weakness in the model. But it is not one I need to pursue here.

In terms of the scalar model, then, suppose two contracting parties enter into a deal in which their actual agreement is (modeled by) the number 50. Schwartz and Scott's central conclusion is that even if a larger base of information reduces interpretive risk and makes it nearly certain that the court will decide on the number 50 in an eventual dispute (rather than some relatively unpredictable value between 30 and 70), using this larger base of information will not be worthwhile to the parties because of its costs: each party will have to search for more

---

[36] *Id.* at 572.

3.3 Contract Interpretation

evidence, introduce it into court, contest the other party's evidence, go through a longer trial, and pay their lawyers more. Because each party is risk-neutral, they didn't care about the risk of imprecision (formally, the variance) in the court's result in the first place, so they would prefer not to pay to reduce it.[37] They'd happily, in other words, take a range of results from 0 to 100, distributed evenly or in some unbiased distribution like a bell curve, rather than pay to make 50 (the value they actually agreed on) a predictable result.

That is the essence of Schwartz and Scott's argument. One simple way to know that it is wrong is that it violates information theory by producing a far more specific "evidentiary base" than its straightforward model justifies. The "minimum evidentiary base" that they have picked happens to correspond roughly to textualism (that is, to contract law's plain-meaning and parol-evidence rules). In form, their argument is indistinguishable from one that risk-neutral firms would prefer a coin flip to a court trial (despite the reality that coin-flip dispute resolution is less commonly chosen as a dispute-resolution technique than trials, if for no other reason than that it would favor those who can manufacture disputes). Virtually nothing in their argument is in favor of the "minimum evidentiary base" as compared to any other specific alternative for an evidentiary base.

Moreover, even if we suppose that a court is not systematically prone to favor one party or kind of party over another, that is not enough to conclude that the meaning the court supplies to a contract will on average be the particular meaning the parties previously reached. Schwartz and Scott in fact assume that there is a particular probability distribution that can model courts' answers to interpretive questions – as I suggested earlier, perhaps it is uniform, or perhaps it is a bell curve centered on the "right" interpretive result – but they have no basis for making this assumption. Instead of probability, there is simply uncertainty – no specific way to model a distribution for courts' potential answers.

To see why this is so, consider the situation more formally, following Schwartz and Scott's abstraction of courts' interpretive decisions as points on a number line.[38] We are told that a court is going to pick

---

[37] Bayern, *supra* note 29, at 954.

[38] Schwartz & Scott, *supra* note 28, at 575.

some number from among all whole numbers (that is, from the range of numbers that looks like "..., −3, −2, −1, 0, 1, 2, 3, ...," where both ends extend to infinity). Furthermore, we are told that there is no more reason to suppose this number will be greater than 50 rather than less than 50. From this, it might be tempting to conclude that the expected value of the number the court will pick is 50; after all, if we have no reason to suppose that the court's number will be higher or lower than 50, then it seems like each possibility is equally likely in fully symmetric ways, and thus the average value appears to be 50. Reasoning in this way, however, is fallacious. Just because we have no reason to believe that the court's number is more likely to be greater than 50 than it is to be less than 50, and vice versa, does not mean that the expected value of the court's number is 50. Consider that we might *also* have no reason to believe the number is going to be higher or lower than 60, or 70, or any other given number.

Simply put, the mere lack of a suspicion of "bias" tells us nothing, alone, about expected values. We need some affirmative reason to think the average decision will be the correct one; otherwise, we could pick any other possible decision and still say, "The court has no systematic reason to veer up or down from this decision." Knowledge of expected values depends on knowledge of the likelihoods of the various possible outcomes; we cannot, from mere uncertainty, determine specific expectations.[39] As economic commentators themselves have nicely put it:

> Uncertainty is not equitable with risk [or probability]. Risk implies the existence of (and the knowledge of) a definable numerical series, the constituents of which can be identified and discounted .... Risk relates to knowledge of the appropriate probability distribution; uncertainty implies that we do not know whether any such distribution exists, and that in fact it may not exist.[40]

---

[39] There is a rich literature on the distinction between probability and uncertainty, but that doesn't stop commentators from assuming that probability distributions are known when they are not. *See, e.g.*, Mark Perlman & Charles R. McCann, Jr., *Varieties of Uncertainty in* UNCERTAINTY IN ECONOMIC THOUGHT 9 (Christian Schmidt ed., 1996) (summarizing several approaches to uncertainty); *cf.* Paul Davidson, *Some Misunderstanding on Uncertainty in Modern Classical Economics in* UNCERTAINTY IN ECONOMIC THOUGHT, *supra*, at 28 ("The current fad in mainstream economics is to argue as if all economic observations are part of time series realizations generated by stochastic processes."); *see also, generally*, FRANK H. KNIGHT, RISK, UNCERTAINTY, AND PROFIT (1921).

[40] Perlman & McCann, *supra* note 39, at 11–12.

3.3 Contract Interpretation

In other words, in cases of pure uncertainty, there are simply no probability distributions to apply and therefore no way to compute expected values sensibly. How much would you pay for a chance at some amount of money, to be determined by an undisclosed procedure? Will there be a nuclear war in the next year? Do we exist in a computer simulation?[41] The answers to questions like these are at best subject to rough *speculation* in subjective probabilistic terms, where probability distributions might be proposed and debated by people with particular intuitions, particular scientific understandings, different experiences with the world, and so forth.[42] But they are not subject to definite probabilistic analysis, as if a known expected value can be computed. Squarely and honestly recognizing uncertainty requires that we avoid resting arguments on the assumption that all uncertainty can be modeled by particular probability distributions. Just because the conflation between probability and uncertainty is convenient does not make it correct.

In considering what you'd rationally pay for a chance at an amount of money to be determined by an undisclosed procedure, infinities come into play and may obscure the analysis. In considering all possible sums of money, ranging in at least one direction toward infinity, there is no midpoint to speak of and thus not even a way to *begin* fixating on any potential "average" in the abstract, in any sense.

Even when there is a midpoint – that is, even when there are upper and lower limits on the possibilities that a case might raise – that alone, too, is insufficient to justify the assumption that the midpoint is the expected value. For one thing, medians (midpoints) routinely differ from means in many kinds of distributions. More generally, it would require specific knowledge, or at least a specific assumption, to associate the midpoint of a range with any kind of average.

For instance, imagine that we know that in a particular contract case, the court isn't really considering awarding all *possible* measures

---

[41] *Cf.* Nick Bostrom, *Are We Living in a Computer Simulation?*, 53 Phil. Q. 243 (2003) (arguing that this possibility is perhaps more likely than typically supposed).

[42] Strictly speaking, determining the expected value of a random variable requires knowing the expected distribution of that variable – that is, the range of possible values and their probabilities. *See* Thomas M. Cover & Joy A. Thomas, Elements of Information Theory 13 (1991). These expectations may be subject, of course, to subjective probabilistic beliefs, determined by intuition and background knowledge, but in the abstract they cannot be derived from scratch.

106   Contract Law

of damages. Suppose instead that the terms of a case make it so that the only reasonably expected range for damages is $20,000–$60,000. In that case, it may superficially seem reasonable to suppose that the expected value of damages – assuming we know nothing more than the range – is $40,000, the average of the upper and lower limits. In some cases that may well be the expected value, but accepting it as a particular expectation requires a further specific assumption – for example, that all values within the range are equally likely, or that they fall into some other distribution that provides the necessary guarantee. Merely assuming that the expected value is in the center of the range is unjustified (and is not required by any kind of rationality or risk-neutrality). For instance, if you're told nothing other than that there are two possible outcomes of an abstract event, it is not required by *reason* alone that you assume the likelihood of each possibility is 50 percent. In fact, with pure uncertainty, 50 percent is just as arbitrary a bet as any other number. You might as well estimate probabilities purely on intuition or superstition or make an entirely arbitrary guess. If you really don't know what the likelihood is of either of the two events, there is simply nothing more to say about the *probabilities* of those two events. The probabilities are unknown.

Indeed, in evaluating economic choices under conditions of pure uncertainty, it is better to say that there is *no expected value* than that the expected value is the average of possible cases' values. For example, suppose you're given the opportunity, for $14, to participate in a game in which you're told you'll be given either $10 or $20, as chosen by an undisclosed procedure. Assuming you're risk-neutral, is it rationally required for you to pay $14 for the bet, given that the average of the two numbers is $15? It may seem intuitive to think so, perhaps because many people have been conditioned to treat cases like this as if they're governed by probabilities; in fact, there is a strong tendency to suppose that, without knowing more, it's appropriate to say that the likelihood of each of the two possibilities ($10 and $20, here) is 50 percent. But this simply isn't true. It is not *irrational* even for a risk-neutral party to turn down the bet.[43] Without knowing or assuming more about it,

---

[43] This sort of reasoning may lead to results that appear counterintuitive. For example, suppose you have choice between two alternatives. In one case, you're told you might

3.3 Contract Interpretation 107

the bet has no expected value.[44] You have little reason, one way or the other, to play or not to play; you might as well make the decision arbitrarily. Indeed, it may well be reasonable on pragmatic grounds to avoid uncertainty when facing artificially constructed bets like this because in the real world, blatantly stated uncertainty may be intended to obscure bad faith or other sorts of practices adverse to the bettor.[45]

The point of this admittedly abstract set of examples is to suggest that there is no reason, theoretically or by default, to assume that events with truly unknown probabilities are equally likely. Similarly, it is not always correct to assume that unknown data spreads evenly through a range of possible values or otherwise produces a known or knowable average. In some cases (as with truly random data), values might indeed be expected to spread evenly through a range. In others, the data may fit a normal distribution (a bell curve). But often it might conform to neither of those preconceived templates.

For instance, suppose we need to determine the average speed at which man-made vehicles are operated and that all we know is that, on one end of the spectrum, there are scooters that move at about 10 miles per hour and that, on the other hand, there are rocket ships that move at about 20,000 miles per hour. It would be wrong to assume from this information that the average speed of man-made vehicles is

---

be given either $10 or $20, to be decided by an undisclosed procedure. In the other case, you're told you might be given either $5 or $21, by another undisclosed procedure. Should you choose the first case over the second case just because the values average to $15 instead of $13? It may seem natural to do so, but this is probably only because we generally have intuitions that uncertainty never governs a case *entirely* – that is, that what's stated as uncertainty actually contains an element of probability too, so that we assume (for instance) that the two possibilities in each case are roughly equally likely (or that all the possible probability distributions favoring either direction somehow cancel out). But in fact, in cases of true uncertainty, you have no *reason* to pick one case over the other. You would not be *irrational* simply to flip a coin or to make an arbitrary decision between the two cases. One way of making an arbitrary decision would be to throw up your hands and say, "Well, I'm just going to assume that all possible outcomes are equally likely!" Whether this is a good way to proceed or not depends on unknown conditions, like what the probability distributions of the events really is (if one exists at all).

[44] We do know, however, that if an expected value exists, it must be between $10 and $20, inclusive. More to the point, the result must be either $10 or $20. Accordingly, a rational, risk-neutral party ought *not* to turn down the bet if it costs $10 or less, and certainly ought to turn it down if it costs $20 or more.

[45] *Cf.* Deborah Frisch & Jonathan Baron, *Ambiguity and Rationality*, 1 J. BEHAV. DECISION MAKING 149, 152–53 (1988) (offering several reasons people may avoid uncertainty).

the average of the two ends of the spectrum that we're aware of – in this case, 10,005 miles per hour. The result, on just the information we're given, is simply *uncertain*; we don't have enough information to answer the question, knowing only the range of possible values. If we're forced to make a decision, choosing the midpoint is not specifically more problematic than any other alternative, but it also has nothing specially to recommend it, except perhaps intuitions that we know more than we initially thought we did about the probability distribution at issue. For example, we might decide that we have some reason to think, perhaps based just on background experience, that normal distributions occur more frequently in problems like these than other sorts of distributions.[46]

Given real uncertainty, there are a variety of approaches we can adopt. We can, similarly to Schwartz and Scott, introduce a new assumption that the distribution of the values that we're interested in happens to conform to a bell curve or another similar shape that centers on the midpoint of an expected range. But for this to be a plausible approach, we need some *reason* to do it. Thus, for Schwartz and Scott's argument in favor of a textualist interpretation to be correct on its own terms, we need to recharacterize its central assumption. It is not sufficient merely for courts to be unbiased. Instead, institutional considerations about courts in general, or courts interpreting contracts in particular, must lead us to believe that in cases where parties present alternative interpretations of a written contract, the court's expected holding will average exactly to the ex ante agreement of the parties. This assumption seems heroic and implausible as a general matter, and for various reasons it is specifically unlikely to be true.

In particular, in the cases Schwartz and Scott have in mind, practical and institutional considerations about courts and contract cases strongly suggest that courts employing the "minimum evidentiary

---

[46] Bell curves – normal distributions – have wide applications in many fields, ranging from pure mathematics and physics to psychology and natural science, because they happen to fit a variety of data well. There are sound theoretical reasons for this (simply put, it is the shape that results, given certain assumptions, from the additive combination of independent random variables), but it is wrong to assume without more that an unknown distribution is necessarily normal. *See* Enders A. Robinson, Statistical Reasoning and Decision Making 61 (1981) ("Despite [the] seeming universality of the normal distribution, we cannot expect it to apply to every measurement ....").

3.3 Contract Interpretation

base" will not, on average, reach the correct result. In contract-interpretation cases generally, we have no practical reason to imagine that courts will center on precisely the result that the parties originally had in mind. Interestingly, Schwartz and Scott occasionally seem to recognize this; for instance, they observe in a somewhat different context that, if a party unduly persuades a court of an incorrect result, the court's result could be anything at all, rather than settling on a specific average that the parties had in mind:

> For example, assume a contract uses the word "red," and a disappointed party persuades the court, wrongly, that the contract was written in a private language in which the word "red" meant "green." Both red and green are vague. In this example, the space of possible judicial interpretations would center around some instance of the concept "green," but the court here could not be right on average. It would be attempting to find the correct shade of green while the parties, ex ante, wanted a court to find the correct shade of red. When courts are mistaken regarding the contract's language, their constructions must be inefficient ....[47]

It is exceedingly difficult to construct a principled basis that allows Schwartz and Scott to separate the two cases – that is, to differentiate ordinary interpretative inquiries from those in which a court has been inappropriately persuaded by a party of an incorrect interpretation. Schwartz and Scott *reach* the two cases differently: in one case, they imagine that courts are interpreting a well-known word; in the other, they imagine that the very choice of an interpretive *language* is at stake, and choosing the wrong language (for instance, a private language of the parties as opposed to what Schwartz and Scott call "majority-talk")[48] will dictate the wrong result. But of course, the only difference here is a question of which particular framing is adopted: we could ask both (1) why, in the case of ordinary interpretation, a court might not be incorrectly persuaded by one of the parties, after which the result will necessarily be wrong and (2) why, in the case of language selection, we don't begin our analysis prior to the point that the court has been led down an erroneous path.

---

[47] Schwartz & Scott, *supra* note 28, at 587.
[48] *Id.* at 586.

110   Contract Law

In any event, in both cases there is simply no reason to suppose that the average result (when using just the written text of agreements and other components of the minimal evidentiary base) is the correct result. Schwartz and Scott's only justification for this proposition is that contracting parties know that if their contracts are too vague, the "mean [interpretation] could be anywhere."[49] As a result, "firms will attempt to write contracts with sufficient clarity to permit courts to find correct answers, though with error." Schwartz and Scott seem to be aiming to justify only the assumption that courts *can* find the correct answer using the minimal evidentiary base (which, recall, includes the contract's written text, a narrative of the contract's performance, a dictionary, and general background knowledge). This could be true. But they offer no justification that it will be at the center of the very specific probability distribution they imagine will characterize courts' decisions. Thus, they more or less assume their conclusion: their argument is that if formalist textual interpretation is good enough, then it is good enough.

Maybe they mean to imply that parties who know about contract law's rules will be able to avoid ambiguity in their drafting, but from experience we know that that is plainly untrue. There are several reasons to suppose that, in fact, parties' incentives to draft agreements carefully are insufficient for the minimal evidentiary base to allow courts' decisions to average to the parties' real agreement. Indeed, these incentives seem mostly irrelevant in the cases Schwartz and Scott have in mind. For cases in which courts need to construct meaning – either for poorly chosen language or unthought-of gaps – whatever incentives the parties had to draft their contract carefully were already insufficient to avoid the lack of clarity that led to litigation. Such cases are not especially susceptible to a suggestion that "[i]t is optimal for risk-neutral firms to invest resources in drafting until the writing is sufficiently clear, in an objective sense, so that the mean of the distribution of possible judicial interpretations is the correct interpretation."[50] That is, it is hard to imagine that parties have precisely enough of an incentive to draft language carefully enough so that courts' average

[49] *Id.* at 577.
[50] *Id.*

3.3 Contract Interpretation

interpretation will be correct but *not* carefully enough to avoid the dispute in the first place.[51]

As a more general matter, even if it were sometimes true that commentators could agree on a specific expected distribution of interpretive responses to text by a court, it is systematically unlikely to be true in contract cases, particularly in the kind of contract cases Schwartz and Scott have in mind. For contract cases generally, compared to cases with more publicly observable regularities (like the rate of foodborne illness as a function of the temperature and duration of food storage), there is little opportunity to aggregate repeated "runs" of the very similar cases in order to build a reliable probability distribution.[52] For the specific kinds of cases Schwartz and Scott have in mind, in which parties intend for language to mean something specific but the language simply fails to achieve its purpose in ways the parties couldn't expect, there is no reason to believe the court can, from this erroneous or sloppy language alone, reach interpretations that average to the correct decision. Indeed, sloppy language is an especially poor candidate for a kind of text that, standing more or less alone, can produce a correct meaning on average.

A related point is that in cases involving significantly sloppy language, which largely approach *mistake* or *mistranscription* cases, the cost of correcting or explaining the contract that is before the court may well be small; the solution may not tend to involve complicated evidence but rather straightforward facts about how the term in the

---

[51] Contract drafting, moreover, has a cost, which is certain – whereas litigation is unlikely ex ante. Indeed, the increased drafting costs under Schwartz and Scott's suggested formalist approach may well be greater ex ante, in expected-value terms, than the extra costs associated with more accurate contract interpretation during litigation.

Similarly, formalism can encourage too much precaution in drafting, and it also might promote sharp drafting practices in bad faith by parties who hope to slip apparently irrelevant text past their counterparties (which in turn promotes further precaution in drafting), perhaps to introduce new clauses where the likelihood of a particular kind of potential sloppiness in drafting might be expected to bias in one's favor, and so on. The result is that drafting every business contract, including small ones, becomes an expensive and unpleasant endeavor – whereas now the most expensive and unpleasant behavior is confined to litigation.

[52] *Cf.* Perlman & McCann, *supra* note 39, at 12 ("[One] kind of uncertainty stresses the absence of enough experiences which will yield a stable probability function. Given sufficient cases, a distribution can usually be found; but just how many cases (how much 'experience') is required cannot be known *a priori*.").

112   Contract Law

contract fails to achieve the parties' intent. To put this differently, sloppy language may often be erroneous as the result of a lapse, or transient mechanical error.[53] It is possible for such a lapse to result in unintended language that the parties could nonetheless plausibly have agreed on (thus making the error more difficult to demonstrate), but given that such plausible agreements are a small set of all possible uses of language, it is more likely that the lapse will be evident and easily correctible.[54] For other contract-interpretation cases, where the court is really filling gaps, the average interpretation forced from text and dictionaries (and a performance narrative and general knowledge of the world) alone is unlikely to happen to correspond to what the parties wanted, or would have wanted had they considered the issue.

To put this differently, in the cases to which Schwartz and Scott's argument applies, we are faced with (1) sloppy language that we already know didn't do what it was intended to do or (2) a contract that is vague with respect to the question at issue. In either case, it seems particularly unlikely that the court's interpretations will average to precisely the right answer from the text (and other minimal evidence) alone. So the proposition that is central to their argument can't be derived theoretically and is unlikely to be true in practice.

3.3.2 More General Problems with Textualist Models

So far, my analysis of Schwartz and Scott's argument has been quite technical, and it has rested on a distinction between the lack of systematic bias and the affirmative assertion of a statistical mean. But a response to Schwartz and Scott's argument needn't be so technical – and, indeed, a technical response could conceivably fail to respond to a more general insight that their model suggests, which is simply that

---

[53] *See* Melvin A. Eisenberg, *Mistake in Contract Law*, 91 CAL. L. REV. 1573, 1584 (2003) (defining "mechanical errors" in "mistake" cases as "physical or intellectual blunders that result from transient errors in the mechanics of an actor's internal machinery"); *cf.* ROBERT COOTER & THOMAS ULEN, LAW & ECONOMICS 232 (6th ed. 2012)(discussing "lapses" in a different context).

[54] *See* COVER & THOMAS, *supra* note 42, at 209–11 (1991) (discussing formal models of error correction).

3.3 Contract Interpretation 113

a contextualist interpretive regime has litigation costs that a textualist interpretive regime might productively avoid.[55] This subsection develops a variety of more general responses to Schwartz and Scott's model.

Recall that Schwartz and Scott's argument depends on the notion that courts, on average, will reach the right interpretive result even if, in individual cases, they will diverge from the parties' initial expectations.[56] This is, after all, what makes their assumption of risk-neutrality relevant; they conclude that risk-neutral parties prefer textualism specifically because they would prefer not to pay for more precise interpretation in individual cases.[57] Under Schwartz and Scott's model, the parties initially contract and have a shared idea of what they have agreed to do, but it is too expensive to draft a contract that covers every possible contingency.[58] A question later arises about the rights and duties of the parties. The parties' original conception could answer this problem in theory, but because of the limitations of the drafting process, this original conception is not verifiable to the court.[59] Because the parties are textualists, they commit the question to the court knowing that the expected value of the court's interpretive distribution is the parties' original conception.[60]

The difficulty with conceiving information and communication in this way is that it assumes that the parties can use, at the time when they produce their contract, language that produces a distribution with a known expected value but is nonetheless ambiguous and leads to different outcomes in courts. Though this is conceivable in theory, it is implausible in practice. I believe the difficulty lies specifically in the translation of Schwartz and Scott's formal model to real cases. It is one thing, in other words, to talk of a mean interpretive result; it

---

[55] Schwartz & Scott, *supra* note 3, at 930. Schwartz and Scott responded to an earlier technical critique I made of their argument. *See id.* at 945 n.47. Their response simply distinguished uniform from normal distributions. It is not clear how that undermines my critique, however, because my argument was that their model justifies no particular probability distribution.

[56] Schwartz & Scott, *supra* note 28, at 605–10.

[57] *Id.*

[58] *Id.*; Schwartz & Scott, *supra* note 3, at 954–55.

[59] "Verifiability" is a term of art in economic contract theory. *See* Schwartz & Scott, *supra* note 28, at 605–07.

[60] *See id.* at 592–93.

114   Contract Law

is another to make the concept operational and tie it to real contract language. Schwartz and Scott never make clear the paradigmatic contract language or specific legal dispute they have in mind, nor do they argue that any particular paradigmatic cases are an appropriate basis on which to construct default legal rules. This abstraction ends up undermining their argument.

Consider more specifically: if the parties can use language that leads to a known and agreed-upon interpretive mean, why does any ambiguity remain? Schwartz and Scott describe the language that generates a known mean as follows:

> It is optimal for risk-neutral firms to invest resources in drafting until the writing is sufficiently clear, in an objective sense, so that the mean of the distribution of possible judicial interpretations is the correct interpretation i^* [i.e., a scalar value corresponding to the correct interpretation]. Contracts sketched out in less detail than this would generate interpretation distributions whose mean could be anywhere.[61]

But if the parties are confident that the language they use will produce a definite mean result – a particular value i^* – why does any ambiguity remain in the language they have used? Why can't the courts settle uniformly on the mean interpretive result, which is evidently public knowledge anyway (because the parties can predict the courts' average result)? In other words, what room in the real world remains for specific purposive language that is characterized by two propositions: (1) there is general (presumably widespread) agreement on the "mean" interpretation, but (2) there is nonetheless symmetrical variance around this mean as a result of uncertainty?

It seems that Schwartz and Scott's model permits a much narrower conclusion than they intend. They wish to show that all risk-neutral parties prefer textualism, but it appears they have shown, at most, that such parties prefer textualism specifically for terms about which there is no possible real-world dispute. This is because, for language with an uncontroversial mean interpretive result that has symmetric variance, no ambiguity remains; there would be little reason for anyone, including parties and courts, to adopt a meaning other than the known mean value.

---

[61] *Id.* at 577.

3.3 Contract Interpretation

To put it differently, how can a legitimate dispute arise out of a publicly known and stable probability distribution? If there is a legitimate dispute about language, why would there be an agreement about the mean interpretive result ex ante; conversely, if there were a general agreement, why would ambiguity remain? Note that this is not simply a case where the parties have a private understanding of terms that they cannot prove to courts,[62] because under Schwartz and Scott's model, the parties' expectation ex ante is specifically that the *courts* will reach a mean interpretive result (with some expected variance).

Even putting this problem aside, as suggested earlier it is hard to discern a meaningful justification for the "minimal evidentiary base" based on theoretical argumentation alone, rather than an argument with more empirical sensitivity. Recall that the "minimal evidentiary base" they promote and consider to be textualist is "the parties' contract, a narrative concerning whether the parties performed the obligations that the contract appears to require, a standard English language dictionary, and the interpreter's experience and understanding of the world."[63] Schwartz and Scott's assertion of this base of evidence as the minimal necessary for courts to reach correct interpretive results on average appears to rest only on their intuitions about the costs and utility of different classes of evidence. It is hard to see how the practical question of evidentiary utility could be decided as a theoretical matter; as noted earlier, there simply isn't enough information in the theory to conclude that "a dictionary" is useful but that trade usage (perhaps even written and widely known trade usage) is not justified by its administrative costs.[64] Schwartz and Scott would presumably agree that flipping a coin – despite incurring administrative costs drastically lower than typical adjudication – is insufficient for courts to reach the

---

[62] Economic contract theorists refer to this case as one in which information is "observable but not verifiable." *See id.* at 605 ("A datum of information is 'observable but not verifiable' if a party can observe it, but cannot verify the information's existence to a third party such as a court at an acceptable cost.").

[63] *Id.* at 572.

[64] I mean this information-theoretic point in a technical sense – specifically, that the information contained in an expression of the theory is insufficient to derive such complex specifics regarding textual sources. *Cf.* Andrei N. Kolmogorov, *Logical Basis for Information Theory and Probability Theory*, 14 IEEE Transactions on Info. Theory 662 (1968) (relating information theory to compressibility and complexity).

right interpretive result on average,[65] but why is a dictionary plus a stochastic resolution sufficient? There is no affirmative argument for the minimal evidentiary base.[66] As another way to put it, if the parties' goal is simply to reduce litigation costs, why not require that all disputes be arbitrated by an AI language model rather than decided in court; why is that better or worse than the specific evidentiary base and litigation procedure that Schwartz and Scott contemplate?

There is another important related problem for Schwartz and Scott's stochastic view of courts.[67] Simply speaking, if the parties agree on the court's mean interpretive result and they are risk-neutral, why would they ever litigate a contract in the first place? In some respects, this is the ex post mirror image of the argument that language with a known mean is unambiguous: language with a known mean is not worth litigating. To put it differently, if Schwartz and Scott's model actually applied to contracting parties, it is difficult to see why they would ever bring a lawsuit – and thus difficult to see why the argument should be the basis for a widespread default rule of contract law. If lawsuits are not brought, parties do not experience the litigation costs that Schwartz and Scott's textualist argument aims to let them avoid. To summarize, then, Schwartz and Scott's model is difficult or impossible to apply in a legal setting.

Nonetheless, in responding as I have done to their argument, I do not wish to minimize their concerns about the costs of dispute resolution. I take those costs to be the chief modern reason that contract textualism is at least plausible in some situations. As Schwartz and Scott put it:

> [A]lthough accurate judicial interpretations are desirable, accurate interpretations are costly for parties and courts to obtain .... If adjudication were costless, courts could minimize interpretive error by hearing all relevant and material evidence .... Since no

---

[65] Given that plaintiffs can specify the interpretive question at issue, an interpretive regime that rests on a coin flip would encourage plaintiffs to ask implausible interpretive questions because they would have a 50 percent chance of being judged "correct" as to those questions.

[66] *Cf. also* Juliet P. Kostritsky, *Plain Meaning vs. Broad Interpretation; How the Risk of Opportunism Defeats a Unitary Default Rule for Interpretation*, 96 Ky. L.J. 43 (2007) (identifying parties' incentives to behave opportunistically under textualist interpretive regimes).

[67] *See also* Bayern, *supra* note 29, at 968–71.

3.3 Contract Interpretation 117

> interpretive theory can justify devoting infinite resources to achieving interpretive accuracy, any socially desirable interpretive rule would trade off accuracy against ... adjudication costs.[68]

This is correct, so far as it goes. My disagreement with Schwartz and Scott arises when they purport to derive a specific default legal rule of extremely widespread applicability (covering, as they wish to do, contracts between all but the smallest firms) on the basis of theoretical deductions. There is also, perhaps, a difference in emphasis. While it is surely right that "no interpretive theory can justify devoting infinite resources to achieving interpretive accuracy," infinite resources were never on the table. In real cases, evidentiary bases are discrete rather than continuous and context-specific rather than context-neutral; the question is not "Can we pick a number corresponding to how much evidence to admit?" but "Is this particular piece of evidence admissible?" Moreover, rules of evidence already serve as a barrier to the possibility that the world will devote all its economic resources to the resolution of contract disputes.[69] Accordingly, while Schwartz and Scott are clearly right to argue that evidence must be cut off at some point, that observation alone does not lead to anything like a widespread textualist default. Perhaps it leads only to a recognition that it is useful to keep, rather than to throw away, evidence law.[70]

And in the context of the overall system of commercial contracting, litigation is vanishingly rare, whereas drafting is commonplace. To put that more directly, most contracts need to be drafted (or at least contracting parties need to engage in some sort of planning efforts), whereas extremely few parties ever litigate their contracts. Even a small increase in the cost of drafting individual contracts would affect large numbers of parties, whereas it is the rare case that needs to be litigated. Even without that recognition, the stability of the overall contracting system is worth far more than any differences that are on the table in litigation costs as a result of slight differences in the "evidentiary base" that litigants might use. I don't mean to say litigation costs

---

[68] Schwartz & Scott, *supra* note 3, at 930.

[69] *See, e.g.,* FED. R. EVID. 102 ("These rules should be construed so as to administer every proceeding fairly, eliminate unjustifiable expense and delay, and promote the development of evidence law, to the end of ascertaining the truth and securing a just determination.").

[70] *See generally id.* 102, 103.

are insignificant, but they pale in comparison to the total value of all contracts – that is, of all gains through trade in the economy of the United States. Tampering with the latter out of excessive concern with the former poses, at the least, a significant danger of economic loss. Though costs are of course a moving target, it appears that, according to one study in relatively recent times, a typical contract case costs between $70,000 and $100,000 if litigated to trial.[71] In 2005, around the same time as the study, state courts in the United States decided 8,917 contract cases,[72] implying that cases that led to resolution in court cost less than $900 million per year. In 2005, the gross domestic product (GDP) of the United States was $14.37 trillion. Of course, $900 million is a significant amount; as the old joke goes, add $900 million here and $900 million there, and eventually you're dealing with real money.[73] Nonetheless, in the year in question (chosen at random), $900 million was 0.006 percent (or one in about 16,000) of the GDP.

Of course, most cases settle, perhaps before being counted in these statistics. The effect of the default interpretive regime in contract law on settlement rates is complicated and contested, but even Schwartz and Scott seem to admit that their textualist proposal would not increase settlement rates.[74] As a result, the only question at stake seems to be: to what extent can we reduce the .006% drain on the economy that contract litigation represents? If the litigation were solely a loss, this might be a productive question for a very small administrative agency to consider; the problem, however, is that the economy receives something

---

[71] Adam J. Eckstein & Matthew P. Gabriel, *Reconsidering the Use of Arbitration Provisions in Contracts*, US LAW, Fall/Winter 2003, at 14, *available at* web.archive.org/web/20141225142433/www.martintate.com/article_Eckstein_Gabriel_USLAW_mag.pdf; Court Statistics Project, 20 CASELOAD HIGHLIGHTS 1 (2013), *available at* web.archive.org/web/20130611032232/www.courtstatistics.org/~/media/microsites/files/csp/data%20pdf/csph_online2.ashx.

[72] Donald J. Farole, *Contract Bench and Jury Trials in State Courts, 2005*, in U.S. DEPARTMENT OF JUSTICE, BUREAU OF JUSTICE STATISTICS BULLETIN (Sept. 2009), *available at* www.bjs.gov/index.cfm?ty=pbdetail&iid=2021 [https://perma.cc/7RRZ-X8WQ].

[73] The joke is often attributed to the American politician Everett Dirksen. *See* www.senate.gov/artandhistory/history/minute/Senator_Everett_Mckinley_Dirksen_Dies.htm [https://perma.cc/NC9R-EGQZ].

[74] *See* Bayern, *supra* note 29 (arguing that more precision in interpretive results should increase the likelihood of settlement if it has any effect at all); Schwartz & Scott, *supra* note 3, at 933 n.21 (apparently agreeing that for risk-neutral firms, the default meta-interpretive rule will not influence settlement rates).

3.3 Contract Interpretation

substantial for that $900 million: it receives a reliable adjudicatory system that backs up the commercial deals of American businesses. How much is it appropriate to risk in order to reduce that cost? Moreover, how much would textualism reduce it; would it even make a significant difference in the total amount, keeping in mind that the typical difference between textualism and contextualism involves only the production of such evidence as trade usage and evidence of course of dealing?[75] Despite general popular rhetoric suggesting the waste associated with litigation,[76] I am aware of no empirical evidence suggesting that the economic savings in reducing the evidentiary base for commercial litigation would be significant.

3.3.3 Risk-Neutrality

A further problem with Schwartz and Scott's model is that their assumptions about the risk-neutrality of contracting parties are stronger than is appropriate for a legal, rather than an economic, analysis. Their model is difficult to apply to real cases, and if it were correct, it would prove too much because it would make litigation unnecessary in the first place.

First, it is important to consider the premises of the argument. Schwartz and Scott intend for their model to apply to all risk-neutral parties.[77] As they recognize, this is not a small limitation on the application of their deductive recommendations because, for example, economists ordinarily understand individual people to be risk-averse rather than risk-neutral.[78] (The terms *risk-averse* and *risk-neutral* are terms of art to economists but have easily accessible meanings: a risk-neutral party would be indifferent between receiving $500 and a 50 percent chance of winning $1,000; a risk-averse party would prefer the certain $500 to the risky bet with an identical expected value.)[79] Accordingly, they intend for their model to apply only to contracts

---

[75] *See* Schwartz & Scott, *supra* note 28, at 574–77.

[76] *See generally* Shawn J. Bayern, Comment, *Explaining the American Norm Against Litigation*, 93 Cal. L. Rev. 1697, 1705–10 (2005) (citing "popular" sources).

[77] Schwartz & Scott, *supra* note 28, at 565 & n.44.

[78] *Id.*

[79] *See* Cooter & Ulen, *supra* note 53, at 44–47.

between companies; they would rule out from their analysis all contracts where at least one of the parties is an individual.[80]

Even this application, however, is questionable, because not all companies are risk-neutral. It is standard in *economic* commentary to treat business firms as if they are risk-neutral, because economists typically model business firms as if they maximize profit. As Schwartz and Scott say, their claim is that "firms maximize expected profits" and "[p]rofit maximization implies risk neutrality."[81] This implication is sound on logical grounds if the premises are correct; if a firm were risk-averse, it would not be maximizing expected profits because it would prefer a lower but definite expected value (e.g., $499) over a riskier but higher value (e.g., a 50 percent chance of receiving $1,000), just as individuals would. The problem, however, is simply that the economic modeling of an entity does not imply that the model matches the entity's properties in the real world or under the legal conceptions of business firms. If Schwartz and Scott's claim is that "firms maximize expected profits," it is trivial to falsify that claim with a counterexample because many firms, in the real world, do not maximize expected profits. Though I don't mean to overstate the point, at least as a purely doctrinal legal matter many organizations, under law, can or must consider values other than profits; for example, Delaware and many other states have passed statutes permitting "public benefit corporations" that balance profits with other goals. The relevant section of the Delaware statute reads as follows:

> The board of directors shall manage or direct the business and affairs of the public benefit corporation in a manner that balances the pecuniary interests of the stockholders, the best interests of those materially affected by the corporation's conduct, and the specific public benefit or public benefits identified in its certificate of incorporation.[82]

This counterexample is admittedly somewhat facile; Schwartz and Scott might happily be willing to exempt the relatively few "public

---

[80] Schwartz & Scott, *supra* note 28, at 544–50.

[81] Schwartz & Scott, *supra* note 3, at 947.

[82] DEL. GEN. CORP. LAW § 365 (2012).

3.3 Contract Interpretation 121

benefit corporations" from an updated version of their analysis.[83] My initial point, however, is only that "firms" is not the right category and requires, at a minimum, further restriction.

As it happens, in their original statement of their argument, Schwartz and Scott did not mean to include all firms in their model; they restricted their argument's scope explicitly to the following group of entities:

> (1) an entity that is organized in the corporate form and that has five or more employees, (2) a limited partnership, or (3) a professional partnership such as a law or accounting firm. These economic entities can be expected to understand how to make business contracts, and the theory we develop applies only to contracts between two such firms.[84]

This category, however, is still far too broad if the goal is to identify risk-neutral entities. More generally, if the goal is indeed to allow parties to choose the interpretive regime that governs them, assuming a preference for textualism in the entire foregoing group would be unjustified for several reasons.

First, as the existence of public-benefit corporations suggests, the role of corporations is broader, in the real world, than economists typically conceive it to be. Again, I do not want to overstate this point; I readily admit that profit-seeking is a major goal – probably the chief goal, and probably appropriately so – of American business corporations. But the economic analysis of entities often misses subtleties in their operational and legal characteristics and structure, and, as a result, "an entity that is organized in the corporate form and that has five or more employees"[85] is unlikely to track risk-neutrality in any meaningful way.

---

[83] Such entities are, however, helpful in pointing out the role that profit-maximization plays in their argument: Schwartz and Scott assume risk-neutrality as a result of profit maximization. As a result, the structure of their argument requires them to exempt public-benefit corporations, which is an odd result because there is little evident reason in the real world that a public-benefit corporation would or wouldn't prefer textualism or contextualism in a contract dispute solely because of its organizational form. In other words, the *form* of an entity is a very poor basis for guessing that entity's preferred interpretive regime, at least once the analysis shifts to real firms rather than modeled, theoretical ones.

[84] Schwartz & Scott, *supra* note 28, at 545.

[85] *Id.*

122   Contract Law

For one thing, the considerations permitted by the statutes authorizing public-benefit corporations are not unique across corporate law and are not limited to a special class of socially conscious corporations. Many states, as a default rule, permit or require boards of directors of regular business corporations to balance a variety of goals in making business judgments. For example, New York's corporate law reads as follows:

> In taking action ... a director [of a corporation] shall be entitled to consider, without limitation, (1) both the long- term and the short-term interests of the corporation and its shareholders and (2) the effects that the corporation's actions may have in the short-term or in the long-term upon any of the following:
>
> (i) the prospects for potential growth, development, productivity and profitability of the corporation;
> (ii) the corporation's current employees;
> (iii) the corporation's retired employees and other beneficiaries receiving or entitled to receive retirement, welfare or similar benefits from or pursuant to any plan sponsored, or agreement entered into, by the corporation;
> (iv) the corporation's customers and creditors; and
> (v) the ability of the corporation to provide, as a going concern, goods, services, employment opportunities and employment benefits and otherwise to contribute to the communities in which it does business.[86]

Despite the prevalence of economists' conceptions of firms as risk-neutral profit maximizers, no lawyer would assume, given this legal structure, that every corporation organized in New York (including small, family corporations) would act in a single, easy-to-characterize way. For one thing, the statute explicitly admits goals other than profit maximization into the calculus of those who oversee the firm. For another, it complicates simple conceptions of "profit maximization" by, for example, permitting directors to consider "both the long-term and the short-term interests of the corporation and its shareholders."[87] Even if risk-neutrality harmonizes with the maximization of the long-term interests of shareholders, it may well be within the "short-term interests of the corporation

---

[86] N.Y. Bus. Corp. Law § 717(b) (McKinney 2015).
[87] Id.

3.3 Contract Interpretation

and its shareholders" to optimize profits subject to constraints upon risk; indeed, it is hard to imagine what the difference between short-term and long-term interests are unless those interests diverge based partly on a tolerance for risk. This is because a fully rational, risk-neutral party facing no time pressure would presumably perceive no differences between "the long-term and the short-term interests."[88]

Second, more importantly, corporations and other legal entities are not simple or easily susceptible to formal modeling; far from being managed by machines or anything resembling an academic conception of rationality,[89] they are human endeavors subject to complex legal and organizational structures. As corporate statutes make clear,[90] even if the board decides on a strategy to maximize profits, it ordinarily pursues that agenda either by voting among people or, more typically,[91] by hiring individual executives who act as agents of the corporation.[92] If humans are risk-averse, it is difficult to conceive the firms they operate as *necessarily* and perfectly risk-neutral. Even if corporate structures mitigate the so-called irrationality of people, nothing guarantees that they do so entirely.

Much of the discipline of corporate law, indeed, aims to address the agency problems that arise between shareholders and directors – that is, between those who residually stand to earn the firms' profits and those who make decisions in pursuit of those profits.[93] Any private goal of the directors, without which there would not be much need for corporate law or the extensive commentary it has generated,[94] undermines the notion that a corporation is necessarily risk-neutral in

---

[88] *Id.*

[89] *Cf.* Shawn Bayern, Autonomous Organizations (2021).

[90] *E.g.*, Model Business Corporation Act § 8.01(b) (2006) (outlining the powers of the corporate board of directors).

[91] *See* Melvin Eisenberg, The Structure of Corporate Law 4–14 (1979) (discussing the evolution of the board of directors from management to oversight).

[92] *Id.* at 20–31.

[93] *Id.* at 31–40; Reinier Kraakman et al., The Anatomy of Corporate Law: A Comparative and Functional Approach 8–16 (2004); John. C. Coates IV, *Explaining Variation in Takeover Defenses: Blame the Lawyers*, 89 Cal. L. Rev. 1301 (2001) (offering an institutional analysis that considers the agency problems in corporate law associated with lawyers); Zohar Goshen, *Controlling Corporate Agency Costs: A United States–Israeli Comparative View*, 6 Cardozo J. Int'l & Comp. L. 99 (1998) (describing the importance and extent of agency costs in a comparative study of corporate law).

[94] *See, e.g.*, ALI Principles of Corporate Governance § 5.01 (1994); Eisenberg, *supra* note 91, at 40–62.

124   Contract Law

anything approaching the sense in which Schwartz and Scott would need it to be for their interpretive argument in contract law to hold. Decisions are made by hierarchies and other groups of humans, each with private pressures; reductive models are too simplistic, particularly in an age when many familiar corporations are controlled by small blocks of special shareholders who can pursue their own conceptions of the corporation's best interests with little practical opportunity for legal challenge.[95] Again, we don't need to dispute that firms care about profits or mostly maximize them in order to challenge Schwartz and Scott's argument; it is sufficient to recognize that firms can be a little risk-averse even while mainly pursuing profits. Their assumption about risk-neutrality has to be fully true or else their model falls apart; as soon as contracting parties care *a little* about risk, interpretive variance in legal cases becomes a problem that parties would pay to avoid.

Schwartz and Scott's categorization of limited partnerships and professional partnerships as necessarily risk-neutral is similarly overbroad, for mostly similar reasons. Like corporations – particularly private or closely held ones – unincorporated business entities often, in practice or even as a matter of legal right, are structured in ways that do not suggest perfect profit maximization or, more to the point, perfect risk-neutrality.[96] For example, the typical limited partnership gives exclusive operational control over the operations of an entity to a single party or a small group of them – the general partners – and these partners can act as they see fit,[97] limited for the most part only by fiduciary duties.[98] The mere organizational status suggests little about risk-neutrality. A general partner might be a single human being, acting with whatever tendencies individual people have.

---

[95] *E.g.*, Matthew Yglesias, *All Hail, Emperor Zuckerberg: How Facebook's IPO Gives a Stunning and Unprecedented Amount of Power to Its CEO*, SLATE, Feb. 3, 2012, www .slate.com/articles/business/moneybox/2012/02/facebook_s_ipo_how_mark_zuckerberg_ plans_to_retain_dictatorial_control_his_company_.html [https://perma.cc/E565-3QG3].

[96] *See* UNIF. LTD. P'SHIP ACT (2001) § 110(a) (permitting the partnership agreement to specify arbitrary provisions that govern the partnership).

[97] *Id.* § 406 ("Each general partner has equal rights in the management and conduct of the limited partnership's activities. Except as expressly provided in this [Act], any matter relating to the activities of the limited partnership may be exclusively decided by the general partner or, if there is more than one general partner, by a majority of the general partners.").

[98] *Id.* § 408 (enumerating fiduciary duties within limited partnerships). For more information, see SHAWN J. BAYERN, CLOSELY HELD ORGANIZATIONS 191 (2d ed. 2020).

3.3 Contract Interpretation

125

Much of my criticism of Schwartz and Scott's argument, on this score, is mainly that it incorrectly identifies firms that are likely to be risk-neutral when they enter contracts. Had they limited their argument to contracts between publicly traded firms, or firms over a certain market capitalization, I would have less to complain about on this particular front, although it still will prove very difficult to draw broad organizational lines aimed at the distinction that their argument needs to draw between risk-neutral parties and those that may act in risk-averse (or, for that matter, risk-seeking) ways. Without substantially more empirical evidence, I do not see how any lawyer could perceive them to have made a plausible case that the organizations they identify are, in the real world, necessarily risk-neutral. To put it differently, for their argument to carry the day, they would need to persuade legal audiences that firms don't care about the outcomes of their lawsuits, a proposition that is surely contradicted by the routine experience of most commercial lawyers!

In the end, one of my principal disagreements with Schwartz and Scott's argument is that the identification of textualist contracting parties cannot proceed along the general lines they have drawn. Importantly, it is probably impossible to derive, from an entity's formal characteristics alone, that the entity was entirely risk-neutral in making all its contracts. To their credit, Schwartz and Scott do recognize this point, but they seem to bury that recognition, perhaps for rhetorical reasons. Thus, for example, they make two telling admissions that suggest they agree that a single firm may act in ways that are occasionally risk-neutral and occasionally risk-sensitive.

First, they admit that firms are not risk-neutral, and thus presumably might prefer a contextualist mode of interpretation for their contracts, when "a correct interpretation is particularly important to them."[99] They dismiss this case, however, merely by saying, "Few business contracts have this 'bet the ranch' character, however."[100] This dismissal is surprising, if only because of the number of firms that fail, that run into trouble, or that for whatever other reasons have a "particularly important" contract or set of contracts that went badly

---

[99] Schwartz & Scott, *supra* note 3, at 947. As they note, they elaborate this point in more detail in their original statement of their argument in Schwartz & Scott, *supra* note 28, at 575–77.

[100] Schwartz & Scott, *supra* note 3, at 948.

126 Contract Law

for them. The force of Schwartz and Scott's argument is essentially that parties are happy to be textualists only when their contracts don't matter to them; maybe few individual contracts matter to the largest corporations, but it is surely not uncommon for firms in general to have "particularly important" contracts.[101] And it would be impracticable or impossible to hinge the operation of a legal doctrine on a determination of the importance of a contract to one of the parties.

Second, Schwartz and Scott note that risk-neutral firms commonly enter into contracts to hedge, assign, or otherwise mitigate risk, which is hard to explain if firms are uniformly risk-neutral:

> A third motive to contract is to transfer risk from more to less risk-averse parties. The legal enforcement of these contracts sometimes is necessary because the transferee of risk has an incentive to breach when large risks materialize. Risk-shifting contracts are not considered here, in part because one of the parties to them commonly is an insurer, and insurance contracts are the subject of a distinct and heavily regulated legal field. Moreover, although many contracts have an insurance component (e.g., commodities contracts, currency hedging), these contracts tend not to give rise to litigation.[102]

The dismissal of this possibility is surprising as well. It is important to note that it is logically incomplete; the possibility of risk-averse parties' entering risk-shifting contracts is ignored because *commonly* one is an insurer (not because one party is *always* an insurer) and because other sorts of risk-shifting contracts *tend not* to give rise to litigation – an unsupported empirical observation that, while probably true for financial instruments like options contracts, is questionable in the case of supply and output contracts that so commonly shift risks.[103] It also narrowly restricts the "insurance component" of contracts to

[101] Reviewing any first-year contracts casebook turns up many cases that would have a "bet the ranch" character for firms. Among interpretation cases alone, LON L. FULLER ET AL., BASIC CONTRACT LAW (10th ed. 2018), a leading contract-law casebook, includes several cases that would have this character. For example, Beanstalk Group, Inc., v. AM General Corp., 287 F.3d 856 (7th Cir. 2002) (Posner, J.), involves a claim to 35 percent of the value of the "Hummer" line of automobiles.

[102] Schwartz & Scott, *supra* note 28, at 565 n.44.

[103] *See, e.g.*, Laclede Gas Co. v. Amoco Oil Co., 522 F.2d 33 (8th Cir. 1975) (granting specific enforcement on a contract for the sale of natural gas because, even though the gas was not "unique," the purpose of the contract was to arrange a supply of gas to avoid the risk of market changes or market failure).

3.3 Contract Interpretation

hyperformal standardized contracts, when in fact business firms routinely enter into insurance contracts that don't involve the formal currency or options marketplaces.

In short, the economic assumption that firms are risk-neutral may work in economic theory, but there is little reason to believe that perfect risk-neutrality is strong enough in the real world to perform the function that Schwartz and Scott need it to perform. Their argument aims to set actual legal policy, not to advance an economic model for the sake of economic discussion. If the goal is to do what commercial parties want, it is not enough merely to assume that they want textualism.

Finally, in view of the discussion earlier in this chapter, it is worthwhile to point out that neutrality toward risk does not necessarily imply neutrality toward uncertainty.[104] Another response to Schwartz and Scott's argument, then, is that even risk-neutral firms may not be uncertainty-neutral. It is reasonable to imagine managers of risk-neutral enterprises preferring certainty to uncertainty on behalf of the enterprise and being willing to pay something for this, particularly given that nobody is really risk-neutral if the stakes are large enough: as just noted, even the most rational firms are not risk-neutral with respect to life-or-death decisions for the firm, and pure uncertainty may imply that there is an opportunity for significantly negative results (or may at least make it impossible to rule out those results).

3.3.4 Empirical Evidence about Actual Contracting Parties

As I noted in Chapter 1, my main focus in this book is on deductive rather than empirical arguments. However, in contract law, the two are not entirely separate because the economists' goal is often to make predictions about what actual contracting parties will want; for example, Schwartz and Scott's model is, at heart, necessarily a prediction about what risk-neutral parties will prefer. To support this way of thinking, many law-and-economics commentators have adduced what they believe is empirical support for a broad default rule of textualism, so in evaluating theoretical economic arguments it is important to evaluate that evidence.

---

[104] *Cf.* Daniel Ellsberg, *Risk, Ambiguity, and the Savage Axioms*, 75 Q.J. ECON. 643, 646 (1961) (proposing that individuals might not ignore uncertainty).

Usually, observational arguments about contracting parties' preference for textualism take the following form: because parties do X, they prefer textualism, so textualism is an efficient default rule. These arguments have, so far, been unpersuasive. It is important to recognize that such arguments have the *capacity* to be persuasive. If it were truly the case that all parties of a particular type always preferred textualism, and if an empirical study could establish this preference convincingly, then the study could be a strong argument in favor of textualism in the cases to which it applied. The problem is not with the enterprise of the empirical analysis of parties' preferences; the problem is simply that those making arguments based on empirics have, so far, generalized too broadly from the available data.

Before considering particular empirical arguments, it may help to lay some general groundwork. The modern empirical economic arguments, like Schwartz and Scott's theoretical one, are attentive to the costs of adjudication.[105] In particular, they seek to balance those costs against the economic benefits of a more informed interpretive method that is more likely to produce a correct answer in individual cases.

As commentators on all sides of the debate seem to agree, empirical evidence of parties' interpretive preferences is extremely limited.[106] Geoffrey Miller and Ted Eisenberg conducted one significant study in which they found that, in contracts with choice-of-law clauses to which public companies are parties, the parties more often choose the law of New York than that of any other state.[107] Schwartz and Scott take this to be significant because, having characterized New York's interpretive law as textualist, they believe the choice of New York reflects a choice by contracting parties in favor of textualism.[108]

There are several problems with such an inference, however. Most importantly, Professors Eisenberg and Miller give several other

---

[105] *See generally* Schwartz & Scott, *supra* note 28.

[106] *E.g.*, Schwartz & Scott, *supra* note 3, at 955 (referring to the "sketchy evidence that exists").

[107] Theodore Eisenberg & Geoffrey P. Miller, *The Flight to New York: An Empirical Study of Choice of Law and Choice of Forum Clauses in Publicly-Held Companies' Contracts*, 30 CARDOZO L. REV. 1475, 1511 (2009) ("Although no state has more than 50 percent of the designations, New York is clearly the dominant state with over 40 percent of the choices of law ... designations.").

[108] Schwartz & Scott, *supra* note 3, at 955.

3.3 Contract Interpretation

explanations for a choice of New York law that confound specific empirical inferences as to parties' motives:

> Since at least the early nineteenth century New York State, and especially New York City, have played a special role in the nation's commercial activity. New York has a keen awareness of the financial benefits of choice of law provisions and has cultivated its role as the choice of law for commercial matters through early efforts to promote enforceability of arbitration clauses, through legislation, and through the creation of specialized business courts.[109]

As Eisenberg and Miller also point out, there are many provisions of substantive New York law that public firms might favor; an inference that they are specifically choosing textualism is unfounded.[110]

There are several further problems with the inference from this study that firms prefer textualism. One is that Eisenberg and Miller have studied only public companies,[111] not all the firms to which Schwartz and Scott intend to apply their analysis.[112] Another perhaps more significant problem is that there is a wide variety in the choices of law that even large public firms have made. New York's law was chosen in fewer than half the cases that Eisenberg and Miller studied, and for particular types of contracts, the choice is even less evident.[113] Thus, public firms chose New York law in only about 25 percent of cases involving the purchasing of assets, only about 20 percent in licensing agreements, only 17 percent in mergers, and, perhaps of special note, only 18 percent of cases involving legal settlements, where regularity of administration is presumably of special importance to at least one of the parties.[114] Indeed, in settlement contracts, parties chose California law – Schwartz's and Scott's paradigmatic contextualist regime[115] – about as often as they chose New York.[116] The picture that the limited empirical data paints is one of variety, not one of consistency.

---

[109] Eisenberg & Miller, *supra* note 107, at 1481.

[110] *Id.* at 1485–87.

[111] *Id.* at 1475, 1511.

[112] Schwartz & Scott, *supra* note 3, at 952–56.

[113] Eisenberg & Miller, *supra* note 107, at 1481.

[114] *Id.*

[115] *See* Schwartz & Scott, *supra* note 3, at 956.

[116] Eisenberg & Miller, *supra* note 107, at 1480–83.

130   Contract Law

More fundamentally, aside from the limitations in the empirical evidence, there are two theoretical reasons to be skeptical of drawing strong inferences, in this particular debate, from studies like Eisenberg and Miller's. One is that if parties particularly want textualism, they can ask for it, so there is little reason to use choice-of-law clauses as a proxy for the underlying substantive choice.[117] Moreover, parties can choose arbitration, in which they can certainly lay out their own rules of evidence. While it may be difficult to arrange, from scratch, for the sort of rich private legal system that Lisa Bernstein describes in several studies,[118] it is not difficult to opt out of the public legal system if it does not provide for parties' desired rules or the opportunity to choose such rules.[119]

There is a deeper and more important problem with the focus on the empirically demonstrated preferences of broad classes of contracting parties. Specifically, in deciding interpretive rules, we are not limited to a single, majoritarian regime. Schwartz and Scott recognize this; indeed, I consider their argument helpful in this regard.[120] But just as the legal system need not answer the interpretive question identically for contracts involving individuals and contracts among firms (as they suggest),[121] it need not answer the question identically for all contracts involving firms. Perhaps the notion of "majoritarian defaults" has caused some confusion on this point. The concept of majoritarian defaults is common in the theoretical legal and economic commentary on contract law.[122] As Russell Korobkin puts it:

---

[117] This is, admittedly, the subject of some debate, because Schwartz and Scott deny that interpretive rules are default rules, rather than mandatory rules, in current law. But regardless, parties can choose arbitration.

[118] *See* Lisa Bernstein, *The Questionable Empirical Basis of Article 2's Incorporation Strategy: A Preliminary Study*, 66 U. CHI. L. REV. 710 (1999); Lisa Bernstein, *Merchant Law in a Merchant Court: Rethinking the Code's Search for Immanent Business Norms*, 144 U. PA. L. REV. 1765 (1996); Lisa Bernstein, *Private Commercial Law in the Cotton Industry: Creating Cooperation Through Rules, Norms, and Institutions*, 99 MICH. L. REV. 1724 (2001).

[119] *See* Jean R. Sternlight, *Mandatory Binding Arbitration and the Demise of the Seventh Amendment Right to a Jury Trial*, 16 OHIO ST. J. ON DISP. RESOL. 669, 696–99 (discussing courts' stated public policies in favor of arbitration); *see also* Marissa Dawn Lawson, Note, *Judicial Economy at What Cost? An Argument for Finding Binding Arbitration Clauses Prima Facie Unconscionable*, 23 REV. LITIG. 463 (2004) (critiquing the ease with which arbitration clauses in contracts can displace the public legal system).

[120] See Schwartz & Scott, *supra* note 3, at 930–31.

[121] *See id.* at 947.

[122] *See, e.g.*, Jody S. Kraus, *The Correspondence of Contract and Promise*, 109 COLUM. L. REV. 1603, 1632 (2009) ("Majoritarian default rules maximize the probability that the

3.3 Contract Interpretation

The traditional analysis concludes that default contract terms should mimic those terms that the majority of contracting parties would agree upon if negotiating and drafting a relevant provision were cost-free. Default rules created according to this process, often referred to as "majoritarian" defaults, minimize the number of occasions in which parties will need to contract around default rules in order to arrive at an efficient outcome.[123]

Used properly, this notion can serve as a useful theoretical device in analyzing default rules in contract law – for example, in distinguishing commonplace rules from "penalty defaults."[124] But the concept may also confuse analysis because it suggests that default rules should be decided by vote, rather than by a sensitive analysis of factors present in particular cases. What is at issue here, in some sense, is improving the "resolving power" of contract law, as with a microscope; a focus on choosing the right "majoritarian default" can easily obscure the more important analytical exercise in which courts are typically engaged, which is to determine which features of a case trigger relevant legal principles. That broader analysis – essentially an attempt to address a reference-class problem[125] – may well produce insights that are absent if cases are grossly lumped together and then decided as a broad majority would decide them.

Perhaps this is why the notion of "majoritarian defaults" has made almost no impact in courts, compared to academic commentary,[126] and why very little common law proceeds based on broad empirical

terms to which promisors are being held correspond with the ones they intended but failed to express or imply, and they save the majority of individuals the costs of specifying those terms, which respects their personal sovereignty by decreasing the barriers to creating promissory obligations.").

[123] Russell Korobkin, *The Status Quo Bias and Contract Default Rules*, 83 CORNELL L. REV. 608, 613–14 (1998).

[124] Ian Ayres & Robert Gertner, *Filling Gaps in Incomplete Contracts: An Economic Theory of Default Rules*, 99 YALE L.J. 87, 102–10 (1989); see also *e.g.*, Richard Craswell, *Contract Law: General Theories*, in 3 ENCYCLOPEDIA OF LAW AND ECONOMICS 1, 3–4 (Boudewijn Bouckaert & Gerrit De Geest eds., 2000); Ian Ayres, *Default Rules for Incomplete Contracts*, in 1 THE NEW PALGRAVE DICTIONARY OF ECONOMICS AND THE LAW 585, 586 (Peter Newman ed., 1998).

[125] In statistical reasoning, there is often a preliminary problem of identifying a reference class for appropriate analysis. See HANS REICHENBACH, THE THEORY OF PROBABILITY 370–90 (1949). For a modern discussion in a legal context, see generally Edward K. Cheng, *Law, Statistics, and the Reference Class Problem*, 109 COLUM. L. REV. 92 (2009).

[126] As of December 2022, the phrase "majoritarian default," according to a search on LexisNexis, appeared in 347 academic articles but in only 3 American court cases.

studies that attempt to infer the legal preferences of contracting parties. When courts interpret contracts, they do not look ultimately to what a "majority" of some arbitrary group of parties would have done. They aim instead to determine what was "reasonable" for the parties "in the circumstances" under which they contracted.[127]

3.4 UNCONSCIONABILITY

A staple of Economics 101-style thinking is that rules that limit voluntary contracts, such as common-law doctrines of unconscionability or statutory rules like those that prevent kidney sales or that impose minimum wages or restrictions on the prices for residential rental property, are necessarily inefficient because they eliminate gains from trade. Most such rules are usually defended on moral grounds, and they have weighty moral reasons in favor of them.[128] But as this section shows, their reputed inefficiency is also not a slam-dunk for the law-and-economics movement. Because this section treats these doctrines and rules – what I call here *contract-limiting rules* – theoretically, as the legal economists do, its goal is not specifically to show that the rules *are* efficient, which would require more factual context and empirical data; it is only to show what amounts to a possibility proof that contract-limiting rules *may be* efficient, despite the classical economic thinking that so readily counsels against them on the simple ground that more trade is necessarily better. Without loss of generality, I focus the discussion here on unconscionability, a common-law rule.

3.4.1 Are Rules of Unconscionability Necessarily Inefficient?

To start with, dating to Arthur Leff's analysis in the late 1960s,[129] unconscionability in contract law has been divided into *procedural*

---

[127] Restatement (Second) of Contracts § 204 cmt. d (1981).

[128] *See* Melvin Aron Eisenberg, *The Role of Fault in Contract Law: Unconscionability, Unexpected Circumstances, Interpretation, Mistake, and Nonperformance*, 107 Mich. L. Rev. 1413 (2009).

[129] Arthur Allen Leff, *Unconscionability and the Code – The Emperor's New Clause*, 115 U. Pa. L. Rev. 485 (1967).

3.4 Unconscionability

unconscionability and *substantive unconscionability*. Procedural unconscionability reflects a simple breakdown of the bargaining process, and a rule that procedurally unconscionable contracts are unenforceable is relatively easy to defend as an efficiency-promoting feature of contract law even within the orthodox law-and-economics framework. If bargains are enforced because private parties are the best judges of terms, then a failed bargain that results in something that looks like a contract should not be enforceable as a bargain contract; it lacks the policy rationales for enforcing bargains and is not constrained to be value-promoting, as seen by the parties ex ante, in the way that bargains are. Procedurally unconscionable contracts have problems similar to those of contracts formed by fraud or duress:[130] because the bargaining process is problematic, the resulting deal is not necessarily a genuine bargain.

Despite this recognition, Chicago-style law and economics often seems to reject rules of procedural unconscionability anyway, ordinarily by deducing that some framework in the background still magically guides parties, or systems of parties, toward efficiency. For example, as Russell Korobkin puts it in describing what he calls the "traditional" view of law and economics and using *Williams v. Walker Thomas Furniture Co,*[131] a famous case involving a very hard-to-understand clause that was struck down, as an example:

> Under the traditional law-and-economics analysis, however, the adhesive nature of the clause does not make it suspect. The store's incentive to include only efficient terms in its contract is guaranteed not by the ability of buyers to bargain for better terms, but by the ability of buyers to shop elsewhere if they don't like the combination of price, product attributes, and terms that Walker-Thomas offers. There is no reason to believe that Williams lacked the choice of shopping elsewhere.[132]

---

[130] *See* J.J. WHITE ET AL., UNIFORM COMMERCIAL CODE § 5:4 (6th ed. 2017) ("Each of these branches of unconscionability has common-law cousins; procedural unconscionability looks like fraud or duress during contract formation ....").

[131] 350 F.2d 445 (D.C. Cir. 1965).

[132] *See* Russell Korobkin, *A "Traditional" and "Behavioral" Law-and-Economics Analysis of* Williams v. Walker-Thomas Furniture Company, 26 U. HAW. L. REV. 441, 452 (2004).

Korobkin adds further deductions that traditional law-and-economics analysts might draw: "Monopolists generally can maximize their profits by providing the efficient combination of price and terms, and then charging a monopoly price, rather than providing inefficient terms."[133] "If Walker-Thomas were one of a small number of neighborhood stores, all of which offered the same terms, the store would have had an even greater incentive to remove the term and raise price: doing so would allow it to steal customers from its competitors."[134] As Korobkin recognizes (in also discussing "behavioral" law and economics), many other factual assumptions would need to be made for all these deductions to hold.

Anyway, putting aside magical forces that more or less assume away the very notion of procedural unconscionability, rules of procedural unconscionability are relatively easy to defend and are not even really contract-limiting rules – not any more than a rule that prevents supposed bargains made under duress or through fraud. The main economic justifications for enforcing apparent bargains that are not in fact actual bargains would likely be administrative: enforcing contracts is important for social efficiency, it is too difficult to distinguish supposedly problematic bargains from real ones, and unfairness in individual cases must be tolerated for the good of the many. That is an empirical argument, not a theoretical one, but it at least could make sense on its own terms. Apart from arguments that pay attention to the costs of administering the contract-law regime, economic arguments in favor of enforcing procedurally unconscionable arguments are extremely weak. And in the real world, even those arguments are extremely weak because procedural unconscionability is not ordinarily too difficult to detect.

The real battle is over rules of substantive unconscionability – which is to say, those that prevent the formation or enforcement of contracts that are extremely unfair as a substantive matter, with very lopsided terms, benefits, or responsibilities.[135] Another way to conceive substantive unconscionability is to recognize that any bargain

---

[133] *Id.* at 453

[134] *Id.* at 454.

[135] *See* 1 E. ALLAN FARNSWORTH, CONTRACTS § 4.28, at 585 (3d ed. 2004). For relatively recent discussions of the merits of rules concerning unconscionability, see Eisenberg,

3.4 Unconscionability

that is efficient ex ante has a contractual surplus – the expected gains from the bargain – and substantive unconscionability reflects an extremely uneven allocation of that surplus. This definition, though narrower and uncritically accepting of some of the legal economists' propositions, is sufficient for our purposes here; in other words, we will assume for the purposes of this discussion that bargains that are substantively (but not procedurally) unconscionable do have a surplus. Again, if our concern were instead that the language of bargains or private ordering is hiding a significant burden to one of the parties that undermines the presence of a contractual surplus overall – for example, if one of the parties is not sophisticated enough to see how much the contract, in the end, will cost them, or if one party is counting on the fact that the other party hasn't read or understood the terms of a form contract – that is procedural, rather than substantive, unconscionability under Leff's dichotomy.

Legal rules that strike down contracts because of substantive unconscionability alone are more controversial and harder to defend against classical economic reasoning than those that rely on procedural unconscionability. If a bargain in question lacks any trace of procedural unconscionability – for example, if it is clear that both parties wanted the contract at the time it was formed, knew what they were doing, and were appropriately informed about the details over which they were bargaining – then Chicago-style law and economics is clearly in favor of it, and it poses at least a prima facie challenge to a doctrine that would strike it down.[136] There are some general responses to the challenge. For example, maybe substantive unconscionability is *evidence* of procedural unconscionability; that is, maybe extremely unfair terms imply some defect in the bargaining process, like the near-fraud or near-duress that counts as procedural unconscionability. Indeed, even those state-court opinions that require both substantive and procedural unconscionability before finding a contract unconscionable tend

---

supra note 128, at 1415–19 (2009); Larry A. DiMatteo & Bruce Louis Rich, *A Consent Theory of Unconscionability: An Empirical Study of Law in Action*, 33 FLA. ST. U. L. REV. 1067 (2006). For a prominent legal-economic view on substantive unconscionability, see Richard Craswell, *Property Rules and Liability Rules in Unconscionability and Related Doctrines*, 60 U. CHI. L. REV. 1, 20–29 (1993).

[136] *See* COOTER & ULEN, *supra* note 53, at 368–70.

136   Contract Law

either to find them both or to find neither of them on the same facts. But recognizing an implication from substantive unconscionability to procedural unconscionability would not clearly explain why courts in other states find substantive unconscionability to be sufficient on its own for a holding of unconscionability.

This brings us back to the need for the "possibility proof" I mentioned earlier, to demonstrate that even despite the classical-economic prima facie case against the legal significance of substantive unconscionability, rules that strike down contracts on that basis alone can be efficient. To demonstrate that possibility, we must first notice that the general economic arguments against contract-limiting rules, just like some of the arguments we have seen already, suffer from what I have called the "neglect of alternatives" pattern in Chapters 1 and 2: the economic argument against striking down unconscionable contracts is an argument that activity that is "efficient," compared to its absence, must go forward. In other words, all classical economics says about enforcing substantively unconscionable contracts is that it would be better for those contracts to proceed than for there to be no contracts at all. What that argument misses is that, because not all possible activity can proceed, rules that permit extremely lopsided contracts may divert effort to extremely lopsided, opportunistic (though productive!) activity at the expense of conduct that would be even more productive. Once we recognize that not all productive activity can occur – because, as in Chapter 2, of limited overall resources and imperfections in factor markets, such as labor markets, supply chains, capital markets, and credit markets – it becomes clear that a general theoretical argument against contract-limiting rules needs to be replaced with a more nuanced analysis. Indeed, recognizing the limitation of resources and the imperfections of factor markets may point the way toward a clearer analysis of contract-limiting rules than those that either the law or legal economists have already used.

Consider, as an example, a simple situation in which the law must decide whether to prevent one party from extracting a large and "unfair" amount of the contractual surplus. Suppose there's a factory owner that would be able to pay its workers up to $40 per hour because the potential workers produce that much value for the factory. But the potential workers have no better options in their locale and

3.4 Unconscionability

cannot easily move, so they would accept wages as low as approximately 50 cents an hour to work. The factory knows this, so it offers 50 cents per hour for the work. Suppose the workers – being plentiful and without a union to organize them – accept the offer.

A basic economic argument against an unconscionability doctrine – or, for example, a minimum-wage law – that would prevent this kind of contract would be that the parties won't enter the contract unless they both benefit from it, and therefore the contract is wealth-producing and should be permitted or even encouraged.[137] The workers wouldn't accept 50 cents an hour if they had better alternatives. Accordingly, as the reasoning proceeds, preventing the contract would make at least one of the parties, and probably both of them, worse off. The contract should therefore be allowed. Maybe there are other reasons in favor of an unconscionability doctrine or a minimum-wage law, an economist might say – such as notions of fairness or broad social concerns about the distribution income and wealth. But allocative efficiency, they would continue, is not among them.[138]

The flaw – the possibility proof against this kind of reasoning – is as follows: the opportunity to extract a large share of contractual surplus may distort behavior, causing people to pursue privately profitable activities that are indeed socially profitable, on their own, but not the best use of their resources from society's perspective. Suppose A can contract with either B or C, but not both. To maximize social welfare, we want the transaction that is most valuable to occur. But A wants the contract that's privately more valuable to A alone. If the contract with B has a total surplus of \$200 and the contract with C has a total surplus of \$250, but A can extract 98 percent of the surplus in the case

---

[137] *See generally* Richard A. Epstein, *Unconscionability: A Critical Reappraisal*, 18 J.L. & ECON. 293 (1975).

[138] *See* Kent Greenfield, *Reclaiming Corporate Law in a New Gilded Age*, 2 HARV. L. & POL'Y REV. 1, 25 (2008) ("Current public policy tools that redistribute wealth and income tend to either take effect after the initial distribution of financial wealth (e.g., taxes, welfare policy) or benefit only those at the lowest rung of the economic ladder (e.g., the minimum wage). These mechanisms are notoriously inefficient."); Mark A. Graber, *Conservative Courts in a Conservative Era*, 75 FORDHAM L. REV. 675, 685 (2006) ("Most conservatives oppose minimum wage laws as economically inefficient."); Herbert Hovenkamp, *Legislation, Well-Being, and Public Choice*, 57 U. CHI. L. REV. 63 (1990) (noting that "the minimum wage statute is clearly inefficient under traditional neoclassical criteria for allocative efficiency" but discussing the possibility that people might draw "social utility" from fairer rules).

138   Contract Law

of B and only 72 percent of the surplus in the case of C, A will choose B (and get 98 percent of $200, or $196) rather than C (and get 72 percent of $250, or $180).

If A can contract with both the other parties, or if other parties like A can contract with both of them, then it doesn't really matter which contract A chooses, at least on economic grounds. But we can be sure that contracts with both B and C will proceed only if we're sure that there are enough parties available to contract with both of them – that is, if the relevant markets are thick enough. To put it differently, we can be sure that the contracts will proceed only if resources are sufficient and macroeconomic features of the situation (capital markets, credit markets, and other factor markets) are all perfect, because that's the only way to ensure that enough parties will be available to contract with both B and C. In the absence of that perfection – in other words, in the real world – it may be less socially efficient for A to pick B (a contract worth $200 in total, but where A gets 98 percent of the surplus) over C (a contract worth $250 in total, but where A gets only 72 percent of the surplus). That choice would be better for A but worse for overall efficiency.

Addressing a few potential complications may be in order at this stage. For one thing, under typical economic theory, surpluses aren't fixed beforehand; the parties can bargain over them.[139] If the contract with C is really more valuable (to both parties, together) than the contract with B, why wouldn't C simply offer a better deal to induce A to make the more efficient contract?[140] For example, why would A be able to extract only 72 percent (or $144) of the contract with B rather than 82 percent (or $205), which would be enough to entice A to choose C over B (because 98 percent of $200 is only $196, which is less than $205)? Surely C would prefer getting *some* surplus rather than *no* surplus, assuming C were rational and perfectly informed; therefore, C would allow A to extract this greater portion of the surplus.

---

[139] *But see* Melvin A. Eisenberg, *Impossibility, Impracticability, and Frustration – Professor Goldberg Constructs an Imaginary Article, Attributes It to Me, and Then Criticizes It*, 2 J. Legal Analysis 383, 392–93 (2010) (suggesting that there could be practical reasons that surpluses are indeed fixed in advance).

[140] This is just a restatement of the Coase theorem. *See* R.H. Coase, *The Problem of Social Cost*, 3 J.L. & Econ. 1 (1960).

3.4 Unconscionability

Bargaining costs, however, may intervene and prevent the contract with C from going forward. Though it is of course correct that divisions of surpluses are not necessarily fixed in advance of contract negotiations, they may reflect typical bargaining patterns in industries, and it may be hard or expensive to vary far from those patterns.[141]

Perhaps more importantly, in the real world, we cannot be sure that it will be worthwhile for A to continue to search for alternatives once finding their privately good deal with B. In other words, the mere availability of a contract with one party can "crowd out" better contracts, because parties don't have unlimited resources to spend searching for contracting partners and then bargaining over contracts.[142] As long as A can contract with only one party, and as long as nobody else will be around to contract with the other, simply providing the *option* of contracting with B makes it less likely, in the real world, that the more socially profitable contract with C will be concluded. But if the contract with B is barely socially valuable compared to its alternatives, it could be a mistake to allow it, particularly where it is so good for A privately that A may stop searching once they find it. In the more general case, putting aside features specific to contract law, unconscionability, and minimum-wage laws, there is no reason to believe that parties will always be able to reach the most efficient result through private bargaining, regardless of the state of the law. To assume that would be to assume that there are never transaction costs great enough to prevent all potentially efficient bargains from proceeding.

Moreover, to emphasize the parties' ability to bargain further here would be to engage in a kind of Coasean bait-and-switch. If bargaining is perfect, minimum-wage laws and unconscionability doctrines have no negative economic effects in the first place: if parties can get around transaction costs in general, then parties can probably get

---

[141] *Cf.* Schwartz & Scott, *supra* note 28, at 554 ("[W]hen bargaining power is determined prior to contract formation, as is common in business contexts, ... [p]arties jointly choose the contract terms so as to maximize the surplus, which the price may then divide unequally.").

[142] *See* Bayern & Eisenberg, *supra* note 14; Peter A. Diamond & Eric Maskin, *An Equilibrium Analysis of Search and Breach of Contract, I: Steady States*, 10 BELL J. ECON. 282 (1979); P.A. Diamond & Eric Maskin, *An Equilibrium Analysis of Search and Breach of Contract, II: A Non-Steady Example*, 25 ECON. THEORY 165 (1989); George J. Stigler, *The Economics of Information*, 69 J. POL. SCI. 213 (1961).

around a minimum-wage law by adjusting other terms. The goal of the legal rules at stake should be to do what makes sense in view of the transaction costs that we know from experience are familiar, and if that is the starting point, then it becomes difficult to say *without more* that minimum-wage laws are inefficient without looking at the potentially redistributive activity they prevent – that is, activity that is more redistributive (in favor of the party extracting a lopsided amount of surplus) than other alternatives available to the contracting parties.

The observation that the contract between A and B is, on its own terms, an efficient contract (because it has a surplus) is, then, insufficient to recommend its validity and enforcement if the goal is to evaluate the normative instrumental justifications for a rule about unconscionability. This, however, hasn't stopped economists from creating the impression that minimum-wage rules, or those preventing unconscionability, are inefficient in broad, almost incontrovertible terms.[143]

In other words, it is clear that there can be simple efficiency-motivated reasons for a substantive-unconscionability doctrine in contract law. It is incomplete to attack unconscionability doctrines and minimum-wage laws on the ground that the contract between A and B should be permitted or encouraged because it makes A and B better off. The absence of a rule preventing unconscionability encourages A to choose B (or at least makes it more likely that A will choose B) as a contracting partner instead of C. Because the contract with C would benefit society more, the increased likelihood of a contract with B reflects a deadweight social loss. Again, if all otherwise efficient transactions could be completed, then there would be no inefficiency at stake here from A's opportunism: A could contract with both B and C. Or if A contracted with B, someone else could contract with C. But because resources are limited and factor markets are imperfect (e.g., A can't get credit to contract with both B and C, and not everyone can become like A merely because there's some value to his position), society loses, overall, from A's "unfair" contract with B.

Allowing a factory owner to contract with ununionized low-wage laborers under harsh conditions might improve (at least in a narrow

---

[143] *See* sources cited *supra* note 138.

3.4 Unconscionability

141

sense) the position of both the owner and the laborers, but it is difficult to know whether, in the abstract, allowing the contract to proceed is more efficient than alternative activities. Perhaps it would be more efficient for society if the owner were in a different business or if the factory were put to a different use – possibilities that might not even arise, without an unconscionability rule or minimum-wage doctrine, because of the redistributive potential of the particular use the factory owner proposes or decides upon first. If a significant motivation of those who engage in activities that these laws prevent is systematically redistributing wealth to themselves and away from others, the absence of these laws encourages more of that activity. That is not necessarily efficient, even if the activity does produce wealth compared to its absence.

3.4.2 Developing Unconscionability Rules in View of the Recognition that Not All Efficient Activity Can Occur

The particular potential inefficiency I have outlined from uncritically permitting parties to make all contracts they desire to make, including substantively unconscionable ones, points the way toward what is perhaps a conceptually clearer view of the law's treatment of substantive unconscionability. As it stands, the doctrine is vague and potentially undertheorized.[144] (I say "potentially" because it may well be that the doctrine should remain vague in order for it to adapt to new, hard-to-predict types of unconscionability.) But the problem I have identified rests on opportunism and on the suspicion that a party is engaging in excessive surplus extraction in ways that divert their attention away from more productive activities. Accordingly, an important test in understanding unconscionability doctrine is whether the allegedly unconscionable party, without the availability of the unconscionable transaction, would have engaged in an activity that is *more* socially productive than the (admittedly socially productive)[145] unconscionable

---

[144] *See* 1 FARNSWORTH, *supra* note 135, § 4.28, at 581 ("Nowhere among the [UCC's] many definitions is there one of unconscionability. That the term is incapable of precise definition is source of both strength and weakness. The comments to UCC 2-302 give only the most general guidance on the meaning of the term.") (emphasis omitted).

[145] Again, I make this concession just for the purposes of considering economic arguments on their own terms.

142   Contract Law

contract. For instance, in the previous section's example, would the factory owner have chosen some other activity that is more productive for society if the law – either a judicially enforced doctrine of unconscionability or a statutory minimum-wage law – did not permit the particular 50-cent-per-hour wage contract that the factory adopted?

On this view, the focus of analysis for a court considering an allegedly unconscionable contract is on the state of the allegedly unconscionable party, not the party that the doctrine would protect.[146] In other words, a court considering whether a contract is unconscionable should not, on economic grounds alone, focus directly on the hardship suffered by the weaker or poorer party. In some sense, this makes sense purely on grounds of efficiency – again putting aside concerns of fairness, other moral considerations, the overall social distribution of wealth, and so on – because on such grounds both parties are (by hypothesis) better off if the contract is permitted than if it is not; the question is not whether the *parties* suffer but whether society overall suffers because of the contract's crowding-out effect on other, potentially more efficient contracts. This requires that we look at the nature and condition of the allegedly unconscionable party, the one that threatens to extract a large amount of the contractual surplus; the danger is that that party's focus on redistribution rather than social efficiency is leading in fact to social inefficiency.

This view, though perhaps counterintuitive as a whole, is consistent with several intuitions that lawyers and law students seem to have about unconscionability doctrine. For example, one popular Contracts casebook[147] once included information about a report by the Federal Trade Commission that found, on limited data, that though retailers in low-income areas charged their customers greater prices and interest, their profit margins were not significantly greater than those of mainstream retailers.[148] To the extent this finding is true, it tends to make students and commentators more, rather than less, accepting of the practices of low-income retailers. That response is consistent with an intuition that the position of the allegedly unconscionable party

---

[146] *Contra* COOTER & ULEN, *supra* note 53, at 368–70.

[147] LON L. FULLER & MELVIN A. EISENBERG, BASIC CONTRACT LAW 69–70 (8th ed. 2006).

[148] U.S. FEDERAL TRADE COMMISSION, ECONOMIC REPORT ON INSTALLMENT CREDIT AND RETAIL SALES PRACTICES OF DISTRICT OF COLUMBIA RETAILERS (1968).

3.4 Unconscionability 143

matters. An economic reason for it to matter is that if the low-income retailers were indeed making supranormal profits by charging extreme prices, those profits would suggest that their activities were chosen in lieu of something more socially efficient: the reason they were low-income retailers, in other words, would be that there was somehow a special opportunity to appropriate the money of people with low incomes, not that there was a commensurately productive opportunity from society's perspective in the business of low-income retail.

The same line of reasoning applies to minimum-wage laws and to rent-control laws. In short, allocative concerns cannot be cleanly separated from distributive concerns, because the opportunity to distribute wealth toward oneself affects choices that have allocative consequences. So if landlords are able to receive supranormal profits by charging high prices to low-income people, their efforts will be inefficiently concentrated in the low-income-housing market. If the activity of paycheck lending is about as profitable as other lending, rather than especially profitable, then it is less likely to be economically problematic. Again, it may be natural for those steeped in traditional law and economics to ask why, if there were supranormal profits in a particular industry, those profits would not go away through competition – but that again assumes that the macroeconomic features of the situation are perfect. In the real world, we see supranormal profits and imperfect competition all the time. It would be interesting, at any rate, if the classical economic attack on unconscionability depended not on the value of bargains alone but on the supposed perfection in all markets that one party uses to exploit another.

As it happens, a similar sort of analysis can explain the law's general distaste for windfalls.[149] A true windfall, if unexpected, may not raise the problems I'm discussing because it is unexpected and therefore does not influence planning or ex ante resource allocation.[150] But those large and apparently unfair profits that can be sought or invested in lead to exactly the sort of distortions as the economic activity that contract-limiting rules would prevent.

---

[149] *See* Christine Hurt, *The Windfall Myth*, 8 Geo. J.L. & Pub. Pol'y 339, 340 (2010) ("[I]n court, once a judge classifies an economic gain as a windfall, that gain is then unlawful and will be prohibited.").

[150] *See* 16 Oxford English Dictionary 439 (2d ed. 1989) (defining "windfall" as a "casual or *unexpected* acquisition or advantage") (emphasis added).

144   Contract Law

Interestingly, then, we seem to reach a sort of convergence between long-term efficiency and fairness. Fairness is particularly concerned with the undeserved appropriation of supranormal profits. Perhaps the intuitions that underlie fairness recognize the economically distortive effects of such appropriation. Ironically, notions of fairness, which economists often diminish in private-law analysis,[151] seem to capture intuitions that address potential efficiency-related problems that would arise from more narrowly economic values.

3.5 EXCUSE FOR UNEXPECTED CIRCUMSTANCES (IMPOSSIBILITY, IMPRACTICABILITY, AND FRUSTRATION)

The general pattern of unexpected-circumstances cases is that one of the parties in a commercial contract agrees to do something, but the thing they've promised to do becomes either impossible, very costly, or otherwise wasteful. For example, a carrier promises to deliver a shipment to a port, but the port is closed because of war, regulation, disease, or some other factor that was hard for the parties to anticipate. Sometimes contracts try to address these situations with force majeure ("greater force") clauses, but it is impossible for contracting parties to address all ways that their contract might go wrong. Parties might aim to make certain all-things-considered guarantees to each other or shift risk very broadly, and over time the commercial world has gotten quite good at accounting for many risks that can arise, but the possibility always remains for the truly unexpected – unusual crimes or terroristic incidents, events that haven't occurred before like nuclear war or a widespread electromagnetic pulse that disables the electrical grid, and so on. It is easy to imagine naively that contracting parties really mean to assign *all* risks of nonperformance to one or the other of the parties, but to assume that parties have done so would be to imply that even small contracts that don't get a lot of attention in their drafting become, necessarily, bet-the-company contracts in the event unlikely scenarios occur. The law therefore excuses some types of nonperformance.

---

[151] *Cf.* COOTER & ULEN, *supra* note 53, at 9–11.

3.5 Excuse for Unexpected Circumstances

The best economic explanations for this area of doctrine come from outside the Chicago-school orthodoxy and focus on the recognition that contracting parties (1) can't plausibly specify and address the risks of all future contingencies and (2) reasonably expect, and benefit from, a limit to their risk on smaller contracts.[152] The leading Chicago-school analysis is much more brittle, however, and entirely unworkable.

That leading analysis comes from Richard Posner and Andrew Rosenfield.[153] Their conclusion is that the party who is in a better position either to reduce or to insure against the risk of unexpected circumstances that develop after a contract is made should be the one to bear the costs of those unexpected circumstances.[154] As Mel Eisenberg[155] and others[156] have pointed out, the argument is almost entirely unworkable, and almost nothing in it can or should be applied to real cases: it requires arbitrary classification of contracting parties' characteristics to determine their ability to bear or insure against risks, and it may still be impossible to distinguish the parties using Posner and Rosenfield's criteria even after making those arbitrary choices.

The argument suffers from two different, specifically analytical problems, both reflecting patterns of failure described earlier in this book. First, it is an example of what I called in Chapter 2 the problem of the *least-cost-avoider avoider*. Posner and Rosenfield's argument is essentially a least-cost-avoider argument: the party who can respond to the risks of unexpected circumstances at a lower cost should be the one to do so. If that is the legal rule, however, then the rule provides an incentive for potential contracting parties to make sure they are not in a position to be able to handle risks at a lower cost than their counterparties.[157]

---

[152] *See, e.g.*, Melvin A. Eisenberg, Foundational Principles of Contract Law 626–64 (2018); for an earlier treatment, see also Eisenberg, *Impossibility, supra* note 2.

[153] Posner & Rosenfield, *supra* note 1.

[154] *Id.* at 88–92.

[155] *See* Eisenberg, *supra* note 152, at 626–64.

[156] *E.g.*, Michael J. Trebilcock, *The Role of Insurance Considerations in the Choice of Efficient Civil Liability Rules*, 4 J.L. Econ. & Org. 243 (1988).

[157] Mel Eisenberg has noted, similarly, that Posner and Rosenfield's rule would discourage parties from attaining "diversification and scale." Eisenberg, *Impossibility, supra* note 2, at 253–54 (2009). For a law-and-economics response to Mel Eisenberg's work on this subject, see Victor P. Goldberg, *Excuse Doctrine: The Eisenberg Uncertainty Principle*, 2 J. Legal Analysis 359 (2010). For Mel Eisenberg's reply to that response, see Eisenberg, *supra* note 139.

146   Contract Law

Second, as I discussed briefly in Chapter 1, Posner and Rosenfield's argument picks one arbitrary consideration among many, leading to arbitrary results. Having chosen to focus on questions of unexpected circumstances, Posner and Rosenfield make a specific descriptive prediction: "Since the object of most voluntary exchanges is to increase value or efficiency, contracting parties may be assumed to desire a set of contract terms that will maximize the value of the exchange .... [T]he more efficiently the exchange is structured, the larger is the potential profit of the contract for the parties to divide between them."[158] In other words, private parties entering into a contract will assign the risk of any contingency, if they had thought about it, to the party who can bear it at the lowest cost; presumably neither party would prefer to bear the cost of the contingency, all else equal, but if one of them has to bear it, the contractual surplus will be greater if the party who can bear it more efficiently is assigned it – and then the parties can negotiate over price in view of the enhanced surplus from the exchange.

Posner and Rosenfield's argument, then, would derive a rule of contact law from terms that parties are predicted, on theoretical grounds, to want. Efficiency in the analysis of legal rules is no more, here, than a drafting of default contractual terms that the parties would have wanted to adopt.

In making their specific prediction about how parties would assign the costs of various contingencies, however, Posner and Rosenfield choose to focus on the assignment of risks of individual contingencies for individual contracts, neglecting the fact that parties in business do not in fact operate that way. Posner and Rosenfield treat the contracting parties as monolithic and analyze their interests for one contract and one contract only. In fact, businesses produce contracts through agents and often have elaborate procedures for managing their agents. It is commonplace to hear from business managers who are terrified of the risks that their agents will agree for the business to cover; this fear is a typical theoretical justification for standardized form contracts.[159] Businesses, in other words, may well be more concerned about not

---

[158] Posner & Rosenfield, *supra* note 1, at 89.

[159] *See, e.g.*, Steven R. Salbu, *Evolving Contract as a Device for Flexible Coordination and Control*, 34 Am. Bus. L.J. 329, 378 (1997) ("[S]tandardization of contractual provisions can reduce agency costs by limiting opportunities for agents to exercise discretion ....").

3.5 Excuse for Unexpected Circumstances 147

agreeing to be responsible for an important class of risks across all their contracts – or about not giving their agents the discretion to do so – rather than about micro-optimizing the assignment of tiny risks in any individual contract.

The importance of the general contracting patterns of businesses over the micro-optimization of individual contracts is even clearer once we recognize that businesses may have made, well in advance of forming individual contracts, general decisions about what insurance to purchase. They might have known they *could* purchase other insurance but made a decision not to do so, instead relying on the adoption of a standard form term – or a general set of negotiation practices or risk-management policies that govern their employees or agents – to avoid certain types of liability or incidence of risk. In other words, a business could have regarded it as cheaper to avoid a class of risks in all its contracts rather than to purchase insurance against that class of risks, even if that means that an individual contract here or there would miss out on the possibility of some marginal optimization in risk assignment between the business and one of its counterparties. For example, a business may routinely contract with one type of party and only irregularly contract with a different type of party, and the business may not consider it worthwhile to adjust its general approach to insurance just because, in those irregular contracts, it might happen (unusually for it!) to be the more efficient bearer of a particular risk than its counterparty.

It may seem as if the possibility of this kind of general risk management is just one empirical factor that a judge applying Posner and Rosenfield's argument might weigh against others in determining whether a contracting party is a lower-cost bearer of risk than its counterparty. But the problem for Posner and Rosenfield's argument is deeper than that because their argument, like many we have seen so far, does not degrade gracefully. That is, their argument requires their descriptive prediction to be perfect. As soon as we recognize that contracting parties in the real world might not *perfectly* assign *every* risk to the party able to bear that risk at lower cost – which is really just the recognition that contracts have transaction costs, in whatever form those costs might take – Posner and Rosenfield's argument falls apart entirely. If we can't assume that any particular assignment of risk is what the actual parties in the real world would have chosen, then a court that

148   Contract Law

assigns a risk to that party by following Posner and Rosenfield's argument may be entirely upsetting the delicate balance of risk, cost, and benefit that the parties to the actual deal came up with.

Admittedly, there is no perfect solution to this problem. A solution requires context-sensitive, open-minded analysis – roughly of the kind that courts already display when they address problems of impossibility, impracticability, and frustration. The goal, ideally, is to be as sensitive as possible to all the factors that business parties might have been concerned with when they negotiated the deal, or alternatively to what is fair and sensible after the fact. This general approach is precisely what Posner and Rosenfield seek to supplant, substituting their brittle set of rules in its place; they describe some of their motivations as follows:

> One commentator has argued that the outcomes in discharge cases are best described as being based on the equities of the particular case, another that "the decision as to be enforced must rest in the end on considerations of policy and expediency," another that "fairness is arguably the foundation of all relief."
>
> ...
>
> In short, one group of commentators argues essentially that no general theory is possible ....[160]

In the absence of a "general theory," the court's answer may be wrong, and answers may be inconsistent with each other, but it is implausible that following Posner and Rosenfield's rule would lead in fact to more efficiency. Instead, it would just lead to arbitrary rules – and still lack a deterministic theory for how to apply the various factors that their argument contains. To put that differently, if decisions are going to be unpredictable anyway, it is better if they are produced with judgment rather than by following arbitrary considerations like those that Posner and Rosenfield urge.

3.6 DISCLOSURE

Contract law imposes no general requirement for one party to disclose private information to the other before forming a contract, although

[160] Posner & Rosenfield, *supra* note 1, at 86–87.

3.6 Disclosure

there are several focused exceptions to that rule.[161] Economists have written much about why they believe efficiency demands nondisclosure of even material information.[162] My goal here is not to rehash that debate but to offer a few specific observations on the legal economists' treatment of disclosure.

First, given that information's economic materiality is not dependent on whether it is asserted or withheld, it is odd in the first place for consequentialists to have drawn such a sharp distinction between fraud (which is impermissible) and nondisclosure (which is generally permissible). Consequentialists, after all, ordinarily reject the conventional distinction between acts and omissions.[163] For economists to want to outlaw fraud but permit nondisclosure seems to require implicitly that they rely on some informal feature of the situation – some deeper sort of cultural norm or expectation among contracting parties. That would be fine, but it's not what they're purporting to do.

Second, economists often defend rules of nondisclosure when those rules provide an incentive for the development of productive information.[164] But often such an incentive is unnecessary, particularly in a market that is functioning relatively well. One typical example of information that a rule that permits nondisclosure is supposed to protect is productive information about minerals discovered underneath land – for example, by a prospective buyer who invests in discovering such minerals and then seeks to buy land from its existing owners, who are not aware of the minerals' presence. But as I pointed out in

---

[161] For a general overview and critique of the modern law of precontractual disclosure, see Melvin A. Eisenberg, *Disclosure in Contract Law*, 91 CAL. L. REV. 1645 (2003).

[162] *See id.* at 1664 & nn. 31–33 (citing sources); COOTER & ULEN, *supra* note 53, at 356–59; MICHAEL J. TREBILCOCK, THE LIMITS OF FREEDOM OF CONTRACT 108–18 (1993); Steven Shavell, *Acquisition and Disclosure of Information Prior to Sale*, 25 RAND J. ECON. 20 (1994); Anthony T. Kronman, *Mistake, Disclosure, Information, and the Law of Contracts*, 7 J. LEGAL STUD. 1 (1978).

[163] *See, e.g.*, Jonathan Baron, *Acts and Omissions*, *in* 18 THEORY AND DECISION LIBRARY 99 (1993) ("[U]tilitarianism and, more generally, consequentialism are notorious for holding that the act-omission distinction in itself is morally irrelevant. Utility theory also implies that the act-omission distinction is in itself irrelevant to all sorts of decisions, not just those that affect others. This claim challenges everyday moral thinking. It implies, for example, that intentionally failing to help the needy is equivalent to harming them.").

[164] *See* sources cited *supra* note 162. There is significant disagreement among economists on the precise sort of information that rules about nondisclosure should protect. *See* Eisenberg, *supra* note 161, at 1663–74.

150   Contract Law

Chapter 1, if the goal is simply to discover the valuable minerals, there are many other ways for that to happen: existing landowners might band together to engage in the same prospecting for valuable minerals; the prospector could offer to provide prospecting services to landowners directly; or the property rights associated with the surface use of the land can be separated from the rights to minerals beneath the land and then traded as a separate economic commodity. The latter of these possibilities is commonplace in the form of mineral leases.[165] Given all these possibilities, it is impossible from theoretical argumentation alone to derive much about the practical efficiency of disclosure rules; Mel Eisenberg puts it nicely:

> It is often explicit or implicit in scholarly discussion of the disclosure problem that a right not to make disclosure is a crucial engine for a prosperous economy, because much less productive information would be developed under a thoroughgoing disclosure regime than under a nondisclosure regime. It is true that *less* productive information would be developed under a thoroughgoing disclosure regime, and therefore something would be lost in the way of efficiency if such a regime was adopted. However, it is speculative whether *much less* productive information would be developed.[166]

Third, weighing any possible advantages of rules that permit nondisclosure against the downsides of such rules requires great sensitivity to detail. The downsides of such rules include the increased costs of duplicate searches[167] and the inability to know if individual contracts are even efficient in the first place in the absence of material information.[168] We shouldn't live in terror at the prospect of doing something inefficient, particularly when – as here – there are efficiencies on the opposite side.

3.7 CONCLUSION

Interpretation, remedies, and the conditions under which contracts can be formed are probably the most significant doctrinal questions

---

[165] *Cf. id.* at 1688 n.93.
[166] *Id.* at 1687.
[167] *See id.* at 1654; TREBILCOCK, *supra* note 162, at 108.
[168] *See* Eisenberg, *supra* note 161, at 1654; TREBILCOCK, *supra* note 162, at 117.

3.7 Conclusion

of contract law. It is perhaps striking how little law and economics has to say that's either useful or decisive about those principal questions.

Apart from the more particular economic models and arguments this chapter addressed, there is a large amount of general treatment – what we might call *economic-style thinking* – about contract law. For example, take Posner's analysis of consideration doctrine. He purports to explain the role of economic reasoning in understanding consideration by introducing five policy arguments with the sentence "Here are some economic functions that the requirement of consideration might be thought to serve."[169] The five policy arguments are (1) avoiding (his term is "minimizing," although nothing in his argument suggests literal minimalization) "phony contract suits"; (2) declining to enforce "inadvertent contractual commitments"; (3) declining to enforce "trivial promises"; (4) declining to enforce vague contracts; and (5) "deterring opportunistic behavior." The last of these is misguided because it is just a halfhearted defense of the preexisting-duty rule, generally regarded as an unjustified rule.[170] The fourth is a mismatch with consideration doctrine and addressed more clearly elsewhere in contract law. The remaining three are the broadest sort of policy concerns, likely covered in most Contracts courses in the country without reference to the law-and-economics movement. In other words, the law-and-economics movement doesn't help us understand anything here; it is just a thin veneer over existing argumentation and analysis with a slight change in terminology toward Benthamite words. Nothing Posner describes here is directly a matter of allocative efficiency; his list merely includes helpful things the doctrine of consideration might do, all things considered. At best, then, economic-style thinking adds little here. At worst, it can distract by drawing our attention away from complex forces toward simple ones, from how people respond in the real world to rules toward the abstract analysis of rules, and from goals or interests for the law other than ones than can be cast in simple instrumental terms (such as the appropriateness and desirability of the law's involvement in certain kinds of conduct, a question that may be relevant to the analysis of

---

[169] POSNER, *supra* note 12, at 103.
[170] *See* EISENBERG, *supra* note 152, at 38–44.

consideration rules).[171] It also is not sufficiently honed or context-sensitive to provide any significant critique of existing doctrine.

Moreover, sometimes economic-style thinking isn't even particularly economic; it is just "thinking." For example, Posner, to his credit, resisted many of the calls for more rigid formalism in contract interpretation. Perhaps the best summary of his general approach to interpretation is, in his own words:

> It would be one thing to impose the efficient solution in the teeth of the parties' agreement. That would be not only paternalistic but also reckless, because it would be rare that a judge or jury had a better sense of what would be an efficient transaction than the parties themselves had. But often, when the parties' intentions are not readily inferable from the written contract, the best, the most cost-efficient, way to resolve their dispute is not to take testimony and conduct a trial; it is to use commercial or economic common sense to figure out how, in all likelihood, the parties would have provided for the contingency that has arisen had they foreseen it.[172]

This is a sensible approach. But nothing – analytical or otherwise – is removed from Posner's proposition by removing the reference to cost-efficiency. Without that phrase, nothing about the analysis sounds in formal economics. The "commercial or economic common sense" to which Posner refers is simply the custom and usage of contracting parties.

---

[171] *See generally* Melvin Aron Eisenberg, *The World of Contract and the World of Gift*, 85 CAL. L. REV. 821 (1997).

[172] Richard A. Posner, *The Law and Economics of Contract Interpretation*, 83 TEX. L. REV. 1581, 1605 (2005).

4 PROPERTY LAW

Unlike the leading legal-economic arguments in tort and contract, the arguments about property tend to be diffuse and broadly justificatory; their goal is often to explain general trends rather than to prescribe legal policy. A negative view of the justificatory theories would hold that they are just-so stories, designed to explain arbitrary rules in an area of law that varies from place to place in a variety of technical details. A more generous interpretation would grant that the arguments have some explanatory force but still are not particularly useful in shaping legal policy.

The legal-economic scholars present several goals for property law, and those goals are mainly administrative, much like procedural rules: perhaps, for example, the rules of property law reduce the general costs associated with making contracts, discerning and responding to torts, and preventing crimes.

Much of the legal-economic treatment of property seeks to demonstrate why we have a law of property at all. For example, Cooter and Ulen's leading and lucid law-and-economics textbook develops a hypothetical bargaining game under which people in the state of nature will transition to having a property regime if they are reasonable, and Shavell's *Foundations of Economic Analysis* demonstrates in detail why recognizing property rights in general enhances wealth. The impulse to do that is curious in a way because there has been no serious question in American law about whether we should abolish the property system. Apart from challenges by communism and anarchism, everyone recognizes the notion that people should be able to own and transfer some property. Instead of defending particular rules

153

154 Property Law

of legal policy, much legal-economic analysis in property law aims simply to demonstrate the capacity of economic analysis to explain a basic feature of our society. But there is a logical problem with observing that property exists and claiming that it is a triumph for economics that economics can explain the existence of property; the problem is that many other techniques may also explain the existence of property, because the existence of property (compared simply to its absence) has many obvious advantages. Much as nearly any conclusion about a social institution can be explained through a hypothesis grounded in some way in evolutionary psychology, Marxism, or feminist theory, an explanation grounded in economic theory proves only that economic theory is flexible enough to provide the explanation.

This chapter for the most part sets aside the general, theoretical justifications of property law as a whole in favor of analyzing the relatively small[1] number of arguments that have been made about either more particular features of the property system or specific property-law doctrines, like adverse possession. It starts, however, with a particularly influential treatment of property theory that is rooted at least significantly in legal economics.

Before going further, it is worth commenting specifically on how thin the economic analysis of property law appears to be, compared to tort law and contract law. Moving past the general discussions that aim to explain why we have property law at all in terms of basic game theory, the feeling one gets when reading economic analyses of property is that they are not really economic analyses in any meaningful sense – they are just attempts by economists to explain the law in familiar ways. For example, it is worth quoting Cooter and Ulen's full explanation for lost-property rules, sometimes called *estray* rules (although that particular term usually applies to lost animals):

> Like registering title, estray statutes discourage the theft of property. Given an estray statute, a thief who is caught with another's property cannot avoid liability by claiming that he or she found it. ("Where did

---

[1] For example, Posner devotes only fifty-five pages of his approximately thousand-page book to foundational property law (though other parts of his book discuss, for example, intellectual property and wealth transfers at death). *See* RICHARD A. POSNER, ECONOMIC ANALYSIS OF LAW 39–94 (9th ed. 2014).

4.1 The Structure of Property Law: Numerus Clausus

you get that watch?" Sherlock asked the suspect. "It fell off the back of a truck," he replied.) Thus, an estray statute helps to distinguish a good-faith finder from a thief. Like adverse-possession rules, estray statutes tend to clear the clouds from title and transfer property to productive users. Like adverse-possession rules, estray statutes also provide an incentive for owners to monitor their property. Finally, estray statutes induce the dissemination of information by finders and thus reduce the search costs of owners who lose or mislay their property.

This sort of justification reads like any that might appear in a noneconomic legal treatise. Indeed, compare this analysis from a law-review note in 1939, which addresses a slightly different legal question at a very similar level of generality:

> [I]t may be said that for the most part the law governing property in these categories is well adapted for the ultimate return of lost or mislaid goods to the owner. However, the rule giving the finder possession as against the owner of the *locus in quo* in the cases involving goods found on the land of another might lead to a different result. The danger of the disappearance of a stranger who happened to find appears to be greater than the danger of the owner of the *locus* disappearing.
>
> .... To preclude the finder from any right therein might lead to his unwillingness to disclose his discovery. To avoid this, the owner of the *locus in quo* should be given the custody of the goods for a period determined by statute, after which he and the finder should share in the goods equitably.[2]

4.1 THE STRUCTURE OF PROPERTY LAW: NUMERUS CLAUSUS

In a novel and in many respects ingenious argument published in the *Yale Law Journal* in 2000,[3] Tom Merrill and Henry Smith attempted to justify what they consider to be a fundamental feature of property

---

[2] *Cf.* Note, *Lost, Mislaid, and Abandoned Property*, 8 FORD. L. REV. 222, 236–37 (1939).
[3] THOMAS W. Merrill & Henry E. Smith, *Optimal Standardization in the Law of Property: The Numerus Clausus Principle*, 110 YALE L.J. 1 (2000).

law that characterizes most or all of the property-law systems around the world: the limited number, or *numerus clausus*, of types of property ownership.

The basic concept of a type of property ownership – or what Merrill and Smith call a *form* of ownership – needs explanation even for most lawyers, and certainly for those who are not familiar in detail with the property system. For the most part, Merrill and Smith do not claim that property law should limit the basic objects of property law. For example, most of their argument is not concerned with the extent to which the law should permit ownership of intellectual property. Instead, they make a more subtle claim: property owners do not have unlimited flexibility to partition (for example, over time or based on legal conditions) what we might think of as the logical rights in their property interests. Merrill and Smith's central example is helpful: property law does and should permit personal ownership of wristwatches regardless of whether they are big or small, novel or conventional, but they claim it should not permit the owner of a wristwatch to sell a property right to possess the watch on Mondays but not during the rest of the week. To be sure, the owner of a watch may make arbitrarily flexible contracts with others under which others may claim the right to use the watch on Mondays, but Merrill and Smith do not want such a contract to affect property law's treatment of the watch. Thus, the owner still owns the watch, may sell or give away the watch, and so on. If the owner can't fulfill a promise to provide the watch on Monday to some promisee because they have sold it or given it away, the promisee would, under Merrill and Smith's view, have a legal claim for breach of contract but not a property-based claim. (To be clear, this distinction is fine, and it matters to the individual promisee only if some parties are insolvent or otherwise unavailable. In other words, what is at stake is only whether a promisee is limited to direct recovery from their contractual counterparty.)

Merrill and Smith's justification for their proposal is subtle: When purchasing watches, buyers' transaction costs – specifically, their costs of processing information – will increase as the complexity in the possible property interests increases. If ownership of watches may be partitioned by days of the week, a potential buyer of a watch has more to

4.1 The Structure of Property Law: Numerus Clausus 157

rule out when buying a watch. The owner and their successors will not pay this cost, so it is an externality. Consequently, owners should be restricted from creating new types of property interests in wristwatches (and, by extension, all property).

Though Merrill and Smith's argument is creative and thoughtful, its potential application to the real world is extremely limited.[4] To start with, the argument is indeterminate. As I noted at the start of this chapter, many economic arguments about property law seek to provide broad explanations rather than identify specific optimal rules, and this argument falls into that same pattern. That is, Merrill and Smith would probably be the first to admit that their economic argument says nothing about the particular number of property forms that would be optimal;[5] perhaps law should support more or fewer than it currently does. It is simply a framework for understanding and justifying, in general, the notion that the optimal number of forms may be limited.

To put that differently, the form of the argument is not a scientific one in the sense that the proposition does not admit of empirical falsification; it is consistent with any number of property rights so long as there is some resistance to creating new ones. Hence, it would be very difficult for a court to apply the numerus clausus principle,

---

[4] Application to the real world does appear to be one goal for the arguments; the role of the arguments is not just theoretical or abstract. For example, based largely on the *Yale Law Journal* article, which contains the argument about externalities I have just laid out and some general thoughts about the institutional capabilities of courts and legislatures, drafts of the American Law Institute's *Restatement (Fourth) of Property*, for which Professor Smith is the Reporter, have included such proposals for black-letter law as "Property interests conform to a limited number of standard forms" and "A court must not recognize or enforce a new type of property right if an owner or transferor attempts to create a new form of ownership." Preliminary Draft No. 3, at 125–32 (Sept. 15, 2017). The updated draft, approved by the ALI membership in 2022, tempers these principles somewhat, reframing them as "Property interests, including the present and future interests, *generally* conform to a limited number of standard forms" (emphasis added) and "An interest contemplated by its creators as a property interest but which does not conform to any standard form does not receive judicial recognition and enforcement, except insofar as recognition and enforcement may involve conforming a nonstandard form or purported new form to one of the standard forms." Tentative Draft No. 3, at 239–79 (April 2022).

[5] *See, e.g.*, Merrill & Smith, *supra* note 3, at 12 ("The point of the discussion is to show that the number of forms is fixed for most purposes, not to offer a substantive account of how we came to have the particular menu of options that exist today."), 17 ("Personal property is restricted to fewer available forms of ownership than real property.").

158   Property Law

because there is no way for the court to determine the empirics associated with extremely broad and speculative externalities. There is perhaps an irony in declaring that the number of something should be limited without telling us what that number is; it is also possible that the particular arrangements of externalities in the real world leads to an *unlimited* number of types of property ownership.

The problems with the economic argument run deeper, however, and mainly result from the fact that the central cost that Merrill and Smith identify – what they call the *information cost* of third-party buyers who must investigate property ownership in order to rule out unusual interests that property owners could create if the number of property forms were unlimited – is purely conceptual and is extremely unlikely to be even noticeable, much less significant, in real cases.

Consider the situation of someone buying an expensive used wristwatch. This person already has some burden to verify that the seller has title, to verify the physical condition of the watch, and in some cases to verify its authenticity (is it a real Rolex or a fake?) or provenance. In that mix of risks (or general information costs) that a potential buyer faces, the fact that a previous owner has encumbered some right associated with the watch does not measurably make the buyer's situation worse. To say that even more simply, the buyer already needs either to trust that the seller owns the watch or to authenticate that ownership; the risks associated with bad title may be more or less significant depending on the precise situation of the parties and the transaction. (Is this a transaction in a back alley or at a reputable storefront? Have the parties worked with each other before?) But it is hard to envision a specific case in which it will add significant costs to the buyer for the law to introduce the possibility of small complications to the watch's title in addition to the major complication that the seller might not even own the watch.

In other words, the buyer already faces significant risks in buying a used good in the first place. The commercial reputation of the seller, the civil and criminal penalties for fraud, the buyer's opportunity to inspect the goods and (if necessary) verify the chain of title all allow the buyer to reach a level of comfort with the deal so that it can go ahead. Into that mix, the risk that someone once sold an idiosyncratic "part" of the right to the watch – or, say, rare painting – is unlikely to

4.1 The Structure of Property Law: Numerus Clausus 159

be significant; it is essentially already subsumed into the verification (or trust) of title that the buyer of an expensive good would conduct anyway.

The risk that a watch would have an unusual property-based restriction is just a slight variation of the risk that the watch isn't actually owned by the seller. We already live with the more general risk (or for example are satisfied with the Uniform Commercial Code's shifting of those risks to the seller via the implied warranty of title);[6] living with a more specific risk is unlikely to be particularly costly. And any concern about the costs of searching for idiosyncratic encumbrances on titles to land can easily be addressed simply by requiring that those encumbrances be recorded along with other official land records. Indeed, the easy availability of those records – and the decreased costs of searching them as a result of modern technology – diminish any concern about third parties' informational costs in the context of land. Title insurance already serves as an indication of the price of those risks, and those costs are relatively small. As applied to land, Merrill and Smith's argument is essentially that allowing property interests like "the right to use this land every year on Bastille Day" would meaningfully increase the systemic costs of title insurance. Given the widespread use of condominiums and homeowners' associations, which can impose ever-changing restrictions on landowners, it is implausible that the costs of investigating new one-off historical restrictions would add much to the economic landscape.

Incidentally, though Merrill and Smith justify the numerus clausus principle in part by pointing to its acceptance around the world in a variety of legal systems,[7] other legal systems adopt different basic property rules that would undermine Merrill and Smith's particular economic justification for numerus clausus in those systems. For example, in many legal systems the good-faith purchaser of a good receives more complete title than that of the purchaser.[8]

---

[6] U.C.C. § 2–312.

[7] *E.g.*, Merrill & Smith, *supra* note 3, at 4–5.

[8] *See, e.g.*, J. G. Sauveplann, *The Protection of the Bona Fide Purchaser of Corporeal Movables in Comparative Law*, 29 Rabel J. Compar. & Int'l Priv. L. 651, 651–52 (1965) ("Whereas most continental legal systems protect the bona fide purchaser, English and American law only exceptionally grant him such protection and, as a rule, uphold the original owner's claims, subject, however, to the rules relating to the limitation of actions.").

160   Property Law

Where that is the rule, there is no concern that novel forms of property ownership pose externalities for potential third-party purchasers; just as with questions of title, any such concerns go away upon a good-faith sale.

Posner expresses a generalized version of Merrill and Smith's point: "people who create excessively complex interests burden the courts as well as themselves and their grantees, so there is some externality that might warrant public intervention."[9] If we were to take this generalized point seriously, however, it would need to apply to contracts as well. There is no general doctrine that courts should not be burdened with difficult or complex questions as long as parties have properly briefed them.

4.2 CONCEPTUAL CLASSIFICATION OF LEGAL PROBLEMS AS AN INFLUENCE ON LAW AND ECONOMICS

Chapter 2 discussed in some detail the economic analysis in tort law of the choice between negligence rules (those that allow the plaintiff to prevail only if the defendant has done something wrong) and strict-liability rules (those that permit the plaintiff to prevail even against an innocent defendant). Many problems conventionally conceived as problems in "property law," like rules that resolve conflicts between the original owner of property and a third-party buyer of that property in good faith (from, say, a thief who stole the property from the original owner), are structurally indistinguishable from tort problems: they raise the same concerns about costs of precautions and costs of harm, and the choice the law faces is between a negligence rule and a strict-liability rule.[10] Consequently, we might expect that law and economics might apply the same analysis it applied there (to that basic question of negligence versus strict liability) to problems with the same structure here. But they do not, having perhaps been distracted by other features of the problems. In other words, the arbitrary level of generality at which economists

---

[9] POSNER, *supra* note 1, at 78.
[10] I am indebted to the late Steve Sugarman's teaching for recognition of this point.

4.2 Conceptual Classification of Legal Problems 161

happen to choose to analyze a question frequently influences or even dictates their results – suggesting that it is illusory that "economics" can decide these questions and instead that economic arguments are simply marshalled as wrappers for intuitive arguments about various legal doctrines.

For example, consider the situation in which a third party buys stolen property from a thief and the original owner seeks damages or return of the property from the third party. The thief would clearly be liable, but in these cases ordinarily the thief is absent, insolvent, or otherwise judgment-proof. In economic terms, this is simply the same kind of bilateral-precaution problem we saw in Chapter 2: the original owner can take precautions against theft, and the third party can take precautions against buying stolen property. For example, if the item is a small good, the original owner can install a burglar alarm or cameras; the third party can try to deal only with reputable resellers, can try to verify the chain of ownership, and so on.

The legal economists recognize these opportunities for precaution, of course, and the law's ability to provide incentives to adopt them. But they do not apply the bilateral-precaution model from Chapter 2, which was supposed to achieve efficient results in tort law, in order to fashion or defend a negligence rule here. The model discussed and critiqued in Chapter 2 proposes to give both parties an incentive to take efficient precaution by judging the fault of each party, making them liable if they fail to take precautions that are reasonable under all the circumstances; having done that, there only remains a decision about which party bears the costs if both parties behave reasonably. Nothing in the facts or the law prevents us from applying that model here. For example, we could adopt a rule of simple negligence and apply it to either party. That is, we could say that the original owner gets their property back (or, alternatively, damages) if, but only if, the precautions they took against the property's theft were reasonable. Or we could say that the third-party buyer gets to keep the property (and owe no damages to the original owner) as long as, under the circumstances, their purchase was reasonable.

Instead, the leading law-and-economics approaches treat the problem as a discrete one and mainly aim to evaluate two competing

162   Property Law

all-or-nothing rules, under which either the original owner or the third party prevails as an all-or-nothing matter.[11]

The same sort of analysis applies to lost (versus stolen) property. For example, discussing the optimum precautions owners of property might take against losing it,[12] Shavell mainly compares two binary rules (which he calls an "original-ownership rule" and a "finders-keepers rule") rather than applying the bilateral-precaution model,[13] although he introduces a new possibility:

> an original ownership rule combined with a *mandatory reward* paid by the owner to the finder. This hybrid rule has the attractive feature that it furnishes incentives to nonowners to recover lost property – because they receive rewards – and it also mitigates the problem of excessive loss prevention efforts by owners, because they retain ownership in lost property. The precise way in which such a rule would influence behavior would depend on the formula for the reward.[14]

At the end of a footnote, he appears to note that this structure reduces to something very similar to the bilateral-precaution

---

[11] *See* ROBERT COOTER & THOMAS ULEN, LAW & ECONOMICS 151–53 (6th ed. 2012); STEVEN SHAVELL, FOUNDATIONS OF ECONOMIC ANALYSIS OF LAW 52–55 (2004) ("Because thieves will find stolen property less valuable, theft will be discouraged more under the original ownership rule than under the bona fide purchase rule. This suggests that the original ownership rule is the superior rule. But when one takes into account the transactions costs of exchange under the two rules ... it is conceivable that the bona fide purchase rule would turn out to be superior."); POSNER, *supra* note 1, at 82–83 (also emphasizing the importance of discouraging theft and concluding "[w]e do not want an efficient market in stolen goods"). As Posner might query his reader at this stage, why don't we want an efficient market in stolen goods but *do* we want an efficient market in goods produced under circumstances that externalize significant costs? It is also never clear how this particular property-law rule is meant to have a plausible effect on deterring theft in the real world or how it is meant to interact with more general criminal-law regimes (and their economic analysis).

Omri Ben-Shahar did once develop, in an unpublished manuscript, a partial application of the bilateral-precaution model to the problem of the resale of stolen goods in that it considers "a rule that conditions the owner's priority on non-negligent protection of the asset prior to the theft." *See* Omri Ben-Shahar, *Property Rights in Stolen Goods: An Economic Analysis*, home.uchicago.edu/omri/pdf/articles/Buyer_In_Good_Faith.pdf [https://perma.cc/YL4K-V9HZ]. Ben-Shahar concludes that "[i]n order to set a feasible and desirable standard, courts have to know more than assumed [under this model].... Therefore, the applicability of this regime is limited, which may explain why legal systems disregard it as a policy instrument." *Id.* at 21.

[12] SHAVELL, *supra* note 11, at 38–40.

[13] *Id.* at 40–43.

[14] *Id.* at 43.

4.3 Adverse Possession

model,[15] but it appears that the only or main reason the bilateral-precaution model didn't organize the whole analysis here is simply that the underlying problem is treated as one of "property law" rather than of "tort law."

A truly economic argument about a problem, however, would not depend on the problem's traditional legal classification. What is striking overall is how much the reasoning of the legal economists tracks the conventional, deep doctrinal divisions in law[16] rather than being led by real-world facts and the methods that economics has purportedly developed to address them. This would not be true of real science. Instead of science, what we see is simply an attempt to give form to particular legal intuitions using economic terminology. In other words, the notion that economics has decided anything about questions like these is an illusion.

4.3 ADVERSE POSSESSION

Though it is probably not an important doctrine for most practicing lawyers, adverse possession is still one of the concepts taught early in many Property courses in the United States. It is striking how much the economic analyses of adverse possession are at odds with each other. Economic analysis clearly is not determinative on the subject, and it is not clear that it has even helped lawyers improve their thinking about the matter.

Cooter and Ulen lay out two economic purposes for adverse possession: "it clears the clouds from title and allows property to move to higher-valuing users."[17] The first of these justifications is of course not really an economic justification; it is just a statement that it may be useful to settle clouds on title. Shavell rejects this explanation in the modern world: "Today, it is doubtful that the rule of adverse possession lowers the costs of land sales because ownership of land is noted in recording systems or in registries."[18]

---

[15] *See id.* at 43 n.21 ("If the reward depends on the optimal recovery effort, it can be shown to lead to optimal behavior for both types of party, and likewise if the reward is paid by the state to the finder.").

[16] For more on the concept of "deep" distinctions drawn by classical legal doctrine, see MELVIN A. EISENBERG, THE NATURE OF THE COMMON LAW 44–47 (1988).

[17] COOTER & ULEN, *supra* note 11, at 154.

[18] SHAVELL, *supra* note 11, at 76.

The second, which as Cooter and Ulen point out is more of a historical justification, is transparently unpersuasive. The argument, such as it is, is that anyone can attempt to use real property for a supposedly productive use, so that if it is otherwise lying "idle" it is available for the taking by those who value it more. Cooter and Ulen nod toward but don't particularly endorse this explanation in their textbook;[19] Shavell outright rejects it.[20] Taken seriously, it would support theft under the banner of "efficient larceny"; after all, if I don't bother protecting my television and am not using it much, a thief who values it more might as well have it.

Posner adds a different strand to the tapestry: someone like an adverse possessor who has been using property for a long time comes to value it more than the original owner, so it would be more harmful to take it away from them now.[21] As Posner puts it:

> Holmes long ago suggested an economic explanation for adverse possession. Over time, a person becomes attached to property that he regards as his own (is this a purely psychological phenomenon or can it be explained in economic terms?), and the deprivation of the property would be wrenching.[22]

Much as with the theory of efficient breach discussed in the previous chapter, however, this suggestion depends on a made-up comparison that assumes its conclusion. The assumption appears to be that just because of the adverse possessor's use and the original owner's failure to sue within a particular interval, we can compare the utility of the parties and determine who values the land more. But this neglects many potential features of the situation, including the original owner's cost of monitoring the land.

In short, the economic analysis of adverse possession comes to very little. Perhaps that is true of all analysis of adverse possession. But the point is that the doctrine does not move the needle forward in any way for those who think that the law succumbs to straightforward economic analysis.

---

[19] COOTER & ULEN, *supra* note 11, at 154.
[20] SHAVELL, *supra* note 11, at 72–75.
[21] RICHARD A. POSNER, ECONOMIC ANALYSIS OF LAW 78–79 (7th ed. 2007).
[22] *Id.* at 78.

4.4 DEAD-HAND CONTROL

An extended treatment of dead-hand control is not worthwhile here,[23] but it may be helpful to note that while the leading books on law and economics all discuss dead-hand control, their analysis of it is not very economic and simply echoes the general discussions about the subject that were commonplace before the law-and-economics movement arose. For example, one general strand of the legal economists' understanding of the problem tends to follow an argument like this: people who own property may have the right to choose to do with it, including at death; however, owners cannot predict all that will happen in the future, particularly in the distant future; therefore, courts are justified in adopting something like a *cy pres* doctrine that adjusts the decedent's instructions based on changing circumstances.[24]

The economic analyses add little to the legal-theoretical morass of the subject except perhaps a general tendency to focus attention on features of the problem that are too abstract and thus unrealistic. For example, Shavell tries to explain why we would expect to see restrictions on dead-hand control even if those restrictions were not efficient, expressing a kind of formalized skepticism of the political process:

> *Why we would* expect *the state to prevent dead hand control of property, independently of the social desirability of such policy.* Quite apart from whether or not there exists sound social justification for the state to prevent dead hand control of property, we would predict that the state will intervene for a simple reason: The generation that is alive always enjoys the power to use property that the dead would have wanted to control and certainly has an interest in doing so. This is especially true when the dead are at least a generation removed from the present generation, which is to say, when the present generation feels few personal bonds to them.[25]

---

[23] The rise of dead-hand control in organizational law may over time make its treatment in property law less important. *See* SHAWN BAYERN, AUTONOMOUS ORGANIZATIONS 133–38 (2021).

[24] *Cf.* POSNER, *supra* note 1, at 711–13; SHAVELL, *supra* note 11, at 67–72; COOTER & ULEN, *supra* note 11, at 156–59.

[25] SHAVELL, *supra* note 11, at 72 (formatting of emphasis adjusted).

But that argument suffers from the same potential shortcoming that Shavell, just four pages earlier, described as an "incorrect argument": the idea that "it would be socially wasteful, a folly, for the dead to control property, interfere with its use, to the detriment of those who are living," which is "incorrect" because "individuals who desire dead hand control will in fact suffer utility losses when they are alive, assuming that they anticipate that property will not be used in the way they want when they are dead. Thus a social policy of ignoring the wishes of the dead will in fact hurt certain individuals when they are alive."[26] Even assuming the "state" were subject to significant lobbying about dead-hand control (and that this lobbying or other sort of influence affected the court system, which decides many of the questions related to dead-hand control), why wouldn't the very individuals that Shavell had just identified – those who care, while they are alive, about their own ability to exert dead-hand control – exert political pressure? In other words, why focus only on one half of the problem when offering a descriptive analysis of the situation?

Cooter and Ulen defend dead-hand control in part by noting the "circumvention costs" associated with rules that would restrict it:

> Any restriction on the owner's choices creates an incentive to circumvent it. To illustrate, imagine an owner who wants to bequeath her land to a particular friend, and imagine that the law will award the property to someone else. The owner can circumvent the law, say, by transferring title to the friend today and leasing it back for $1 per year until her death. Circumventing the law usually requires the assistance of a good lawyer. In general, owners use costly legal resources to circumvent restrictions on the use of property.[27]

But that argument would generalize to one that is anti-regulatory in all respects and in all contexts. It also appears to assume that all the law's restrictions can in fact be circumvented by lawyers, which is plainly not true in the general case and raises a question: why focus on the private parties' cost to circumvent the rules rather than on developing the rules in such a way that they can't plausibly be circumvented even with "the assistance of a good lawyer"?

---

[26] *Id.* at 68.

[27] COOTER & ULEN, *supra* note 11, at 171.

4.5 CONCLUSION

The overall picture that this chapter paints is that the economic analysis of property law is diffuse; it serves more as an example of how economic progress in law has been illusory than of how (as in contract law and tort law) it has been erroneous. Elaborate models lay an unfalsifiable theoretical foundation for why we have property rights rather than avoiding them entirely, although whether to abolish all property rights has never been a question that the common law has seriously entertained. Nods toward economic reasoning do not satisfactorily explain more particular details in the structure of property law, such as the alleged principle of numerus clausus. Purported economic insights into other legal subjects that ought to apply to analogous questions in property law are not applied simply because those questions are labeled "property" questions – a problem that the law itself has faced and that the "external" or interdisciplinary analysis of rules hasn't solved. Rich and difficult problems like dead-hand control remain rich and difficult.

5 AFTERWORD

Ways Forward

5.1 A REVIEW OF THE PROBLEMS

What I hope will be clear from the main three subject-specific chapters of this book is that at least very often the following propositions about the law-and-economics movement are true.

First, on many specific questions, the law-and-economics movement adds little to preexisting legal debate or legal rules and instead is just an attempt to force discussions of law into a particular terminological or conceptual template. From that perspective, it is just a particular kind of legal formalism – admittedly, a new and peculiar one because it purports to speak of functionalist, instrumental ends – and it carries little argumentative weight. This sort of pattern is most evident in Richard Posner's early work, where his goal seems to be to show that everything in law is susceptible to economic reasoning – but, read carefully, extensive parts of the analysis are just a general survey of law couched in economic terms. In other words, from this perspective the law-and-economics movement is an empty vessel – a matter of terminology or style rather than substance. Or if it has any role, it is just one that would encourage an inappropriate tendency to reduce, simplify, and ignore context – vices of any legal formalism.

Second, relatedly but more specifically, as a number of my analyses here have shown, what is thought of as "law and economics" is in fact indeterminate in that it could easily defend both sides in most traditional legal arguments. If it is taken to defend a particular side, that is often because of the arbitrary assumptions its adopters have made.

168

5.1 A Review of the Problems 169

Third, many of the particular prominent arguments simply fail as arguments for specific reasons internal to the arguments themselves – not just because they make implausible assumptions about human behavior (though they do) but because they exhibit specific analytical problems, like the inability to degrade gracefully.

Cutting across these categories, it is accurate to say that the law-and-economics movement faces both descriptive problems and pre-scriptive ones. It fails to *explain* law because it acts as a just-so story; most or all legal arguments can be put into an economic form or can be reframed with economic or social-scientific words. It fails to *defend* legal rules because of the analytical problems I have described throughout this book. The best kinds of legal arguments can both explain legal rules and promote reform,[1] and the Chicago-style law-and-economics movement certainly aims to do both. But for the reasons I have described in this book, it fails at both.

In the end, it is hard to see any clear explanation for why the move-ment would ever have been compelling. It should not have been. In the Preface, I gave some very general guesses about psychosocial motiva-tions for people to accept the rule, but I'm not sure any of them are compelling either. Maybe the explanation is simply that lawyers, who until recently rarely had prior educational or professional grounding in more technical subjects, were dazzled by the advertised rigor and pre-cision of Chicago-style thinking – and legal academics were pleased to ground their field in other disciplines that their universities understood. Alternatively, the explanation could be as simple as a craving for order or a tendency for many people to adopt what might be seen as the cyni-cal core of economic thinking – that harsh tradeoffs in the allocation of the world's resources have to be made, so we might as well get on with doing that, conscience, human judgment, or emotion notwithstanding.

It would be a very significant mistake, however, to ignore con-science, judgment, and even emotion in fashioning law. To be clear, I am not arguing for an *inefficient* law in positive terms. The cumulative

---

[1] *Cf.* Stephen D. Sugarman, *Assumption of Risk*, 31 VAL. U. L. REV. 833, 835 (1997) ("My argument here is something of a mixed positive and normative one. On the one hand, I offer what I believe to be a parsimonious explanation for most of the existing cases .... On the other hand, by offering a better way of thinking about the cases, my analysis helps cor-rect the mistakes that I believe some courts have made.").

weight of this book's analysis of individual law-and-economics arguments suggests, for me, the importance of using factors beyond formal, narrow analysis in order to achieve efficiency. As I said at the outset, I believe efficiency is *one* important goal of the law, and it can be a very important one. But the arbitrary identification of two or three forces, particularly in the rich subjects of tort law, contract law, and property law, is no way to go about achieving it. Fairness, intuition, experience, judgment, and efficiency should, and normally do, all pull in the same direction, and neglecting informal sources of propositions about what is best for the law to do, taking into account all possible parties and considerations, is ordinarily a mistake. A law professor who graduated from the University of Chicago's law school has told me that his Contracts professor, upon hearing a student make an argument about what was "fair," said something to the effect of, "In this class, 'fairness' is the 'f-word' and should never be spoken." But because actual contracting parties have and depend on a sense of what is fair – transactionally fair in the real world, not "fair" in some more abstract sense in use among philosophers or those who focus on society-wide income redistribution – it is a profound mistake (even on grounds of efficiency alone) to ignore fairness in analyzing and setting contract rules.

It is no accident that common lawyers are generalists; the proper function of the law demands a wide view and sensitivity to factual context and social propositions that may be unpredictable in advance. We might envision a broad, polycentric view of the law as *synoptic functionalism* – a mode of analysis that depends on generalism and the opportunity for courts and commentators to be comprehensive. The required mental discipline is much the same as for those who care about responding to cybersecurity attacks: anything might matter, and the weakest link in the chain can be decisive. Law and economics, as a movement, is instead aimed at reduction and specification. The problem with law and economics is not that it is necessarily insensitive to any particular sort of fact; indeed, even moral considerations can be processed as personal preferences to be aggregated. The problem is instead that, in reducing and specifying, it aims to deny the need to be comprehensive. Genuine utilitarians or consequentialists would care about many factors that Chicago-style legal economists avoid – say, the role of education in society, the destruction of productive

5.2 Alternative Legal-Economic Approaches

motivation that may come from large amounts of inherited wealth,[2] the perspective-altering potential of the arts, the potential but hard-to-quantify benefits of investment into pure science, or the prevention of tyranny. They would also be open to a variety of means and processes – for example, valuing collaboration, competition, diversity, and robustness rather than a reductive sort of efficiency.[3] The harder edge of the Chicago school – the people who subscribe most to hyper-optimization of individual variables in models, even at the expense of widely accepted social norms – poses a threat that even the coldest utilitarian should, on reflection, recognize.

5.2 ALTERNATIVE LEGAL-ECONOMIC APPROACHES

What is to be done, then, for those of us who believe that instrumental concerns are not irrelevant for common-law judges but who also believe that the leading instrumentalist analyses are unpersuasive?

My sense is that the best way forward is not to ignore the legal-economics movement but to try to extract useful principles from it. Economic thinking is not and should not be irrelevant to law. Much can be learned from consensus positions that are modest in scope and tied to particular effects of rules that lawyers can evaluate in context. For example, consider the general observation (probably a

---

[2] For recent reporting on these last two subjects, see Andrew van Dam, *It's Better to Be Born Rich than Gifted*, WASH. POST. WONKBLOG, Oct. 8, 2018, www.washingtonpost.com/business/2018/10/09/its-better-be-born-rich-than-talented [https://perma.cc/QZD4-M2VS] ("A revolution in genomics is creeping into economics. It allows us to say something we might have suspected, but could never confirm: money trumps genes .... Using one new, genome-based measure, economists found genetic endowments are distributed almost equally among children in low-income and high-income families. Success is not.").

[3] For recent reporting on this subject, see David Dayen, *Larry Summers Shares the Blame for Inflation*, N.Y. TIMES, Feb. 28, 2022, nytimes.com/2022/02/28/opinion/larry-summers-inflation.html [web.archive.org/web/20230314042725/nytimes.com/2022/02/28/opinion/larry-summers-inflation.html] ("The transformation reflects how elite economists in both parties reached a rough accord on the importance of free markets, free trade, and restrained regulation .... And there was little disagreement about the means."). The article also quotes Summers as saying: "In general, economic thinking has privileged efficiency over resilience, and it has been insufficiently concerned with the big downsides of efficiency .... Going forward we will need more emphasis on 'just in case' even at some cost in terms of 'just in time.'"

172 Afterword: Ways Forward

rough consensus among modern American instrumentalists) that the illusory-promise rule in contract law, and indeed most applications of classical ideas of mutuality, are unproductive and antagonistic to the notion that commercial bargains should be enforced. That recognition forms the basis for a useful critique of the formalism of classical consideration doctrine. An instrumental analysis of the preexisting-duty rule in contract law, focused on the possible gains in efficiency from enforcing modifications to contracts, should at least cause a lawyer or judge to question the superficial appeal of that rule. Similarly, as a more focused example, an instrumental "economic" analysis of a particular proposed rule of contract law that shows that the rule would permit one party to speculate at the expense of the other party may highlight important weaknesses in a rule – weaknesses, it is important to say, that amplify "noneconomic" concerns like the transactional unfairness of that sort of speculation.

In other words, lawyers should not be closed off to *policy* arguments or to the notion that legal rules have consequences and that those consequences matter. Rejecting all instrumentalism – an approach more common in the past and more common outside the United States, where the legal-realism movement was particularly strong in the mid-1900s – leaves us with nothing but dry formalism – with doctrine or legal concepts for their own sake, as if the goal of the law were to make law professors or philosophers happy by aiding them in reconciling the real world with their preexisting categories. Indeed, there is one particularly dysfunctional response to the analytical failures of law and economics: the relapse into legal formalism or its various philosophical veneers – or, equivalently, the abandonment of all attempts at instrumentalism or the notion that consequences or human happiness matter.[4] It is increasingly common to see scholars who speak of all instrumental reasoning as if it has the same problem as overly broad law-and-economic arguments, or who define very

---

[4] *E.g.*, C.C. Langdell, A Summary of the Law of Contracts 20–21 (2d ed.1880) ("It has been claimed that the purposes of substantial justice, and the interests of contracting parties as understood by themselves, will be best served by holding that the contract is complete the moment the letter of acceptance is mailed; and cases have been put to show that the contrary view would produce not only unjust but absurd results. The true answer to this argument is, that it is irrelevant ....").

5.2 Alternative Legal-Economic Approaches 173

broad functional concepts like "justice" in narrow, limited ways and then attempt to analyze those definitions in purely conceptual terms. That response misunderstands the problems with law and economics, and it threatens to impose similarly contextless, regressive, and stale methodologies on the law. The main problems with the aggrandizement of narrow instrumentalism are aggrandizement and narrowness, not instrumentalism; the solution is less narrowness and singlemindedness, not less concern about the policy of the law. An informal sort of instrumentalism – "law and economics" without the Chicago school's restraints, without the need to proselytize the discipline, and without the artificial assumptions or the instinct to press toward harsh, counterintuitive conclusions – certainly has much to offer modern courts and commentators.

That prescription may sound too general for some, however. While law is not susceptible to singular methodologies, perhaps we can be more specific here in a way that will be helpful. Economic reasoning or analytical "rationality" in the pursuit of instrumental goals can, as I have said, be helpful to law. Apart from providing general reasons to be weighed casually against other reasons, perhaps legal-economic argumentation can, if done well and sensitively, be reoriented to provide ranges of options instead of definite purported policy prescriptions.

A tendency of today's rationalism, in many areas, is to approach decisions as if rationality demands singular answers. As an analogy, in personal finance it is common to model the behavior of asset classes as random variables based on past performance – indeed, to emphasize this approach with Monte Carlo simulations, which are a sort of trial-and-error way to mimic formal conclusions in order to make predictions in cases where formal analysis is too complicated. This is fine as long as it is used as one source of potential information – for example, to tell an investor, "If the variances we have seen in data in the past continue into the future, here is a range of possible outcomes along with their probabilities." The difficulty is that the future may not mirror the past, and risky assets expose the owner to uncertainty rather than just probability distributions. Assuming the opposite runs into the same analytical problem discussed in Chapter 3, and very roughly speaking it is why we have periodic financial collapses that models told us in advance were extremely unlikely. That is, models do not

174   Afterword: Ways Forward

capture everything, but we nonetheless act as if they do, as if rationality demands that we pretend they do. Rationality imposes no such requirement. For an individual investor, a wide range of asset allocations is consistent with "rationality" – much in the way, just as a loose analogy, that the law recognizes that an extremely wide range of state action may have a "rational basis."[5]

But a wide range is not an infinite range, and maybe that is the lesson. In other words, maybe economic reasoning can delimit ranges beyond which instrumental consequences are likely to be extremely poor. For example, *at least* a standard of negligence is *ordinarily* efficient; a tort system that systematically undershoots that standard is *capable* of systematic underdeterrence of unsafe conditions.

To put this differently, it is misguided for commentators to offer fragile models to try to show why a particular rule is "optimal" in the abstract in ways that are never likely to translate into practice. Perhaps more work should be done to show that particular candidate rules are likely, in the real world, to be very problematic. Focusing on ranges and not points – and focusing on preventing worst-case or very problematic outcomes rather than achieving an elusive and false optimum of a hypothetical "expected value" – could be very helpful to legal policymakers.

5.3 STUDYING HUMANITY

Regardless, economics should never forget that its object of study is humanity. Humans are surprisingly diverse and complex. Isaac Asimov once described the human brain as "the most complex and orderly arrangement of matter in the universe,"[6] a conclusion shared by modern scientists and doctors.[7] The most sophisticated economics

---

[5] *Cf.* Raphael Holoszyc-Pimentel, *Reconciling Rational-Basis Review: When Does Rational Basis Bite?*, 90 N.Y.U. L. Rev. 2070, 2070 (2015) ("Rational-basis review, the most deferential form of scrutiny under the Equal Protection Clause, rarely invalidates legislation. Between the 1971 and 2014 Terms, the Supreme Court has held laws violative of equal protection under rational-basis scrutiny only seventeen times ....").

[6] Isaac Asimov, *In the Game of Energy and Thermodynamics, You Can't Even Break Even*, 1 J. Smithsonian Inst. 4, 10 (1970).

[7] *E.g.*, BBC News, *The Brain Is the 'Most Complex Thing in the Universe,'* May 29, 2012, bbc.com/news/uk-scotland-18233409 [https://perma.cc/QFV6-FSHW] (attributing the

5.3 Studying Humanity 175

still feels like trying to approximate very complex objects with lines and simple mathematic functions – or like comparing ancient computer graphics to high-resolution photographs. Perhaps it would be sounder to start with psychology, knowing its limits, rather than to start with economics. This is what "behavioral law and economics" purports to do, but it would probably be better to think of that sort of analysis simply as "analysis that applies psychology to law and the incentives that legal rules create"; *behavioral law and economics* isn't terrible terminology, but it puts the cart before the horse.

Sometimes simple lines or curves are enough to approximate a real-world function, and sometimes low-resolution images provide insight – or are at least better than nothing. The main failure of law and economics is in extending the techniques of economics beyond their range. As I briefly noted in Chapter 2 in discussing the leading legal-economic conception of negligence rules, the economists behind the original models were much more aware of their limitations than were the lawyers or law-and-economics scholars who applied them.

Maybe what we need is something more like what Lon Fuller called *eunomics*[8] – which he "defined as the science, theory or study of good order and workable arrangements."[9] As background, one proposition that Fuller rejected was "the infinite pliability of social arrangements, the view that, given a sufficient agreement on ends or a dictator strong enough to impose his own ends, society can be so arranged as to effectuate (within the limits of its resources) any conceivable combination or hierarchy of ends ...."[10] Law in general, much less the law-and-economics movement, has not paid enough attention in recent years to the sort of limitations that Fuller had in mind. Even if Fuller's belief is not true – for example, the modern philosophical transhumanists would probably deny it – the gulf between abstract, extreme legal positivism and reality is still "drawing attention away from the most vital

---

quotation to psychiatrist Professor Sir Robin Murray, whom the article also reports to have said, "We won't be able to understand the brain.").

[8] *See, e.g.*, Lon L. Fuller, *American Legal Philosophy at Mid-Century*, 6 J. Leg. Educ. 457, 473 (1954).

[9] *Id.* at 477.

[10] *Id.* at 473.

176 Afterword: Ways Forward

problems of social order and welfare."[11] This is perhaps truer of grand ideological economics (in forms like extreme libertarian academic and political theory) but it is also true of models that don't start meaningfully with humans or human societies as their objects of study. In general, lawyers need to pay attention to more and richer perspectives on humanity – like sensitive applications of behavioral psychology, Fuller's work, Iain McGilchrist's fascinating account *The Master and His Emissary*,[12] and other scholarship and interdisciplinary research that rejects or sheds light on the limits of formalistic hyperrationalism.

5.4 CONCLUSION

The general problems of law or of politics do not have easy answers, and one of the most important things we can do in analyzing those problems is to avoid the patterns of thought that lead us to oversimplify important questions. In the end, this book's goal has been to show that the law-and-economics movement is guilty of exactly that kind of oversimplification.

It may at first sound unfair, but the law-and-economics movement suffers from twin problems: when it is too specific, it is wrong; when it is too general, it adds little to the debate apart from reorienting our terminology and attention toward a particular arbitrary subset of the things that law would need to do even to meet utilitarian or other consequentialist goals. But it has set itself up for that pair of problems. Its models fail to model reality for internal reasons and because they adopt implausible assumptions. Its general discussions – which are surprisingly common – essentially serve as introductory treatises on law but with new terminology. Neither of those types of contributions has offered much to the law. When legal-economic analysis restricts itself to offering general guidance, it can be helpful in framing legal questions, but cautiously shedding light has been at odds with a general goal to proselytize the movement and present all legal questions

---

[11] *Id.* at 474.

[12] Iain McGilchrist, The Master and His Emissary: The Divided Brain and the Making of the Western World (2d ed. 2019).

5.4 Conclusion

as reducible to economic analysis. If the movement were content with providing partial, limited answers, it could make a very strong contribution; when it tries to do more than that, it threatens to destroy deeper efficiencies in law and to mimic only an arbitrary, limited subset of legal reasoning.

That is not to say that instrumentalism isn't important, that economic reasoning has never shed light on legal problems, or that we should abandon the economic analysis of law entirely. But it is long past time to stop taking it as seriously as its proponents and practitioners want it to be taken.

INDEX

activity levels. *See under* tort law
act-omission distinction, 80, 149
administrative law, 7
adverse possession, 163–64
agency costs, 15, 147
allocative efficiency
   versus broader instrumental notions, 23
allocative negligence
   definition, 72
American Law Institute, 87
"antipatterns", 12
antitrust law, 7
arts, 171
Asimov, Isaac, 174
asset allocation, 174
assumptions
   of economic models, in general, 10
autonomy, 70

B < PL. *See* Hand formula
bargain contracts
   efficiency of, 84
Bastille Day, 159
battery, 82
battle
   trial by, 22
beauty contest game (in game theory), 54
behavioral law and economics, 6, 134, 175
bell curve, 108
Bentham, Jeremy
   use of terminology, 151
Bernstein, Lisa, 130
bilateral precaution, 14, 36–59, 80, 162
   definition, 37
   discrete *versus* continuous model, 58
   fragility of model, 52–53

Blackburn, Colin, 5
boards of directors, 122
bona fide purchaser. *See* property, bona
   fide purchaser of
brain, complexity of, 174
breach of contract
   deliberate, 88
   precaution against, 94
Buddha, 23

Calabresi, Guido, 76
California
   contractual choice of law, 129
causation, in negligence. *See under* tort law
changed circumstances. *See under* contract
   law
climate change, 23
Coase theorem, 22, 28, 138–39
Coase, Ronald, 28, 71
comparative negligence, 43
conceptualism, legal, 8
conscience, 169
consent, implied, 82
consequentialism, 170
   and act-omission distinction, 149
conservation easement, 23
contextualism
   definition, 99
contract law. *See also* breach of contract;
   efficient breach, theory of
   changed circumstances. *See* unexpected
     circumstances
   consideration, 151–52, *See also*
     preexisting-duty rule
   disclosure, 16–18, 148–50
   duress, 133–35

179

Index

empirical evidence of parties'
preferences, 127–32
expectation damages, 87–90, 94–96
fraud, 133–35, 151
frustration, 144–48
impossibility, 14, 144–48
impracticability, 14, 144–48
interpretation, 99–132
mistake, 111
new-business rule, 96–99
nondisclosure. *See* disclosure
political dimensions of, 99
preexisting-duty rule, 5, 151, 172
remedies, 4, 86–99
unconscionability, 19, 132–48
unexpected circumstances, 14, 144–48
contract risk management
by businesses, 146
Cooter, Robert, 17, 23–25, 28–29, 35,
37–40, 42–47, 49–52, 55, 58–63, 65,
69, 74, 82, 112, 119, 135, 142, 144,
153, 154, 162–66
corporate law
board's duty, 122
counterintuitiveness
as a false virtue, 21
Craswell, Richard, 94
cy pres, 165

damages, 4
dead-hand control, 165–66
default rules, 5, 116, 122, 127–28, 130–31
degradation, of formal models, 12–16
descriptive arguments
versus prescription, 169
dictionaries
as interpretive aid, 102, 110–16
distribution, normal, 108
distribution of wealth, 70
doctrinalism, 8
duress. *See under* contract law
duty, in negligence. *See under* tort law
duty to rescue. *See under* tort law

economic harms
in tort law, 81
education, 170
efficient breach, theory of, 4, 86–94
Eisenberg, Melvin, 2, 9, 18, 70, 79, 85, 90,
92, 94, 112, 123, 134, 138, 142, 145,
149–52, 163
Eisenberg, Theodore, 128

emotional harms, 81
environmentalism, 23
eunomics, 175
evidentiary base
in contract interpretation, 103
evolutionary psychology, 154
expectation damages. *See under* contract
law
externalities, 20–21, 69–80, 157–60, 162
definition, 20

fairness, 1, 3, 11, 70, 96, 137, 142, 144,
148, 170
false imprisonment, 81
Farber, Daniel, 21
Farnsworth, Ward, 87
Federal Trade Commission, 142
feminist theory, 154
Fiat justitia ruat caelum, 10
finders-keepers rule. *See under* property law
flourishing
human, 10
foodborne illness, 111
fraud, 149. *See also under* contract law
frustration. *See under* contract law
Fuller, Lon, 8, 175
f-word
fairness as, to legal economists, 170

game theory, 54
Goldberg, Victor, 96–98, 145
growth
versus allocative efficiency, 24

Hand formula, 26–27, 32, 34–35, 65–67
extended form, 66
Hand, Learned, 26, *See also* Hand formula
happiness
human, 10
harms, dignitary, 81
hedonic psychology, 7
Holmes, Oliver Wendell, 164
horses, 23
Hylton, Keith, 78

ideal gas law, 13
impossibility. *See under* contract law
impracticability. *See under* contract law
incentives
redundant, 18
information
productive *versus* redistributive, 149

Index

181

injunctions, 4, 92–95
innovation
versus efficiency, 23
instrumentalism
role of in law, 171–74
insurance, 27, 126, 147
title, 159
intentional interference with contract, 87
intentional torts. *See under* tort law
intergenerational restrictions. *See* dead-hand control
internal critique of law and economics
description, 3
interpretation, contract. *See under* contract law
irrationality
of humans, 2

Korobkin, Russell, 130, 133
Kronman, Anthony, 17

Landes, William, 80
Langdell, Christopher Columbus, 8, 172
Learned Hand, 29
leases, 92–94
oil-and-gas, 18, 150
least-cost avoider arguments, 76–78, 145
Leff, Arthur, 2, 132
legal conceptualism. *See* conceptualism, legal
legal realism. *See* realism, legal
legal-duty rule. *See* contract law, preexisting-duty rule
libertarian theory, 176
lost property. *See under* property, lost

majoritarian defaults, 131
management, of organizations, 1
mandatory rules, 85
marketing, academic, 1
Marxism, 154
McGilchrist, Iain, 176
Merrill, Thomas, 20, 155
metrics, 1
Miller, Geoffrey, 128
minimal evidentiary base
in contract interpretation, 103
minimum wage, 19, 132, 140
mislaid property. *See under* property, mislaid
Model Code of Professional Responsibility, 89

Model Rules of Professional Conduct, 89
Monte Carlo simulation, 173

naivete, 1–6
negligence, 14, 26, 160
definition, 27
versus strict liability, 27–36
New York
contractual choice of law, 128
corporate law, 122
new-business rule. *See under* contract law
nondisclosure. *See under* contract law
numerus clausus, 21, 23, 155–60, 167

omissions
versus actions, 79, 149
opportunism, 71, 77, 140–41
opportunity costs, 18–20
optimal precaution, 49
organizational law
and dead-hand control, 165

Perlis, Alan, 13
physics, 13
pluralism
in legal theory, 23
Pope, 23
Pope, Alexander, 11, 31
possession
adverse. *See* adverse possession
positivism, legal, 11, 175
Posner, Richard, 4, 5, 14–16, 29–30, 32–34, 72, 75, 80–81, 89–93, 126, 144–48, 151–54, 160–168
precaution, bilateral. *See* bilateral precaution
precontractual investigation, 95
prescriptive arguments
versus description, 169
private law
as focus of book, 7
probability
versus uncertainty, 105–11
procedural unconscionability. *See also* contract law, unconscionability
definition, 133
profits, supranormal, 142–43
property
bona fide purchaser of, 161
lost, 162
mislaid, 162

182　　Index

property law
　finders-keepers rule, 162
　limited forms of ownership. *See* numerus
　　clausus
　relation to tort law, 160
property rules, 79
provenance, 158
public-benefit corporations, 121
purchaser
　bona fide, 161

random variables, 97, 108, 173
rational-actor hypothesis, 9, 13, 54, 100
rational-basis test, 174
realism, legal, 8
reciprocity
　in tort theory, 79
redistributional negligence
　definition, 73
remedies. *See under* contract law *or*
　particular remedies
rent control, 19
rescue, duty to, 79
Restatement (Second) of Torts, 46
Restatement (Third) of Restitution and
　Unjust Enrichment, 88
Restatement (Third) of Torts, 26, 78, 87
Restatement (Fourth) of Property, 157
rights, 70
risk aversion
　definition, 119
risk neutrality, 119–27
　definition, 119
robustness
　versus allocative efficiency, 171
Rosenfield, Andrew, 14–16, 144–145
rules
　default. *See* default rules
　mandatory. *See* mandatory rules

Schwartz, Alan, 100. *See also* interpretation
science, investments into, 171
Scott, Robert E., 99, 100. *See also*
　interpretation
self-driving cars, 23
settlement, of lawsuits, 116–19
Shavell, Steven, 3, 10, 17, 20, 37–40,
　42–46, 49–51, 55–66, 76, 80, 83, 153,
　162–66
simulations, of reality, 105
singularity, mathematical, 95
Smith, Henry, 20, 155

social cost
　versus private cost, 47, 71
specific performance, 4
standardized form contracts, 146
static-efficiency analysis, 23
stolen property, 161
strict liability, 160
　definition, 27
　versus negligence, 27–36
substantive unconscionability. *See also*
　contract law, unconscionability
　definition, 133
Sugarman, Stephen, 64, 78–79, 160, 169
supranormal profits. *See* profits,
　supranormal
surplus, contractual, 15, 135
synoptic functionalism
　definition, 170

tax law, 7, 77
terminology, economic
　versus substance, 151
testator
　power of. *See* dead-hand control
textualism
　definition, 99
theft, 161, 164
theory of efficient breach. *See* efficient
　breach, theory of
tort law
　activity levels, 44–47, 59–67
　causation, 80–81
　duty, 78–80
　duty to rescue, 79
　incentives in, 25
　intentional interference with contract, 87
　intentional torts, 81
　professional sports, 79
　relation to property law, 160
transaction costs, 22, 71–75, 91, 99, 139,
　147, 156
transhumanism, 175
trespasser
　flagrant, 80
trial by battle, 22
tyranny, 171

Ulen, Thomas, 17, 25, 35, 39, 43–46, 51,
　52, 58–62, 74, 82, 112, 119, 135, 142,
　144, 153, 154, 162–66
uncertainty
　versus probability, 105–11

Index

183

unconscionability. *See under* contract law
Uniform Commercial Code, 159
unilateral precaution, 48, 52
unexpected circumstances. *See under*
    contract law
utilitarianism, 170
    in and act-omission distinction, 149

verifiability
    in contract theory, 113

virtue, 70
Voltaire, 19

wealth, inherited, 171
welfarism, 3
well-being, 3
windfalls, 143
wristwatch
    right to use periodically, 20,
        156

Printed in the United States
by Baker & Taylor Publisher Services